BIBLE
FINANCIAL
PURPOSE
DRIVEN

OUT OF DEBT AND POVERTY
INTO GOD'S WEALTH

BRUNO CAPORRIMO;
DOMINIC CONTRERAS

authorHOUSE®

AuthorHouse™
1663 Liberty Drive
Bloomington, IN 47403
www.authorhouse.com
Phone: 833-262-8899

Published by AuthorHouse 02/12/2024

ISBN: 979-8-8230-2218-7 (sc)
ISBN: 979-8-8230-2217-0 (e)

Print information available on the last page.

This book is printed on acid-free paper.

Because of the dynamic nature of the Internet, any web addresses or links contained in
this book may have changed since publication and may no longer be valid. The views
expressed in this work are solely those of the author and do not necessarily reflect the
views of the publisher, and the publisher hereby disclaims any responsibility for them.

Scripture quotations are from the NKJV™ & The Amplified
Bible (AMP)™ unless otherwise stated.

Emphasis within scripture verses is the author's own.

CONTENTS

INTRODUCTION

We recommend that you read one chapter a week so that on this 52-lesson journey with God, towards your reconstruction recovery in life, God will anoint you and transform your mind, body and soul so that you can walk by faith and be a good steward for His prosperity spiritually, mentally, physically and materially.

This theme is found throughout the bible. Note the following scriptures:

Isaiah 14:24
Amplified Bible (AMP)
²⁴ The Lord of hosts has sworn, saying, Surely, as I have thought *and* planned, so shall it come to pass, and as I have purposed, so shall it stand—

Psalm 33:11
Amplified Bible (AMP)
¹¹ The counsel of the Lord stands forever, the thoughts of His heart through all generations.

Isaiah 55:10-11
Amplified Bible (AMP)
¹⁰ For as the rain and snow come down from the heavens, and return not there again, but water the earth and make it bring forth and sprout, that it may give seed to the sower and bread to the eater,

11 So shall My word be that goes forth out of My mouth: it shall not return to Me void [without producing any effect, useless], but it shall accomplish that which I please *and* purpose, and it shall prosper in the thing for which I sent it.

Hebrews 6:16-17
Amplified Bible (AMP)
16 Men indeed swear by a greater [than themselves], and with them in all disputes the oath taken for confirmation is final [ending strife].

17 Accordingly God also, in His desire to show more convincingly *and* beyond doubt to those who were to inherit the promise the unchangeableness of His purpose *and* plan, intervened (mediated) with an oath.

The passages above will enable you to come into God's purpose for your life, to receive all the fullness and understand the blueprint He's prepared for your inheritance. At the end and during this process of learning how to receive and make the right decisions, you will start to recover all of the pieces of your life as they begin to fit together as God's word shapes you for the new beginning, as a new vessel equipped to inherit the abundance that's awaiting you. Receive it all as you learn now to be blessed with success. This process will help you to reduce your stress as you become aware of all the benefits of God's word and this will give you immediate satisfaction. Most importantly, you will be prepared for God's wisdom and strength, by making Him your partner in this great journey.

8 PRINCIPLES FOR FINDING YOUR PURPOSE

How do you discover what is right? The next 8 points will reveal some purposes so that you can successfully fulfill goals in every area of your life.

1. God does nothing without a purpose
2. God created everything with purpose.
3. Not every purpose is known to us because we have lost HIS understanding & purpose intended for us.
4. Where purpose is NOT known, abuse and destruction is inevitable.
5. We will never discover HIS purpose unless we read and ask from HIS book.
6. Our purpose in God is revealed to us, not only in creation, but in asking the Creator.
7. We find our purpose only in the mind of our maker.
8. God's purpose is the only KEY to the door which brings us fulfillment.

EYE-OPENER

If you are sincere and do not know your purpose, you will be sincerely wrong. These examples demonstrate that if you do not know the purpose of something, that you will misuse or abuse it in someway. That is why it is possible to be sincerely wrong. It is possible to be faithfully wrong. It is possible to be seriously wrong. You can be serious but still wrong because you do not know the purpose for the thing that you are involved in! This principle holds true for everything, including people. Often, we see people break contracts, break their word and use and misuse friendship. People go to the church and stand before the altar and say to their brothers and friends, "I will love you until I die".

Many people go into marriage very seriously and men and woman make a vow to each other to be together until the end and then they fail the contract because they do not understand the purpose of marriage, or a mate, or family or union and commitment to the binding promise. People abuse things because they just don't know the purposes or because they disregard those purposes and that's when men and women fail. By doing so, they end up abusing each other, even if they do not mean to. If men and woman want to resolve their current identity crisis and fulfill their purpose in life, as men, husband, father, women, wife and mother, then they must REDISCOVER God's plan for them. Otherwise they will hurt those around them, even if it is unintentional.

In these 52 chapters, I strongly encourage the reader to read at least one chapter a week, by reading and meditating and applying each purpose to your life, daily, for 7 days. Don't you think it would be wise for you to determine how you are going to manage the rest of your life? Take these 52 lessons with God as a practical guide, to show you how to know how to spend the rest of your days and to understand your potential to receive the blessings of God so that you can be a blessing to others!

The Bible is full of illustrations of those who consecrated themselves to receive a breakthrough. The first example was Moses for 40 days and 40 nights. This revelation was given to Moses while he was on the mount with God for 40 days and another 40 days and how he came down with instructions to liberate his people from the Egyptian slave mentality. Remember, as they obeyed His instructions they came out wealthy and healthy on their journey to the promised land that flowed with milk and honey. Houses they didn't have to build and yet they were established because they followed the instructions of God. Simply put, if you do it His way you will not fail and you will walk in the provision that is already there and belongs to you.

Day after day, you will have time to think and meditate about the implications of the daily contents of your life. The Bible declares that God transforms people to have new lives, just like he transformed Abraham, Isaac, Jacob, Ruth, Esther, Boaz, Samson, Joseph, David, Christ Jesus, the disciples, Apostle Paul and millions upon millions of people who have been changed from rags into riches. Now it's your time to seize this opportunity and the journey out of Debt and Poverty into God's Wealth.

Don't just read this like any other book; but pray, meditate, underline it and apply and confess out loud as we take you chapter by chapter. We will break it down for you, so that the journey becomes an adventure as you apply all the instructions which will manifest the blessings, during the 52-week journey. At the end of each chapter, there is a section where you will be given the opportunity to declare and confess what you have learned, so you can easily put into practice what you have read. Practice these lessons until you see the manifestation coming to you. Don't give up! Continue to confess and pray and meditate for each day's provision and for all that you will be learning on this journey as we take you through all 52 chapters in 52 weeks. You WILL grow stronger and stronger in faith and be driven by faith that cannot fail you!

BRIEF TESTIMONY BY
THE AUTHOR

This book has been written for one specific purpose and that is to glorify God in His eternal plan and will for mankind. Whosoever trusts in His plan and will, whether a person is in Africa, South America, Bombay, India or in the worst areas of Russia or China, God can reach out to a person and transform and change their life and supply all of their needs in abundance. The scripture comes to mind, John 10:10 where Jesus said:

John 10:10
King James Version (KJV)
[10] The thief cometh not, but for to steal, and to kill,
and to destroy: I am come that they might have life,
and that they might have it more abundantly.

As I look back to 1985, just before I came to Christ, I was busy in my life working 12 hours a day, running a restaurant, delicatessen and pizza shop and most of my leisure time was spent gambling, drinking and traveling back and forth to Las Vegas and fishing. The more money I made, the more money I spent. I owned property in Las Vegas and wanted to build a casino and I owned a restaurant and a home. My financial value in property and stock was at least 2 million dollars but I was carrying a triple mortgage. The more I worked the more money I needed to fulfill my ego. Everything was working, but my life was not working. In fact, it was a mess. There was emptiness in my life, which I did not know then, but I know now. It was God's plan and will into my heart. When I began to take inventory of my loneliness, depression and gambling habits, I began searching for something greater that I knew existed for my life. By God's grace and mercy, He sent one of His servants who was a missionary and evangelist, into my restaurant. Now, the time came for this heroic confrontation. My day of deliverance had arrived in the form of a courageous and loving Christian man named Roy Lang.

He confronted me in my restaurant with the gospel. He looked straight into my eyes, into my soul, and declared that I was a sinner. He explained to me that God had a plan and that He was my only salvation. Many people in the past had tried to witness to me about the Lord and I always responded with pride and ignorance to the gospel. I would say things like, "Look, you do not see the crucifix around my neck?" or, "Do you not see the crucifix on the wall? I have God", I would say. But, the truth was…. I had religion, not a relationship. I was worse than a Sadducee or a Pharisee. I was nothing but a self-righteous hypocrite. There was something special about this man. His character and his love toward me became more than I could handle. I felt guilty and unworthy and ashamed of my conduct. I began to experience my filth and unworthiness and my lack of value.

I started to listen to him. I knew that he was a messenger from God. I wish that I could take back the nasty, self-righteous attitude that I had towards this man. I thank the Lord everyday for sending this great Christian man to me. Roy told me that I must get on my knees with a contrite heart and to have true sorrow for my sins. I remember him being gentle, but firm and there was something special in his eyes. His words were like a command. Now I know that it was the Holy Spirit in him trying to draw me to the Master. My friend, I wish that this would have happened to me when I was a boy. Unfortunately, through wars and afflictions of men like Hitler and many false leaders in Europe, people became victims, with no way out and without God. Perversion, danger, fear, rejection, loneliness, darkness and poverty occupy people's lives and that was the way I was raised and maybe this could be the same path and circumstance in which you were raised.

Several days later when I finally cried out to the Lord and invited him to come into my life. The Lord Jesus supernaturally baptized me with the Holy Spirit and began to work in my life. Instantly the Lord delivered me from drinking and gambling and gave me great peace and wisdom. I began to see His ways. Within a few months I sold the restaurant, property home and business. I paid off all the debts and had enough money to move to Arizona and build a three-bedroom home for $85,000 and I had $110,000 left and lived off it for five years. It was a wise investment as my living income from this was $1,500 a month and it was more than enough because the only bills I had were the utilities and food. Praise the Lord! What a blessing. He took a 200lb monkey of debt off my back and that freed me to serve Him and enjoy life more abundantly by fishing, swimming and I had enough time to seek Him and enjoy reading the bible and other spiritual books and witness of His goodness to me everywhere that I went.

He taught me to live by faith and trust Him for every need. His plan and His purpose have been working in my life ever since. My wife and I have experienced His grace, His mercy, His laws and His rules and His abundance and provision. They have never left us and even today we see His hand upon us to bless us and prosper us as we continue to live by faith, moment by moment, day by day, week by week, month by month and year by year. This is truly the heart and love of God for all mankind.

Now, 33 years have gone by and God has carried me out of debt, foreclosure and poverty and God has anointed me and carried me into HIS prosperity. He has taken me, 246 times, to China and Asia on the Mission fields and to 42 nations. I have written

14 books and have built a curriculum for a bible college. This began when I learned God's principles on how to make God my partner and how to give and receive tithes and offerings and how to reach out and bring the gospel and His laws to the nations of the world for the witness and purpose of making disciples. God has been faithful with His treasure from heaven by releasing His anointing into our lives and by making provision to pay all the expenses and bills and HE has given my wife and I abundant joy and faith to trust in him.

Now, I get to write this book for YOU and if you apply the principles in these lessons, you cannot fail! You will experience a debt free life and freedom from poverty and YOU will come into God's prosperity! If you want to know more about my testimony, and about my life prior to coming to the Lord, I encourage you to read, <u>Honeymoon with the Holy Spirit</u> and <u>From Mafia Boss to the Cross</u> which are now available in bookstores and online.

- Dr. Bruno Caporrimo,
  Chancellor, ECM
  La Puente, Ca.

LESSON ONE

Galatians 3:13-14
Amplified Bible (AMP)
¹³ Christ purchased our freedom [redeeming us] from the curse (doom) of the Law [and its condemnation] by [Himself] becoming a curse for us, for it is written [in the Scriptures], Cursed is everyone who hangs on a tree (is crucified);

¹⁴ To the end that through [their receiving] Christ Jesus, the blessing [promised] to Abraham might come upon the Gentiles, so that we through faith might [all] receive [the realization of] the promise of the [Holy] Spirit.

UNDERSTANDING AND OBEYING COVENANT RULES

I wonder if the thought of you doing something for society and God, like helping the poor, has ever entered your mind? If so, you might find it quite difficult when you have nothing to offer. The main question in your mind is "How can I help the poor when I am poor?" Therefore, you must gain God's wealth and provision for HIS vision and mission, in order to walk in the blue print of God's destiny for your life and obey His laws. Right now, our ministry is lead to help the poor and the orphans in China, a mission from the heart of God. The scripture above illustrates a beautiful truth.

Do you see that what God did for us He can do for anyone? Jesus took on the cross, sickness, disease, depression, oppression, our sins, EVEN debts and poverty. You can see that the cost of the law involved complete separation from God and all the blessings of Abraham required substitutional sacrifice for sins, holy and acceptable to God.

TODAY Christ is the perfect, holy, pure, redemptive sacrifice for all mankind! A scripture that comes to my mind is Ephesians 2: 10-13. Let's read it together:

Ephesians 2:10-14
Amplified Bible (AMP)
10 For we are God's [own] handiwork (His workmanship), [a]recreated in Christ Jesus, [born anew] that we may do those good works which God predestined (planned beforehand) for us [taking paths which He prepared ahead of time], that we should walk in them [living the good life which He prearranged and made ready for us to live].

11 Therefore, remember that at one time you were Gentiles (heathens) in the flesh, called Uncircumcision by those who called themselves Circumcision, [itself a [b]mere mark] in the flesh made by human hands.

12 [Remember] that you were at that time separated (living apart) from Christ [excluded from all part in Him], utterly estranged *and* outlawed from the rights of Israel as a nation, and strangers with no share in the sacred compacts of the [Messianic] promise [with no knowledge of or right in God's agreements, His covenants]. And you had no hope (no promise); you were in the world without God.

13 But now in Christ Jesus, you who once were [so] far away, through (by, in) the blood of Christ have been brought near.

**14 For He is [Himself] our peace (our bond of unity
and harmony). He has made us both [Jew and
Gentile] one [body], and has broken down (destroyed,
abolished) the hostile dividing wall between us,**

Dear friend, it does not matter where you were born or what religion you were raised with. Now all the above is for you and I. Hallelujah!! It is crystal clear that Christ Jesus is our champion. We just read that He made peace through the blood of His cross. By the way, the word peace in Hebrews has over 18 different meanings. Here they are as follows:

*Love, Joy, Peace, Long suffering, Kindness, Goodness,
Faithfulness, Gentleness, Self-control, The Blood,
Redemption, Sanctification, Restoration, Reconstruction,
Wholeness, Liberty, Destination, Heaven.*

RICHES

Dear reader, these 52 short chapters are written for one purpose only, to turn you around and bring you into God's prosperity and riches; mentally, physically, spiritually, emotionally, materially and financially. It's up to you. If you doubt and don't believe then put this book down and send this book back and you will be refunded. You deserve the best! God has a wonderful plan and purpose for your life.

Riches and Wealth

**Deuteronomy 8:18
King James Version (KJV)
18 But thou shalt remember the Lord thy God: for it is he that
giveth thee power to get wealth, that he may establish his
covenant which he sware unto thy fathers, as it is this day.**

1 Chronicles 29:12
King James Version (KJV)
¹² Both riches and honour come of thee, and thou reignest over all; and in thine hand is power and might; and in thine hand it is to make great, and to give strength unto all.

Proverbs 8:18-19
King James Version (KJV)
¹⁸ Riches and honour are with me; yea, durable riches and righteousness.

¹⁹ My fruit is better than gold, yea, than fine gold; and my revenue than choice silver.

Proverbs 22:4
King James Version (KJV)
⁴ By humility and the fear of the Lord are riches, and honour, and life.

Ecclesiastes 5:19
King James Version (KJV)
¹⁹ Every man also to whom God hath given riches and wealth, and hath given him power to eat thereof, and to take his portion, and to rejoice in his labour; this is the gift of God.

Isaiah 45:3
King James Version (KJV)
³ And I will give thee the treasures of darkness, and hidden riches of secret places, that thou mayest know that I, the Lord, which call thee by thy name, am the God of Israel.

2 Corinthians 8:9
King James Version (KJV)
⁹ **For ye know the grace of our Lord Jesus Christ, that, though he was rich, yet for your sakes he became poor, that ye through his poverty might be rich.**

Now let's do what Joshua 1: 8 says:

Joshua 1:8
King James Version (KJV)
⁸ **This book of the law shall not depart out of thy mouth; but thou shalt meditate therein day and night, that thou mayest observe to do according to all that is written therein: for then thou shalt make thy way prosperous, and then thou shalt have good success.**

We will take you from chapter to chapter, beginning here with chapter one. I am recommending you to read aloud, carefully and slowly until these words become revelation to your spirit so that you experience _Rhema_ knowledge. At the end of each chapter we are going to give you the opportunity to exercise what you have learned. This will enable you to become more proficient in declaring these statues. So that your mind will be renewed according to Romans 12:2:

Romans 12:2
Amplified Bible (AMP)
² **Do not be conformed to this world (this age), [fashioned after and adapted to its external, superficial customs], but be transformed (changed) by the [entire] renewal of your mind [by its new ideals and its new attitude], so that you may prove [for yourselves] what is the good and acceptable and perfect will of God, _even_ the thing which is good and acceptable and perfect [in His sight for you]**

We ask you to focus on the prayers and the scriptures that you have learned daily, 7 times in one week. They will help you to continue, in a devotional commitment, towards your 52-week journey for YOUR financial breakthrough. The first twelve days are designed to prepare the foundation of your journey. They are based on:

rules, provisions and promises to give you the benefits of God's laws.

It is crystal clear that God wants to bring correction to all of us, to eliminate the older ideas among Christians that God is against His children having material wealth for fear they will lose their souls. Many teach this and it is unscriptural. The Bible is full of records of God blessing men with prosperity - (Gen. 13:3-9; 26:12, 16; 33:11; 39:2-23; 41:40-44; I Kings 10:7; 2 Chron. 1:12' 9:22; 17:5; 3:27; Job 1:3; etc.). God has promised in both testaments, riches and blessings untold to those who will serve and obey Him (Lev. 26; Deut. 28; 29:9; Josh. 1:7-9; I Kings 2:3-4; I Chron. 20:20; 24:20; 26:5; Ps. 1:3; Prov. 10:22; I Cor. 16:1-2; II Cor. 8:9; 9:6-11; I Tim. 6:17; III John 2).

God, Himself, is the richest person in the universe; so, if it would be a sin to be rich then He would be the greatest sinner of all. The very streets of heaven are paved with gold. Jewels of all kinds garnish the foundations. The gates are solid pearls and every house is a mansion (John 14:1-3; Rev. 21). If God has promised us these things in the next life, why would it be a sin to have some of these things in this life? It should be clear to you that having wealth is not a sin, and the reason God's children are so poor is that they do not ask and receive as He has promised. Money is all right to have, and it is a great blessing that can be used to help God's work and others in their needs.

This is the purpose of asking God for prosperity. It is true that men are warned not to trust in riches and permit them to destroy their souls, but saved men can get victory over the wrong use of money as they can get victory over other sins (Ps. 62:10; Prov. 11:28; Luke 8:14; I Tim 6:17-19). Such warnings were not given to cause God's people to desire poverty in order to be saved, but rightly to regulate the right use of money when one is saved and is prospered.

God has provided abundance and has made no limitation to His children in getting all that they want in this life. But here we may say that what you need of this world's goods you should begin to pray for and believe the promises, and even before you get the laws of prosperity you can receive many benefits of this kind. Thousands of Christians are in total ignorance as to the Bible doctrine of power for believers. We want you to know the truth about this so that you can start, from the first of these 52 lessons, to get what you want from God and to get power over the devil. The Old Testament saints had great power and did great acts that are seldom heard of today among Christians. Abraham had power to heal a whole nation at one time (Gen. 20). Moses and Aaron did great wonders in Egypt (Ex. 7:10-11:10) and in the wilderness (Ex 15:22-26; Num. 11:2, 29-30; etc.). Moses healed the whole nation of Israel, and there was not a feeble one in all their tribes (Ps. 105:37; 107:20).

Joshua and many of the judges, kings and prophets did many signs and wonders by the power of God. For example, Elijah did fifteen miracles and Elisha did thirty, such as raising the dead, shutting the heavens against rain, bringing rain, calling fire from Heaven, dividing Jordan, healing people, helping people get out of debt, making iron to swim, and other kinds of miracles (I Kings 17:1-2; II Kings 13:21).

We are bringing many truths to you that you will seldom get in modern churches. We want you to know that everything that God ever promised to Christians is for you and that God has not changed. If there has been any change, it is on man's part. If you will accept truth as you can plainly read it in all of these Scriptures, you can help us give to the world a new type of Christianity that it has not seen since the days of the early church, except in a measure here and there.

We want you to know that you are receiving lessons that will wake up the Christian world. <u>Especially in the very sensitive area of money and finances</u>. When you get to know the next few lessons, which are not just the same old teachings that you can get in any book but are bible driven truths with a purpose that are new to modern Christians, you will begin as a believer, to enjoy these blessings to the fullest. You might say, "But all books on financing are more or less the same?" Well, stay tuned, we will make it clear to you in the forthcoming chapters.

TAKE TIME TO LOOK INSIDE

Scripture To Focus On:

Psalm 86:11
King James Version (KJV)
¹¹ Teach me thy way, O Lord; I will walk in thy truth: unite my heart to fear thy name.

Jesus always restored health and always gave (paid taxes, fed the people, cooked for his disciples). What do you do to maintain good health? How do you use your abundance for God's kingdom? We speak to God about health, relationships and finances and it seems like there is always a request before Him. Sometimes His answer takes a little longer than you expected.

How do you wait for His reply? Quietly? Pacing? Mumbling? Expectantly? Worrying? When we fail to love we break God's law. But when we love, God smiles. What have you done to make God smile? Share something good to others!

LESSON ONE

**Bible Purpose Driven
Daily Wisdom Key for Today:**

UNDERSTANDING AND OBEYING COVENANT RULES

**Verse to Remember: Galatians 3:13-14
Amplified Bible (AMP)**

13 Christ purchased our freedom [redeeming us] from the curse (doom) of the Law [and its condemnation] by [Himself] becoming a curse for us, for it is written [in the Scriptures], Cursed is everyone who hangs on a tree (is crucified);

14 To the end that through [their receiving] Christ Jesus, the blessing [promised] to Abraham might come upon the Gentiles, so that we through faith might [all] receive [the realization of] the promise of the [Holy] Spirit.

Question to Meditate On: Say this out loud:

TODAY IS MY TURNING POINT I CHOOSE TO AGREE WITH THE WORD OF GOD FOR ME.

Prayer of faith and recognition: Father, I thank you for making known, through your word, how I can prosper and be in health. I repent from going the world's way and chose to declare what you have already decreed for me. My needs are met and I'm out of debt and there is much more in the storehouse; in my Father's house. I ask You, Lord, to be my partner in all that I do and to guide my steps into new opportunities in work, which will bring your blessings my way mentally, physically, and financially so that I will have an abundant supply to extend to others so they too can fulfill YOUR purpose. In Jesus' name, amen!

LESSON TWO

3 John 1:2
King James Version (KJV)
**² Beloved, I wish above all things that thou mayest
prosper and be in health, even as thy soul prospereth.**

PROSPERITY FOR BODY, SOUL AND SPIRIT

Believe that it is God's will for you to prosper and that you are in His will. Contrary to common opinion, God wants you to be prosperous. If this is a fact, and it is, then God will see to it that you are prosperous if you will learn the laws of prosperity and co-operate with them and with God in all things. Why should it be God's will for you to lack the things you need in life if you are His child, and then give them to rebels against Him? This does not make sense, and until Christians wake up to believe the whole Bible and demand that their leaders teach the whole truth or quit, we will never see prosperity, happiness, and success among all Christians.

God has created in the world an abundance of everything that men need, and there is enough for all. He laid down certain laws of life and of prosperity and all He asks us to do is to obey these laws. These laws are plainly revealed in the Bible and they are given for all men to follow. Those who follow them will surely reap the benefits promised to all alike. God's providence is over all His creation and He has given abundant promises for all the needs of men. One cannot read all the many promises listed in the bible without being convinced that it is the highest will of God to bless His children with prosperity and all they need and want in life here and now. Let it be firmly settled then that you are in harmony with the will of God when you desire to prosper and be in health and have victory over sin and failure in life.

If you obey and think right and do right you will not fail in your life. Remember that all the wealth that God put on the earth is still on the earth and has not fallen out into space or vanished. I am hoping that you begin to catch on that God loves you so much that He gave up His only begotten Son to redeem mankind back to Himself and He wants to bestow upon you, His unlimited blessings until you cannot contain it any longer so that you will overflow and begin to touch other nations. Wouldn't you like that? Then continue to follow the way of the cross and follow the boss!

While you are meditating and prayerfully waiting on the Lord and listening to His voice begin to proclaim out loud and declare all His benefits that you will receive today through His word. Write them down and make a note of any revelations you receive here:

NOTES:

_____

_____

_____

_____

_____

_____

_____

_____

_____

_____

_____

_____

_____

_____

_____

_____

_____

_____

_____

_____

_____

_____

GETTING WHAT YOU WANT IN LIFE

Have you ever wanted something and got something else, a substitute? The more we get used to the substitutes the more we deny ourselves from getting what we really want. We don't get the right job that we really want. We do not finish the goals that we want to accomplish and we don't get to marry the one we really want, so we marry a substitute. We don't have enough finances for steak and lobster at dinner; so, we settle for less than the best. Our lives become full of substitutes.

So, you get sometimes what you chose, and if you think in terms of substitutes you become accustomed to saying things like "Oh, it doesn't matter, whatever" and you will settle for less every time. Go for what you want. You don't have to sell out anymore for the substitute. You can have what you want. Having what you want is being wealthy. Being wealthy is not being extravagant or wasteful. It is having exactly what you want for the present need and it includes health and wealth, which is prosperity and that is success.

Verse to remember:

Job 36:10-11
King James Version (KJV)
[10] He openeth also their ear to discipline, and commandeth that they return from iniquity.

[11] If they obey and serve him, they shall spend their days in prosperity, and their years in pleasures.

God has already, before the foundation of the world, preordained and predestined in His providence for the abundant promises for the needs of man. We must focus and believe that God says what He says and means what He means. Our purpose is to disprove the false and nonsensical theories in many modern churches that it is God's will for His children to suffer disease, sickness, poverty and lack every good thing in life so as to keep them humble and continue saved to the end.

All the promises of God reveal that He has provided for man here and now despite the curse. Every man can enjoy to the full all the benefits of these promises if he will but surrender his life to God and get the genuine new birth and live a godly life in this present world according to the gospel of Christ. Many of these things are even for the unsaved so as to prove to them that God provides for all creation in spite of their rebellion. The purpose of such goodness to the unsaved man is to lead him to repentance (Rom. 2:4) and preserve him until he either repents or rejects God for the last time and is cut off from all eternal hope in Hell.

If many of these things are for the unsaved, certainly all of them are for the saved. So why should Christians worry about which ones are for which class? Do the wise thing—get right with God and stay right with Him so there will be no need to question what God desires for you to have and how He wants you to be blessed in this life. This fact will be forever settled and we can go on to get ALL OF HIS PROMISES which are YES and AMEN.

GOD CREATED MAN IN HIS IMAGE & GAVE HIM THE KEYS TO BE THE LANDLORD

God created man that he might be prosperous, healthy, successful, happy, wise and blessed with all the good things that he could wish for in this life. He created all things and gave them all to man to use for his own good and pleasure. If it were sinful for man to have these things God would not have promised them for man to enjoy. The sin of man was not in being prosperous, healthy and happy, but it was in eating of the forbidden fruit. The world of abundance here and now proves that God wants man to have an abundance of all good things that are here. God made enough for all and every person can have all they want if they will follow certain laws to get what they need. What parent would not desire and will for all his children to have the best things of life and that in abundance? Is God less loving and good than man? Jesus said, "If ye then, being evil, know how to give good gifts unto your children; how much more shall your heavenly Father give good things to them that ask him?" (Mt. 7:7-11). Certainly, God will give every child of His what he wants.

The people that backslide when prosperous, healthy, and happy would backslide anyway, so if a few do backslide when God blesses them with prosperity, let us not lose faith in the abundant love and providence of God. We must all learn to live Christian lives under all conditions of life. Some people backslide over food, clothes and other things of life that we all must have. Shall we quit eating? Shall we go naked? Shall we quit doing every good thing in life that men backslide over? Shall we conclude that such things are not the will of God just because a few people backslide? Then do not argue this way about prosperity, health and the abundant blessings of life that God wants all His children to enjoy. Stay saved and use prosperity wisely to help others and God will bless you in greater abundance.

It is the trick of the devil to propagate false and slanderous ideas about God and His infinite Fatherhood in order to turn thousands of sane men away from such a God. If one will read the Bible he can see for himself that many of these false ideas of modern teachers are entirely unscriptural. The scripture abundantly promises everything to man that is good and legitimate and that would be for his best enjoyment. Note the following plain scriptures teaching that it is God's will for man to be blessed and have many things that the average church member has been led to believe are not for the child of God:

PROSPERITY DEMANDS WEALTH & MONEY WITHOUT IT YOU ARE CRIPPLED

This is what God said to Joshua in the beginning of his leadership and journey to the promised land and wealth:

Joshua 1:5-9
Amplified Bible (AMP)
5 No man shall be able to stand before you all the days of your life. As I was with Moses, so I will be with you; I will not fail you or forsake you.

6 Be strong (confident) and of good courage, for you shall cause this people to inherit the land which I swore to their fathers to give them.

7 Only you be strong and very courageous, that you may do according to all the law which Moses My servant commanded you. Turn not from it to the right hand or to the left, that you may prosper wherever you go.

8 This Book of the Law shall not depart out of your mouth, but you shall meditate on it day and night, that you may observe *and* do according to all that is written in it. For then you shall make your way prosperous, and then you shall deal wisely *and* have good [a]success.

9 Have not I commanded you? Be strong, vigorous, and very courageous. Be not afraid, neither be dismayed, for the Lord your God is with you wherever you go.

"The Lord maketh poor, and maketh rich: he bringeth low, and lifteth up. He raiseth up the poor out of the dust, and lifteth up the beggar from the dunghill, to set them among princes, and to make them inherit the throne of glory" (1 Sam. 2:7-8); "And keep the charge of the Lord thy God, to walk in his ways . . . that thou mayest prosper in all that thou doest, and whithersoever thou turnest thyself" (1 Ki. 2:3-4); "Both riches and honour come of thee, and thou reignest over all; and in thine hand is power and might; and in thine hand it is to make great, and to give strength to all" (1 Chron. 29:12); "The hand of our God is upon all them for good that seek Him: but his power and his wrath is against them that forsake him" (Ezra 8:22); "If they obey and serve him, they shall spend their days in prosperity, and their years in pleasures" (Job 36:11); "Blessed is the man that walketh not in the counsel of the ungodly, nor standeth in the way of sinners, nor sitteth in the seat of the scornful. But his delight is in the law of the Lord; and in his law doth he meditate day and night. And he shall be like a tree planted by the rivers of water, that bringeth forth his fruit in his season; his leaf also shall not wither; and whatsoever he doeth shall prosper (Ps. 1:1-3).

In Deuteronomy alone, according to the Fenton translation, the word "prosper" is used many times in place of "well with thee," as in the King James Version (Deut. 5:16, 29, 33; 6:3, 18; 12:28; 19:13). In Deut. 30:15 this translation reads, "I put before you today life, and prosperity, and sin, and death." Thus, prosperity is promised if men will quit the sin business. It is true sinners sometimes prosper, but they generally get rich through wrong dealings with their fellow men (Ps. 73).

PRINCIPLES FOR THOSE WHO
TEACH A POVERTY GOSPEL

Those who teach that the Christians should be poor, sickly and suffering all their days would naturally argue that these passages are in the Old Testament and refer to those under the Law of Moses, but we reply, we are under a better covenant and have greater and better promises in the New Testament; so, if these things were promised under the Old Covenant, they are for us in a greater way under the New Covenant. In 2 Cor. 3:6-15 Paul argues that the glory and blessings of the Old Covenant were not as great as those under the New Covenant; so, if men could get prosperity under the Old, then it is certain they can get it under the New Covenant.

In Hebrews Paul argues that the New Covenant is a "better testament . . . established upon better promises" (Heb. 7:22; 8:6) and that the law was a "shadow of good things to come" (Heb. 10:1); so if a mere shadow produced prosperity, how much more will the realities of the New Covenant do the same? Apart from this argument there are plain promises in the New Testament concerning prosperity: "What things soever ye desire, when ye pray, believe that ye receive them, and ye shall have them" (Mk. 11:22-24); "Ask, and it shall be given you . . . For everyone that asketh receiveth . . . If ye then, being evil, know how to give good gifts to your children; how much more shall your Father, which is in heaven, give good things to them that ask him?" (Mt. 7:7-11); "For after all these things [good things of life] do the Gentiles seek: for your heavenly Father knoweth that ye have need of all these things. But seek ye first the kingdom of God, and his righteousness; and all these things shall be added unto you" (Mt. 6:31-33); "He that soweth sparingly shall reap also sparingly; and he which soweth bountifully shall reap also bountifully . . . God is able to make all grace abound toward you; that ye, always having all sufficiency in all things, may abound to every good work" (2 Cor. 9:6-8); "But my God shall supply all your need according to his riches in glory by Christ Jesus" (Phil. 4:19); "If ye abide in me, and my words abide in you, ye shall ask what ye will, and it shall be done unto you" (Jn. 15:7, 16); "Beloved, I wish above all things that thou mayest prosper and be in health, even as thy soul prospereth" (3 Jn. 2).

What could be more clear? How could God express His highest will any other way? Why should we limit God and His bountifulness to us just because we fear we may backslide? Why not make up our minds that we will watch any danger of riches and prosperity and act sensibly with what God blesses us with? Why not use it for God's glory and the good of others and there will be no limitation concerning blessings?

LESSON TWO

Bible Purpose Driven
Daily Wisdom Key for Today:

PROSPERITY FOR BODY, SOUL AND SPIRIT

Verse to Remember: III John 1:2
King James Version (KJV)
**2 Beloved, I wish above all things that thou mayest
prosper and be in health, even as thy soul prospereth.**

Question to Meditate On: Now that you have completed the
second day, step out by faith and open the door of your room
and say this prayer out loud............

Prayer of Agreement: In Jesus name sickness, diseases and
poverty and false wants you're not welcome or allowed in my life
anymore: take a hike! get to flight, you are no longer my plight,
I chose to do what's right in God's sight. Blessings, prosperity,
wonder no more. You are welcome here in my life for evermore.
In Jesus' name, Amen.

PLEASE REPEAT THIS PRAYER 3 TIMES UNTIL
IT SINKS INTO YOUR BODY, MIND & SOUL.

(Congratulations, you have completed your second
chapter and we believe that God is going to give you
incredible peace as you continue to walk by faith.)

LESSON THREE

John 15:7
Amplified Bible (AMP)
7 If you live in Me [abide vitally united to Me] and My words remain in you *and* continue to live in your hearts, ask whatever you will, and it shall be done for you.

MAKE GOD YOUR PARTNER IN YOUR LIFE

In everything that you do, in every breath that you take, walk with HIM and do not lean to the left or the right. Work with Him, abide and obey in His laws of prosperity. Make Him the Senior Partner in your business. Give him the seat at the head of the table in all your business conferences. Recognize Him in all that you do. Keep in touch with Him concerning His guidance in every business deal. Recognize His presence with you always. Talk to Him about your problems as you would talk to your best friend. Turn all your problems over to Him. Do not make a move without feeling sure that it is the will of God and for the best interest of all concerned. Remember the words in:

1 Peter 5:7
Amplified Bible (AMP)
7 Casting the [a]whole of your care [all your anxieties, all your worries, all your concerns, [b]once and for all] on Him, for He cares for you affectionately *and* cares about you [c]watchfully.

If you will give all your hard problems to God to solve; if you will simply stop fretting and worrying over them and trust God with all your heart to work out things to His glory and for your good, He will do it. After turning things over to God to handle them for you, don't interfere and spoil things. Stay out of them until God works them out. Do not be impatient and unbelieving. If God is your Senior Partner and He is running your business, trust Him, for it could not be operating by anyone better. Since you believe that God can handle all your problems better than you can, let Him do it. He will remove all obstacles. He will work for your good. Believe His Word that "all things work together for good to them that love the Lord, to them who are called according to his purposes (Rom. 8:28)." Since, God cannot fail, you cannot fail if you keep all things committed to Him and trust Him to keep you and make you a success in every area of your life.

PROMISES TO WIN

God never meant for His children to become failures, as such failures are a reflection upon Him, just as any failing, sinful, and rebellious child would bring disgrace upon his parents. God is no different than any other father. He doesn't glory in the failure of His children. He is not abnormal. He does not desire the worst for His children instead of the best. Is He the only Father that gets pleasure in the failures of his children? No! Jesus taught us that God loved us more than we love our own children (Matt 7:7-11).

We are the only ones that hold back the floodgates of God's abundant blessing; and, as long as we believe that God is a hard, unloving Father, we cannot hope to receive these benefits. The truth is that nothing makes God happier than to see His people blessed, happy and successful in all that they do in life. Let it be remembered that we said *His children*, not rebels against Him, for they are children of the devil (John 8:44; Eph. 2:1-3; I John 3:8-10). Real children of God will not get into any business that is sinful. So, we say that any legitimate business and anything that is worthwhile, God will prosper in this phase of life.

Making God your partner implies full surrender of your life to Him and obedience to His Word daily and in all things. It requires a total dependence upon God to know His will and the ways that would cause you to prosper. Without God's approval and God's help, you are already headed for failure, but with Him guiding you at every step you cannot fail! Be sure that your plans, ambitions and your undertakings are all in harmony with the best will of God and then go ahead, fearing nothing.

If you want to overcome the obstacles that have been holding you back, start right now to take God into your life and obey Him and He will lead you into prosperity. Right where you leave off your self-efforts and stop leaving God out of your life, right there, you will begin to experience God and His life, His wisdom. His power will begin to be manifest all around you. Christ came to give life and give it more abundantly, so there is no limitation in God unless you limit Him by your unbelief and failure to appropriate the promised benefits. Think about this scripture for your breakthrough and meditate on it:

John 10:10
Amplified Bible (AMP)
[10] The thief comes only in order to steal and kill and destroy. I came that they may have *and* enjoy life, and have it in abundance (to the full, till it [a]overflows).

WORD OF PROPHESY AND ENCOURAGEMENT

Creativity is an expression of wisdom – let's read:

Proverbs 8:22
Amplified Bible (AMP)
22 The Lord formed *and* brought me [Wisdom] forth at
the beginning of His way, before His acts of old.

James 1:5
Amplified Bible (AMP)
5 If any of you is deficient in wisdom, let him
ask of [a]the giving God [Who gives] to everyone
liberally *and* ungrudgingly, without reproaching
or faultfinding, and it will be given him.

Proverbs 2:3-6
Amplified Bible (AMP)
3 Yes, if you cry out for insight and raise
your voice for understanding,

4 If you seek [Wisdom] as for silver and search for
skillful *and* godly Wisdom as for hidden treasures,

5 Then you will understand the reverent *and* worshipful fear
of the Lord and find the knowledge of [our omniscient] God.

6 For the Lord gives skillful *and* godly Wisdom; from
His mouth come knowledge and understanding.

NOW IF WE ARE SERIOUS ABOUT INCREASING OUR
CREATIVITY, WE SOULD NOT ONLY ASK FOR WISDOM
BUT ALSO CRY OUT FOR IT.

The <u>ultimate source of wisdom</u> is the scriptures. The more we study, memorize and meditate on them, the greater foundation we will have for true creative ideas for financial breakthrough and for every need of our lives and the life to come.

10 POINT PERSONAL EVALUATION YOU CAN USE TO DETERMINE WHERE YOU ARE AT, SO YOU CAN START MOVING IN THE RIGHT DIRECTION TOWARDS YOUR SUCCESS.

How creative are you?

- Do you have the power to conquer the temptations Satan brings to you?
- Do you thank God for times of suffering and rejoice in them?
- Do you acknowledge your weaknesses to the Lord in order to experience His power?
- Do you cultivate wise thoughts by meditating on Scripture day and night?
- Do you find creative ways to encourage members of your family?
- Do you spend time in planning strategies to effectively present the Gospel?
- Do you seek to motivate others to carry out good works?
- Do you look at obstacles as hindrances or opportunities for creative solutions?
- Do you conquer boredom by finding new and challenging ways to do things?
- Does a lack of results motivate you to try a new and better method?

GET INTO THE LIFE WORK THAT YOU FEEL GOD WOULD HAVE YOU IN OR THAT FOR WHICH YOU ARE BEST SUITED.

God has a lifework for you and you can be extremely happy and successful if you find that work and then make God your life-long partner. If your life's work is not clear to you then get this settled once and forever. At least you can know what your present work is and if ever there comes a time when your work should be changed, you will move in the will of God, as you have been doing. As you go along, God will guide you and open up doors of opportunity for you to step into. You are capable of filling your own place in life and you can do your work better than anyone else can.

Put your whole life into your work, realizing it is for God and others that you do your work. The thing God considers is, not our success but, whether we work honestly and faithfully at our calling in life. This is all that He asks and then He will begin to reward us accordingly. Real happiness lies in genuinely liking to do what we do as an occupation, not in doing what we think we would like to do or should do because somebody said so. You can be very unhappy if you realize, upon taking inventory, that you are in the wrong kind of life work. Thousands of people are even in the right kind of work and are unhappy because they yearn for the wrong kind of work. Being in the right kind of work, work that is fulfilling and satisfying, should make it clear to you that that type of work is what will suit you.

When plans do not materialize or when doors close for you in one occupation, look to God, who will open doors for you in another. Hallelujah. Become content with your lot and make a success of what you are doing and then you will be capable of success in other ways. On the other hand, if you do not make a success at any one thing and are always dissatisfied with every kind of work, it is not the work that is wrong. It is you who may have the problem. You must get a hold of yourself and conquer that shiftless spirit and God will help you become stable, content, successful and happy in His will, in any kind of honest work. An honest day equals a honest pay.

Ask God to guide you into your lifework and in His best plan for you. Talk things over with Him and wait for His guidance, which will come in many ways you may not at first understand. If you are in the right work, seek God in order to open up even greater fields of service. If you are in the wrong work, much prayer will open the right door for you. Be constantly in tune with God and praise Him for His help in life. Thank Him for the work you already have. Act as if God is guiding you. Be happy and contented in your work, and you will be a success. Also remember that, without faith it is impossible to please God (Heb. 11:6).

LESSON THREE

Bible Purpose Driven
Daily Wisdom Key for Today:

MAKE GOD YOUR PARTNER IN YOUR LIFE

Verse to Remember: John 15:7
Amplified Bible (AMP)
**7 If you live in Me [abide vitally united to Me] and My
words remain in you *and* continue to live in your hearts,
ask whatever you will, and it shall be done for you.**

Question to Meditate On: We highly recommend you to go into the closet and shut the door behind you and pray to the Father in secret and God will reward you in the open. Be specific and be clear in your prayer to Him and you will see and watch God work for you. Even in the same day, God will guarantee you results. (Matthew 6:6). Now go forward and activate your faith. Remember to PRAY and PLAY not PLAY and then PRAY.

Congratulations, you have completed your third lesson. Now, shout 3 HALLELUJAH's out loud.

LESSON FOUR

1 John 5:4
Amplified Bible (AMP)
⁴ For whatever is born of God is victorious over the world;
and this is the victory that conquers the world, even our faith.

HAVING FAITH THAT CANNOT FAIL

You must believe that God loves you and that He is with you, giving you strength to overcome all hindrances to your happiness and success in life. All men who have made a success in life have had to overcome ALL opposition to their progress. The lives of successful people abound in stories of how they overcame obstacles and finally succeeded. This life of overcoming obstacles will continue through life even in success and happiness. It is in such struggles in life that you need faith in God. All your obstacles are small and shrink to nothingness when compared to the PROMISES of God and the faith in God which they create.

When your troubles seem like giants, steal away always in secret prayer. Get a good night's rest. Read the promises of God and have faith in God and they will become very small. If your problems persist, get your mind off them and turn them over to God. Forget them for the time being and you will find that God will take care of your concerns better than you ever could. We are told in:

Psalm 37:5
Amplified Bible (AMP)
⁵ **Commit your way to the Lord [roll and repose each care of your load on Him]; trust (lean on, rely on, and be confident) also in Him and He will bring it to pass.**

This law of success will work without fail because God's Word cannot fail. The more you do this and the less you think of the hindrances in your life the more you will overcome them. God is your Father, if you have surrendered to Him, He can be trusted. He will keep His promises better than any earthly friend will. Allow His promises to abide in you as you abide in Him and then:

John 15:7
Amplified Bible (AMP)
⁷ **If you live in Me [abide vitally united to Me] and My words remain in you *and* continue to live in your hearts, ask whatever you will, and it shall be done for you.**

What a blessing to know that God is with you and that by faith in Him you can do all things and can get what you want! Your enemies cannot triumph. Your problems cannot defeat you. God cannot fail. The minute you are tempted to worry and fret about some problem, turn it over to God. He can see further than you can. He can work out things that are invisible to you. Throw your worries away and become wreckless in faith and confident in God and accept what comes with peace and thankfulness.

Psalm 1:1-6
Amplified Bible (AMP)

Book One

Psalm 1[a]

¹ Blessed (happy, fortunate, prosperous, and enviable) is the man who walks *and* lives not in the counsel of the ungodly [following their advice, their plans and purposes], nor stands [submissive and inactive] in the path where sinners walk, nor sits down [to relax and rest] where the scornful [and the mockers] gather.

² But his delight *and* desire are in the law of the Lord, and on His law (the precepts, the instructions, the teachings of God) he habitually meditates (ponders and studies) by day and by night.

³ And he shall be like a tree firmly planted [and tended] by the streams of water, ready to bring forth its fruit in its season; its leaf also shall not fade *or* wither; and everything he does shall prosper [and come to maturity].

⁴ Not so the wicked [those disobedient and living without God are not so]. But they are like the chaff [worthless, dead, without substance] which the wind drives away.

⁵ Therefore the wicked [those disobedient and living without God] shall not stand [justified] in the judgment, nor [b]sinners in the congregation of the righteous [those who are upright and in right standing with God].

⁶ For the Lord knows *and* is fully acquainted with the way of the righteous, but the way of the ungodly [those living outside God's will] shall perish (end in ruin and come to nought).

Psalm 37:23
Amplified Bible (AMP)
²³ **The steps of a [good] man are directed *and***
established by the Lord when He delights in his way
[and He busies Himself with his every step].

YOU MUST EXERCISE YOUR FAITH

By exercising your faith you will cause it to grow.

Romans 1:17
'For in it the righteousness of God is revealed from faith
to faith; as it is written, "The just shall live by faith."

One of the best secrets of how to increase faith is for the person to begin using the faith he already has. For instance, Jack LaLanne began to build his body up 60 years ago. He went from a skinny guy to an incredible body-builder and he became a legend. While he was working everyday to build his strength, he used faith, day after day, to become a great leader and a champion. It took days of hard work, persistence and a 'never-give-up attitude' to build his muscles.

Faith is God's muscle into our very lives. There should never be a doubt about receiving from God. If a believer will see to it that he has faith without doubting and questioning anything about the answers. The answer is part of God's work, and why should mere man worry so much about the phase of answered prayer, leave all such worry to God who is responsible for such answers and who WILL ANSWER if true faith is exercised by men. Man's part is to ask and simply believe and refuse to doubt after prayer to the Lord. Again, leave all such worry to God who is responsible for the answer and who will answer if true faith is exercised by men.

GOD NEVER REBUKES FAITH

Man's part is to ask and believe and then refuse to doubt. If a man will take care of his part of the program, God will take care of His part and there will be no failure. When man begins to meddle in God's business, the answering part, then God lets him sweat. God leaves him alone until he takes care of his own part in the deal, then the answer is granted. If the law of faith is that no answer is granted until all doubting, fear, worry, unbelief and questioning cease let it be settled once and for all. God is not going to break His law to please some whining wimps and unbelievers who look more to criticism of God for not answering than to his praise and promises for the answer.

Let those who want answers cease from worry about how and when God is going to carry it out his part of the contract. Permit God to run His own business in His own way and time. Be patient and faithful to God until He does answer. Jesus says in:

Luke 18:1
Amplified Bible (AMP)
18 Also [Jesus] told them a parable to the effect that they ought always to pray and not to [a] turn coward (faint, lose heart, and give up).

KNOW THE WORD OF GOD AND OBEY IT

The second step in getting faith is to get totally familiar with the word of God.

Romans 10:17
Amplified Bible (AMP)
[17] So faith comes by hearing [what is told], and what is heard comes by the preaching [of the message that came from the lips] of Christ (the Messiah Himself).

Acts 10:44
Amplified Bible (AMP)
[44] While Peter was still speaking these words, the Holy Spirit fell on all who were listening to the message.

Acts 15:7
Amplified Bible (AMP)
[7] And after there had been a long debate, Peter got up and said to them, Brethren, you know that quite a while ago God made a choice *or* selection from among you, that by my mouth the Gentiles should hear the message of the Gospel [concerning the [a]attainment through Christ of salvation in the kingdom of God] and believe (credit and place their confidence in it).

After getting into Christ the next thing to do is to start reading the word of God and meditating on it day and night. We are promised that if a person will do this: He will be like a tree planted by the rivers of water that will bring forth its fruit in due season and that whatsoever he doeth shall prosper.

Joshua 1:1-8
Amplified Bible (AMP)
[1] After the death of Moses the servant of the Lord, the Lord said to Joshua son of Nun, Moses' minister,

[2] Moses My servant is dead. So now arise [take his place], go over this Jordan, you and all this people, into the land which I am giving to them, the Israelites.

[3] Every place upon which the sole of your foot shall tread, that have I given to you, as I promised Moses.

[4] From the wilderness and this Lebanon to the great river Euphrates—all the land of the [a]Hittites [Canaan]—and to the Great [Mediterranean] Sea on the west shall be your territory.

5 No man shall be able to stand before you all the days of your life. As I was with Moses, so I will be with you; I will not fail you or forsake you.

6 Be strong (confident) and of good courage, for you shall cause this people to inherit the land which I swore to their fathers to give them.

7 Only you be strong and very courageous, that you may do according to all the law which Moses My servant commanded you. Turn not from it to the right hand or to the left, that you may prosper wherever you go.

8 This Book of the Law shall not depart out of your mouth, but you shall meditate on it day and night, that you may observe *and* do according to all that is written in it. For then you shall make your way prosperous, and then you shall deal wisely *and* have good [h]success.

So many people, in praying, never think about what God says about what they are asking. If one should ask the average person what promise of God that he was depending on as the basis of his faith, to get what he was asking, he would not have in mind any particular scripture. It is no wonder that such people are seldom heard of God. As we saw prior, Jesus said in:

John 15:7
Amplified Bible (AMP)
7 If you live in Me [abide vitally united to Me] and My words remain in you *and* continue to live in your hearts, ask whatever you will, and it shall be done for you.

The word of God and prayer are to go together if definite results are to be expected. There are no grounds for answered prayer outside of the word of God. It is the bible that reveals what God says on ALL things and promises certain benefits through

Christ and by faith. No man can get prayers answered normally who does not know the truth. Jesus declares,

John 17:17
Amplified Bible (AMP)
[17] Sanctify them [purify, consecrate, separate them for Yourself, make them holy] by the Truth; Your Word is Truth.

Finally, 7 POINTS TO GET GREAT FAITH

1. Get into Christ.
2. Know the word of God.
3. Have faith only in God.
4. Listen to good preaching.
5. Reject all bad teaching.
6. Obey the word of God.
7. Yield to the Holy Spirit.

Faith is not only natural ability or exercise of the creative faculty of man, but it is the fruit of the Spirit and a gift from God.

Galatians 5:22-23
Amplified Bible (AMP)
[22] But the fruit of the [Holy] Spirit [the work which His presence within accomplishes] is love, joy (gladness), peace, patience (an even temper, forbearance), kindness, goodness (benevolence), faithfulness,

[23] Gentleness (meekness, humility), self-control (self-restraint, continence). Against such things there is no law [[a]that can bring a charge].

1 Corinthians 12:4-11
Amplified Bible (AMP)

[4] Now there are distinctive varieties *and* distributions of endowments (gifts, [a]extraordinary powers distinguishing certain Christians, due to the power of divine grace operating in their souls by the Holy Spirit) and they vary, but the [Holy] Spirit remains the same.

[5] And there are distinctive varieties of service *and* ministration, but it is the same Lord [Who is served].

[6] And there are distinctive varieties of operation [of working to accomplish things], but it is the same God Who inspires *and* energizes them all in all.

[7] But to each one is given the manifestation of the [Holy] Spirit [the evidence, the spiritual illumination of the Spirit] for good *and* profit.

[8] To one is given in *and* through the [Holy] Spirit [the power to speak] a message of wisdom, and to another [the power to express] a word of knowledge *and* understanding according to the same [Holy] Spirit;

[9] To another [[b]wonder-working] faith by the same [Holy] Spirit, to another the extraordinary powers of healing by the one Spirit;

[10] To another the working of miracles, to another prophetic insight ([c]the gift of interpreting the divine will and purpose); to another the ability to discern *and* distinguish between [the utterances of true] spirits [and false ones], to another various kinds of [unknown] tongues, to another the ability to interpret [such] tongues.

¹¹ All these [gifts, achievements, abilities] are inspired *and* brought to pass by one and the same [Holy] Spirit, Who apportions to each person individually [exactly] as He chooses.

When a man uses his own powers of faith in God and His word properly he makes contact with God in a supernatural way and he becomes a partaker of the divine nature and of His promises.

LESSON FOUR

**Bible Purpose Driven
Daily Wisdom Key for Today:**

HAVING FAITH THAT CANNOT FAIL

**Verse to Remember:1 John 5:4
Amplified Bible (AMP)
⁴ For whatever is born of God is victorious over the world;
and this is the victory that conquers the world, even our faith.**

Question to Meditate On: CONGRATULATIONS, SAY OUT LOUD 3 TIMES – HALLELUJAH, HALLELUJAH, HALLELUJAH,

Focus on this prayer this week:

I have the faith to rebuke every mountain of darkness and to rebuild the mountain of prosperity and blessing of God which is coming down into my life, ministry, job, financing and every area of my needs. In Jesus' name, amen.

LESSON FIVE

1 Thessalonians 4:11-12
Amplified Bible (AMP)
¹¹ To make it your ambition *and* definitely endeavor to live quietly *and* peacefully, to mind your own affairs, and to work with your hands, as we charged you,

¹² So that you may bear yourselves becomingly *and* be correct *and* honorable *and* command the respect of the outside world, being dependent on nobody [self-supporting] *and* having need of nothing.

FOLLOW BUSINESS PRINCIPLES TAUGHT IN SCRIPTURE

Paul laid down some business principles when he said, "Let love be without dissimulation. Abhor that which is evil; cleave to that which is good. Be kindly affectionate one to another with brotherly love; in honour preferring one another; not slothful in business; fervent in spirit; serving the Lord; rejoicing in hope; patient in tribulation; continuing instant in prayer; distributing to the necessity of saints; given to hospitality; bless them which persecute you; bless, and curse not; rejoice with them that do rejoice, and weep with them that weep...Be not wise in your own conceits. Recompense to no man evil for evil. Provide things honest in the sight of all men...Be not overcome of evil, but overcome evil with good" (Rom. 12:9-21). If one will obey these principles in business he cannot help becoming happy, prosperous, and successful in all that he undertakes.

Solomon said, "See thou a man diligent in business? He shall stand before kings; he shall not stand before mean [obscure, or unknown] men" (Prov. 22:29). These passages teach that a man should be constantly at the job of making a success. Do not let any grass grow under your feet. Use every legitimate means and opportunity to make and be successful and do not neglect even one opportunity to reach your goal. This may mean self-sacrifice to begin with. It will mean many hours of hard work. It will mean much prayer to God for guidance. It will mean being honest with all men and living to serve others by your business.

Some people do not care to succeed in life enough to obey the laws of prosperity. They are naturally shiftless, careless, indifferent, and unconcerned about their responsibilities.

They would not put forth the least effort, beyond what they feel like doing, in order to succeed. They are like sinners who know that they are lost and doomed to hell and who do not care. Or they are like some sick people who know how to get well but will not put forth the effort to meet the necessary conditions to get healing. If sinners cared whether they go to hell or not, not one of them would neglect his salvation for even one minute. So, would some men succeed in life if they cared to put forth the best effort that is in them to make a success? If you do not put forth the proper effort to prosper, do not expect God to bless you with prosperity.

DO NOT BE AFRAID TO LAUNCH OUT INTO NEW VENTURES AND MAKE THE BEST OF OPPORTUNITIES THAT COME

Proverbs 19:15
Amplified Bible (AMP)
¹⁵ Slothfulness casts one into a deep sleep,
and the idle person shall suffer hunger.

Many men could have been prosperous in life if they had not been afraid to take hold of opportunities that came to them. Have no fear. If you have been praying for things to happen that would cause you to be prosperous, God is sure to open up many doors of opportunity. You must not be afraid to enter into opportunities while under the guidance of God. Have confidence in yourself and know that God is leading you to success.

As you enter into new ventures, be led of God. Ask Him how far you should go and how much you must invest. Do not go into debt beyond your ability to pay. Do not become wreckless and act unwisely. Be led of God and go as far as you feel He would have you to go and as far as common sense dictates. Do not focus your eyes on sudden riches; be careful to not over-step yourself. You can always develop a steady and healthy business.

Your business will be secure and better than blowing a bubble beyond the bursting point. We have seen throughout the recent decades, men and women in business who have made this mistake and have had the 'bubble' burst just when things seemed nearly invincible for them. For some it was the 'dot-com' bubble, for others the 'real estate bubble' and even the 'monetary crisis' in the Asian countries. These people were not praying and asking God to lead them. Instead, they were being led by their own greed and desire to acquire. In each crisis, it created a greater problem than what existed before and caused economic damage to the nations, families and regions in which they did business. That is why you and I should be willing to ask God to lead us in the area of business, because our decisions affect so many more people than just you and I. Act sensibly and wisely and you will succeed. Let the law of increase work for you normally. Stay within your ability to take care of business and build on a solid foundation that will last, HIS FOUNDATION!

ALL MANNER OF BUSINESS INVOLVEMENTS MUST BE ON A SOLID FOUNDATION

Obey the Golden Rule. This means that you will always do unto others, as you would have them do unto you. If you do this you will never take advantage of any man in order to prosper. You will always be fair and square in all of your business dealings, giving your customers value for money received. You will never skimp in making products or cheat in selling them. You will never misrepresent one item you sell or service you perform. You will not put off on the public what you would not use. You will never be dishonest to any man. You will always tell the truth. You will never be selfish. You will always be friendly, courteous, helpful, happy and consecrated to serve your fellowmen and to please God. You will always let your customers know how much you appreciate their business and show them how you seek to be of service to them.

In more simple terms, you must be a real human being and make people feel that they would like to be around you. You can be that kind of man or woman. No matter what your age, appearance, education or position in life, you can be real and attractive in your personality. If you will let Christ live in and through you, He will make you free from all dullness and will fill your life with charm and influence. Power and radiance come from a change of heart and from Christ's living in you. Regardless of age, one can have charm, attractiveness or influence. These qualities cannot be put on in the beauty parlor. They must come from the inward man. It is all right to be as attractive as you can be outwardly and this will help you, however, scripture says:

1 Peter 3:4
Amplified Bible (AMP)
4 But let it be the inward adorning *and* beauty of the hidden person of the heart, with the incorruptible *and* unfading charm of a gentle and peaceful spirit, which [is not anxious or wrought up, but] is very precious in the sight of God.

SEEK YE FIRST THE KINGDOM OF GOD, AND HIS RIGHTEOUSNESS

If we do this we are promised in the word:

Matthew 6:33
Amplified Bible (AMP)
33 But seek ([a]aim at and strive after) first of all His kingdom and His righteousness ([b]His way of doing and being right), and then all these things [c] taken together will be given you besides.

The truth is that, by doing this, this puts the interests of the Kingdom of God and of others before our own. In doing this, we must recognize that a man's life does not consist in the abundance of the things he possesses (Luke 12:15). If we can ever learn this lesson, we can easily be free from covetousness which makes us selfish and self-centered so that we live only for self. Jesus said:

Matthew 10:39 (Amplified Bible)
[39] Whoever finds his [[a]lower] life will lose it [the
higher life], and whoever loses his [lower] life
on My account will find it [the higher life].

In other words, the man that will be so selfish as to hold on
to those things of life to please self and satisfy only self, will
lose the reality of true living and will be banished from eternal
society where everyone consecrates himself like God to do
those things that are for the best of all in society. But if we will
give up our selfish living and seek first the Kingdom of God
and His righteousness, we will receive a hundredfold in this
life and in the life to come, everlasting life. That is assured us
by Christ Himself

Matthew 19:27-30
Amplified Bible (AMP)
[27] Then Peter answered Him, saying, Behold, we have left
[our] all and have become [a]Your disciples [sided with Your
party and followed You]. What then shall we receive?

[28] Jesus said to them, Truly I say to you, in the new age [the
[b]Messianic rebirth of the world], when the Son of Man shall
sit down on the throne of His glory, you who have [become
My disciples, sided with My party and] followed Me will also
sit on twelve thrones and judge the twelve tribes of Israel.

[29] And anyone *and* everyone who has left houses or
brothers or sisters or father or mother or children or
lands for My name's sake will receive [c]many [even a
hundred] times more and will inherit eternal life.

[30] But many who [now] are first will be last [then],
and many who [now] are last will be first [then].

WE WERE BORN TO SERVE EACH OTHER

Giving up self-interests for those of the kingdom of God means consecration to living for the good of all men and the betterment of the society of which we are a part. We are a part of society now, and we cannot cease being a part of it. If everyone would live for the best good of all concerned, we would have a Heaven on Earth. Paul said,

Romans 14:7-11
"For none of us liveth to himself, and no man dieth to himself. For whether we live, we live unto the Lord; and whether we die, we die unto the Lord: whether we live therefore, or die, we are the Lord's. For to this end Christ both died, and rose, and revived, that he might be Lord both of the dead and living. But why dost thou judge thy brother? Or why dost thou set at naught thy brother? For we shall all stand before the judgment seat of Christ. For it is written, As I live, saith the Lord, every knee shall bow to me, and every tongue shall confess to God"

LESSON FIVE

FOLLOW CERTAIN BUSINESS PRINCIPLES TAUGHT IN SCRIPTURE

Verse to Remember: I Thessalonians 4:11-12
"That ye study to be quiet, and to do your own business,
and work with your own hands, as we commanded
you: that ye may walk honestly toward them that are
without, and that ye may have lack of nothing"

Question to Meditate: By faith begin to confess and say this out loud 3 times:

HALLELUJAH, HALLELUJAH, HALLELUJAH,
I AM OUT OF DEBT AND POVERTY AND IN
GOD'S WEALTH AND THERE IS MUCH MORE
WHERE IT CAME FROM, THE STOREHOUSE – MY
FATHER'S HOUSE, IN JESUS' NAME, AMEN.

LESSON SIX

Genesis 1:1
Amplified Bible (AMP)
¹ In the beginning God (prepared, formed, fashioned,
and) created the heavens and the earth.

WE HAVE BEEN INSPIRED BY GOD TO BE CREATIVE

That includes you and I because, in creation, God created all of us and in His wisdom, He gave US wisdom to create, rebuild and restore. Of course, we know that everything comes from God and we are not questioning that. Only God can and has brought into being that which previously did not exist. In fact, Genesis 1:1 declares that it is only He who creates and no other.

But we must be careful not to neglect the fact that God gave Adam the keys and made him the landlord to rule the earth. We see that the Hebrew word 'bara', used in Genesis 1:1 to refers to creation out of nothing, also has a different significance. In addition to carrying the meaning of absolute creation, the word means "to renew", "to produce" or "to do something new".

In all of these places the ideas of newness, productivity and forming are fundamental. And it is just those ideas that, in part, adhere to the modern English usage of the word "creativity." To speak of a Counselor, Preacher, President, Governor, Engineer, Doctor and many more as 'being creative' means that they have the ability to produce new forms, concepts, etc., out of previously existing ones. We learn from Solomon who spoke to the Lord and said, "Lord, I am a young boy and I need wisdom." And the Lord replied:

I Kings 3:11-12
'Then God said to him: "Because you have asked this thing, and have not asked long life for yourself, nor have asked riches for yourself, nor have asked the life of your enemies, but have asked for yourself understanding to discern justice, behold, I have done according to your words; see, I have given you a wise and understanding heart, so that there has not been anyone like you before you, nor shall any like you arise after you."

We see from the scripture that God gave Solomon the ability to be creative and he was so creative that he wrote 3,000 proverbs and over 1,000 songs. How much more will God want to give you and I through His Son Jesus Christ? Creativity is the art of making old things new. I must confess that I am not altogether happy about the use of the English word 'creativity' to describe activities attributable to man. My reservation comes from the fact that, in addition to the idea of newness, productivity and forming in the biblical use of 'bara' there also seems to be another reference and we choose to go deeper in the scriptures and look at the passage to see the power of God in His element in all creation.

We see that God created a man and gave him the ability because he was made in His image. He possessed certain characteristics that animals do not have such as creation. Man is quite different. He devises tools and appliances, invents new ways of doing things, alters routines, abandons past ideas and practices in favor of new ones, builds on the past, and so forth. Man is constantly forming new ideas and producing new things. He has a great capacity for newness. Indeed, man can even undergo the utter transformation called the new birth. Though he is passive in that transformation called the new birth, nevertheless, it demonstrates that there is human potential for radical change. Animals cannot experience regeneration and conversion. The fact that regeneration in no way alters man's humanness so that he is rendered something other than human by it plainly shows that man, as man, has a large potential, in his God given abilities, for change.

These new things are new because they did not exist before, even though the ideas and the materials from which they come did. New things are the product of new thoughts. God gave Solomon, in his creative wisdom, the ability to build temples and a city, with his perfect design. But God did not yet give him the ability to create a television because electricity was not discovered yet and now, in 2017, man has the DVD player, plasma tv's, and cell phones that communicate globally in mere seconds. We ourselves have little idea of what man will be doing with some other yet undiscovered force, even 5 years from now. All this, and much, much more has resulted from a God-given ability in man to conceive of and to produce new things that are adaptations of old ones. The new is built on older discoveries and so progress occurs. That ability to produce and form new ideas, and those things which flow from these ideas, as a dim reflection of the absolute creative ability of God, not too unfairly we call creativity.

I know of no other english word that closely captures the essential factors at work conceptualizing and subduing activities of man. Creativity is what is involved in arranging, shaping and adapting the elements of the original creation that God gave us and told us to bring under control. That is the meaning of the command in Genesis 1:28. Man was commanded to bring the world completely under God's power by discovering the ways and means that He provided.

Remember, NOW IS YOUR TIME TO BE CREATIVE in every area of your life. YES, YOU CAN! As long as it is honest, just and good for all mankind, God will not fail you if you apply these principles which are taught in these chapters. You will not fail if you continue to make God your partner by abiding in HIM and He will make you successful and wealthy. Solomon said:

Proverbs 8: 21
"That I may cause those who love me to inherit wealth, That I may fill their treasuries."

Biblical creativity requires our use of God's Wisdom in action and within the framework of, and according to, biblical principle. God's creative wisdom will cause you to create things which were not before and to bring them to existence today which will create an abundance of supply for public need in your city and community and nation which will equal wealth.

LESSON SIX

Bible Purpose Driven
Daily Wisdom Key for Today:

WE HAVE BEEN INSPIRED BY GOD TO BE CREATIVE

Verse to remember: Genesis 1:1
Amplified Bible (AMP)
¹ In the beginning God (prepared, formed, fashioned, and) created the heavens and the earth.

Question to meditate on: I will, I will, I will pray for God's wisdom by making God my partner and activate my activity to be creative too. We call these the 5 Big R's:

Rebuild: if your house burns rebuild it

Repair: if your car crashes repair it

Restore: if your relationship suffers restore it

Renew: if you lose your business renew it

Redeem the time that God gave you under the sun!

Repeat these 5 statements out-loud 3 times and then shout Hallelujah 3 times.

LESSON SEVEN

Hebrews 9:27
**'And as it is appointed unto men once to
die, but after this the judgment.'**

THE END OF MAN'S JOURNEY

There are a whole lot of people that do not relate to Matthew, Mark, Luke and John and that need to know Jesus and that He came to warn and confirm that we all have to face the great white throne judgment before God. We have to reach them before we can teach them. We have to catch them before we can clean them. Some try to clean-up people whom they have not yet caught, and others try to teach people that haven't been caught – we've got to reach them first.

This may even be you today as you read these chapters you might come to a conclusion to say, "I'm blessed with my god. My god takes care of me financially and with my money" And you are convinced and you might be thinking that you have the right savior and the right religion and road to success. And you think that you have eternal life with your religion. It might be Buddhism, Islam or a New Age concept. Very well, but remember that the bible is the ultimate God-inspired book and contradicts and condemns all these new religions that are inspired by Satan and his demons. Moses and the prophets always warned the people to forsake and abandon and turn away from these so-called inspired religions and himself and all the prophets declare the soon coming of the Messiah! We read below now that the disciples in the book of Acts stated very clearly that there is no salvation under the sun but only through Christ. He are five points to illustrate this:

1. Introductory – Joel's prophecy fulfilled

    Acts 2:14-21:
    "But Peter, standing up with the eleven, lifted up his voice and said unto them, Ye men of Judea, and all ye that dwell at Jerusalem, be this known unto you, and hearken to my words: For these are not drunken, as ye suppose, seeing it is but the third hour of the day. But that is that which was spoken by the prophet Joel; And it shall come to pass in the last days, saith God, I will pour out my Spirit upon all flesh: and your sons and your daughters shall prophesy, and your young men shall see visions, and you old men shall dream dreams: And on my servants and on my handmaidens I will pour out in those days of my Spirit; and they shall prophesy: And I will shew wonders in the heaven above, and signs in the earth beneath; blood, and fire, and vapour of smoke: The sun shall be turned into darkness, and the moon into blood, before the great and notable day of the Lord come: And it shall come to pass, that whosoever shall call on the name of the Lord shall be saved."

2. The Works of Jesus prove that He is the Lord and Christ
3. David foretold Messiah's kingship after resurrection.
4. His resurrection proves that he is Lord and Christ
5. What Israel must do

Not only did the disciples fulfill the prophecy but they demonstrated with signs and wonders and even today God is still manifesting, around the nations of the world and through

His people, SIGNS and WONDERS which follow them who believe and who have accepted Jesus Christ as their Lord and Savior.

Mark 16:16-18
'He who believes and is baptized will be saved; but he who does not believe will be condemned. And these signs will follow those who believe: In my name they will cast out demons; they will speak with new tounges; they will take up serpents, and if they drink anything deadly, it will by no means hurt them; they will lay hands on the sick and they will recover.'

In the next few chapters we will expand on God and His angels and also prove that the doctrine of Satan and His demons are real and cause false religion in the world because we want to make sure that you know that you know that all of the wealth that you will accumulate in life cannot buy happiness, love, peace and joy. God wants you to be happy and full of joy, successful, prosperous and healthy and to know God's plan for your very life, from the beginning to the very end.

At this point the chapters above have introduced you to prosperity and wealth and have shown how you can obtain everything that you want in life. However, we want to bring deep inspirational teaching about the deity of God and all of His creation so that you can know definitely and for sure the direction that you need to take to get all of these rich benefits, which are the rewards of allowing God to lead you in business and finance, so that you can fulfill God's plan for you, which is to be bible purpose driven in your reconstruction on the road map of your life!

Apostle Paul declares in scripture:

Acts 16:31
'Believe in the Lord Jesus Christ and you will be saved.'

This is not a myth. We want to show that the word SAVED has more than one meaning and this very book is written to reveal to you chapter by chapter that SALVATION indicates God's Plan complete for every need of your life, mentally, physically, financially and in every other area. We will be very careful to give you, in this book, an opportunity to make the right choice by discovering that you are a sinner and in need of God's Plan for you and all of your family.

GETTING TO HEAVEN

On a recent Mission trip to Thailand I visited an Orphanage of 9 and 10 year olds. While we were distributing gifts to them I asked them if they can tell me how a person can get to heaven. It was interesting to hear what these 9 and 10 years olds said. Many were clear that salvation was through faith in Jesus Christ. But, some were not yet equipped to explain the gospel. One said, "You have to be good and go to Sunday school." Another boy said tentatively, "You have to pray to God." Another said, "If you are nice to your friends and obey your mom and dad."

As I gently tried to direct the thinking of each child to the central element of salvation – faith in Jesus who died to pay for our sins and then rose again – I thought that these kids represented so many others in our world who do not yet understand the gospel simply because, in different parts of the world, they've been brought up to believe different. How about you? As you read this chapter today, are your ideas about salvation based on biblical truth? Think about the importance of what Jesus did for you. There is so much more at stake than getting a free gift for answering a question. We finally explained to them John 3:16 which says:

"For God so loved the world, that He gave His only begotten Son, that whosoever believeth in Him should not perish, but have everlasting life."

We had the opportunity to bless the children because more than 50 of them carry AIDS through infected blood transfusions from their parents. They gladly received the gift of God.

Ephesians 2:8
'For by grace are ye saved through faith; and that not of yourselves: *it is* the gift of God:'

LESSON SEVEN

**Bible Purpose Driven
Daily Wisdom Key for Today:**

THE END OF MAN'S JOURNEY

**Verse to remember: Hebrews 9:27
'And as it is appointed unto men once to
die, but after this the judgment.' –**

Question to Meditate: Am I going in the right direction?

LESSON EIGHT

Psalms 14:1-4:
'The fool hath said in his heart, *There is* no God. They are corrupt, they have done abominable works, *there is* none that doeth good. The Lord looked down from heaven upon the children of men, to see if there were any that did understand, *and* seek God. They are *all* gone aside, they are all together become filthy: *there is* none that doeth good, no, not one. Have all the workers of iniquity no knowledge? Who eat up my people *as* they eat bread, and call not upon the name of the Lord.'

DOES GOD EXIST?

We can see that David was confronted by many government leaders, Kings from different regions and there is no difference in time from then until now. The enemy is always at the door to disqualify the things of God. The first and most basic question that every human being on earth must answer for him or herself is this: Does God exist? Whether or not we choose to ponder this greatest of all questions, it still sits, demanding attention, in the conscience of all people, even in children. The very meaning and quality of your life is affected by your view of God. Are you the god in your world or do you acknowledge the Divinity and Lordship of an Almighty Supreme Being? Are you among those who regard the Divine as a mere philosophical concept, just interesting fodder for intellectual debate, or do you worship a real, personal and living God?

God is a holy God and God is a gentleman. God is not going to force anyone to accept Him. It is all done by faith and free will. The answer to this second question is as important as the first. While we cannot prove or disprove the existence of God by a purely scientific manner, we do have solid evidence that points to His existence. Research carried out for more than a century by anthropologists around the world indicates that every known human society throughout history has held a belief in an afterlife and a divine source of creation. This same research has also found that most primitive societies began with a belief in a single God, or "monotheism." Some of these societies, as they grew, developed "polytheism" (the belief in several gods or deities), but returned later in their histories to accepting the concept of "one God."

When we ponder this most important of questions concerning the existence of our Creator, we have to bear in mind that we are approaching Him with a very limited human viewpoint. The following are only a few of the theological inquiries that have been made about God. Let's take the law of cause and effect into consideration. No "effect" can exist without a "cause." Every physical thing in our Universe that was ever created, including ourselves, can be thought of as an effect. Therefore, we must have a cause. This line of logic leads inevitably to an ultimate creator who is a "cause with no cause" or, in other words, to an Almighty God, the Alpha and Omega, the Eternal One. God is by His very definition, eternal and uncreated. If He was anything less than that, for instance a finite being with a beginning, He simply would not and could not be God.

Colossians 1:15- 17
15: "Who is the image of the invisible God,
the firstborn of every creature:

16: For by Him were all things created, that are in Heaven, and that are in earth, visible and invisible, whether they be thrones, or dominions, or principalities, or powers: all things were created by Him, and for Him:

17: And He is before all things, and by Him all things consist."

The infinitely complex and delicately balanced order of the universe clearly indicates the necessity of an infinite Creator. It requires the "eternal cause" in back of all causes and effects. Many eminent scientists of the 20th century from Albert Einstein to today's astrophysicists and astronomers have been awe-struck by the astounding and incomprehensible universe that Our Lord has created for us to inhabit. The mathematical probability against the universe having formed as it has "by chance" is staggering. The analogy that some have stated is this:

"Scientists have spent centuries scaling a mountain of ignorance and just as they have reached the peak, they find that theologians have been sitting there waiting for their arrival."

When I said before that it isn't possible to devise a scientific method of proving or disproving the existence of God, it's because in order to prove something by a scientific method, you must be able to repeat it under controlled experimentation. As an example, we cannot prove that Julius Caesar existed by the same means, but we know by history that he was a real individual. While we can observe the stars using such advanced devices as the Hubble Space Telescope, we simply cannot re-run the beginning of the universe. My point is that ultimately our belief in God becomes a matter of faith. Few, however, seem to consider that it takes the same degree of faith to not believe in Him.

Nearing the middle of the (20th) last century, most scientists still held firmly to a "belief" in "spontaneous generation" (accidental creation). Way back in the 1980's and 90's, scientists discovered very compelling evidence to the contrary. Today, the creation story as stated in Genesis seems a great deal more plausible to those in academic circles. So much so that many of our finest scientific minds (people who have traditionally been agnostic or atheistic) are rapidly losing their faith in His non-existence. God has created us with a free will. We have the freedom of choice, to love Him and obey His Will or not to. If we had no free will, we would be less than fully human. We could only operate on instinct, much like a dog. A dog has no choice in the matter; he has to behave exactly as God says a dog should behave. Think about it -would you really want a husband or wife who loves you by no choice of his or her own? In other words, a robot? I think not. The "fall" of mankind is man exercising his free will to choose evil over good. The Lord does not demand that we love Him or even that we understand everything. He wants us to love Him willingly and with a childlike faith.

2 Peter 3:9
"The Lord is not willing that any should perish,
but that all should come to repentance."

In today's world, our Christian faith is being attacked from all sides. One may expect, and even accept, doubt and open hostility from the secular world, but the most fundamental of Christian tenets are being assailed by some schools of Theology and even from the pulpit. Various sectors of so-called Christianity, in these early days of the 21st century are claiming, "God Is Dead." The very concept of an eternal, loving, omnipotent deity is no longer necessary. My objective in this lesson is to state, in the clearest and strongest terms, Christian teaching as it is presented in Scripture.

Worldwide, nations have developed educated and sophisticated cultures. Competing theologies and challenges to our faith are everywhere. It is no longer adequate that Christians simply know WHAT we believe, but now, it is imperative that believers know WHY we believe as we do. Our beliefs are as likely to be challenged by secular humanists, as they are by Muslims, Hindus, Buddhists and atheists, among others. We can no longer afford the comfort of merely conforming to a pat set of answers and from that basis try to argue our assailants into the Kingdom. One of the chief methods the Holy Spirit uses to bring enlightenment is a sound and reasonable presentation of the truth of God's Word. The Lord has commanded us to be well-versed and intelligent in our faith.

1 Peter 3:15
"Be ready always to give an answer to every man that asketh you a reason of the hope that is in you, with meekness and fear."

If, by our own ignorance, we cannot give sound reasons for our faith and if we are defeated in conversations and debate with non-believers, then we are merely confirming their unbelief and the commonly held opinion that Christians believe blindly like children. We must be able to show non-believers and ourselves that Scripture is objectively true, regardless of who told us so that we are not just echoing our religious background or the beliefs taught by our parents and our culture.

Some non-believers do not take the Word seriously because no one has ever shown them the facts in an evident and conclusive manner. Believers and non-believers alike need to know that being a Christian does not mean we have to "check our brains at the door." The Gospel can be successfully and triumphantly defended as the Lord calls us to do, because it is the Word of God and is therefore inherently reasonable and true.

In early 2000 while doing a radio program a skeptic called me and strongly made a stand that he was an atheist and that God did not exist. My reply to him, on national radio was, to both him and all of the skeptics who tuned in and who have embraced their leader's teachings, like Charles Darwin and Issac Asimov and many others whom we described above, was to go ask Moses, David or Pharoah concerning the historical fact that God threw the Egyptian army into the Red Sea and through Moses liberated over 3 million people.

The listener replied to me if he could get there phone numbers to contact them. I replied, "Sure, You want to talk to Moses, Pharoah or David?" He responded, "Hold on, wait one second, I'm going to get a pen." Quickly he got back on the line and said ok, I'm ready' I said, 'Good news, David just happened to come into the studio right now, listen to what he says, are you ready" He replied, "Yeah" I then quoted to him out loud, on the radio, in a singing tone Psalms 136:1-26. Here it goes:

Psalm 136:1-26
New International Version (NIV)

Psalm 136
¹ **Give thanks to the Lord, for he is good.**
His love endures forever.

² **Give thanks to the God of gods.**
His love endures forever.

³ **Give thanks to the Lord of lords:**
His love endures forever.

⁴ **to him who alone does great wonders,**
His love endures forever.

⁵ **who by his understanding made the heavens,**
His love endures forever.

[6] who spread out the earth upon the waters,
His love endures forever.

[7] who made the great lights—
His love endures forever.

[8] the sun to govern the day,
His love endures forever.

[9] the moon and stars to govern the night;
His love endures forever.

[10] to him who struck down the firstborn of Egypt
His love endures forever.

[11] and brought Israel out from among them
His love endures forever.

[12] with a mighty hand and outstretched arm;
His love endures forever.

[13] to him who divided the Red Sea[a] asunder
His love endures forever.

[14] and brought Israel through the midst of it,
His love endures forever

[15] but swept Pharaoh and his army into the Red Sea;
His love endures forever.

[16] to him who led his people through the wilderness;
His love endures forever.

[17] to him who struck down great kings,
His love endures forever.

[18] and killed mighty kings—
His love endures forever.

¹⁹ Sihon king of the Amorites
His love endures forever.

²⁰ and Og king of Bashan—
His love endures forever.

²¹ and gave their land as an inheritance,
His love endures forever.

²² an inheritance to his servant Israel.
His love endures forever.

²³ He remembered us in our low estate
His love endures forever.

²⁴ and freed us from our enemies.
His love endures forever.

²⁵ He gives food to every creature.
His love endures forever.

²⁶ Give thanks to the God of heaven.
His love endures forever.

LESSON EIGHT

**Bible Purpose Driven
Daily Wisdom Key for Today:**

DOES GOD EXIST

Verse to Remember: Psalms 14:1-4:
**'The fool hath said in his heart, *There is* no God. They
are corrupt, they have done abominable works, *there
is* none that doeth good. The Lord looked down from
heaven upon the children of men, to see if there were
any that did understand, *and* seek God. They are *all* gone
aside, they are all together become filthy: *there is* none
that doeth good, no, not one. Have all the workers of
iniquity no knowledge? Who eat up my people *as* they
eat bread, and call not upon the name of the Lord.'**

Question to Meditate On: If I die today where would I go?

LESSON NINE

Revelation 1:5-6
'And from Jesus Christ, who is the faithful witness, and the first begotten of the dead, and the prince of the kings of the earth. Unto him that loved us, and washed us from our sins in his own blood, And hath made us kings and priests unto God and his Father, to him be glory and dominion forever and ever. Amen.'

GOD IS REAL AND ROYAL

Webster's dictionary explains that the English word 'real' comes from the latin root word *'reale'* which means real or royal meaning KING. I suggest that you please review John 1:1-14 and 1 John 1:5 in God's Word to better prepare for this chapter. Many people who profess a belief in God begin by apologizing for their ignorance of Him. Preachers, theologians and writers, almost without exception, tend to speak of God in vague terms or as being incomprehensible and beyond human understanding.

There is no excuse for thinking of our Lord as a mysterious and unknowable God. The Bible contains thousands of passages that define very clearly who He is. In today's lesson, we intend to look at God exactly as He is defined in the Bible and believe what it says. In today's modern technological world, the view of God tends to be that He is only a spirit or merely a set of universal principles or physical laws. This is not scripturally correct.

1. THE BIBLE TELLS US THAT HE IS A LOVING FATHER AND A REALPERSON

   a. The Bible gives God personal names (read Exod. 3:13-15, 6:3).
   b. Scripture contains personal statements about God, as with other persons. His personal body, soul and spirit are described. Evidence of God on Earth is given in:

Genesis 3:8-9
Amplified Bible (AMP)
8 And they heard the sound of the Lord God walking in the garden in the cool of the day, and Adam and his wife hid themselves from the presence of the Lord God among the trees of the garden.

9 But the Lord God called to Adam and said to him, Where are you?

Further evidence of God as man is in:

Ezekiel 1:26-28
Amplified Bible (AMP)
26 And above the firmament that was over their heads was the likeness of a throne in appearance like a sapphire stone, and seated above the likeness of a throne was a likeness with the appearance of a Man.

27 From what had the appearance of His waist upward, I saw a lustre as it were glowing metal with the appearance of fire enclosed round about within it; and from the appearance of His waist downward, I saw as it were the appearance of fire, and there was brightness [of a halo] round about Him.

²⁸ Like the appearance of the bow that is in the cloud on the day of rain, so was the appearance of the brightness round about. This was the appearance of the likeness of the glory of the Lord. And when I saw it, I fell upon my face and I heard a voice of One speaking.

2. GOD IS A LOVING SHEPHERD WHO TAKES CARE OF HIS SHEEP. JESUS CHRIST, AS THE SECOND PERSON OF THE TRINITY, IS THE GREAT SHEPHERD

The shepherd is a man or woman who takes care of his flock. The term can also describe a spiritual father, a comrade or a friend. This is descriptive of a shepherd's duty in the natural world. His is the role of protector, provider and guide of the flock. A spiritual shepherd performs the same role of protector, provider and guide of God's people in the spirit. Scripture refers to our Lord as the Shepherd of His flock many times. He is the model and the very definition of what He desires of us as shepherds in the Body of Christ. Jesus Christ is the Good Shepherd of our souls. The following is a list of scriptural references to the Lord as our Shepherd. Read Psalms 23:1, Ezekiel 34:12, Isaiah 40:11, Psalms 77:20 for a more thorough understanding of this material.

a. Action of the Great Shepherd -
The Lord of the Old Testament is the Great Shepherd to His flock Israel, and more. He also illustrates, to all spiritual shepherds throughout all ages, the proper attitudes and actions of a shepherd of God's people. The list below names some of the actions that rose from the Shepherd's heart of the Lord in the Old Testament:

Ezekiel 34:11-16 "Searched out the lost sheep."

Ezekiel 34:13 "Gathered the dispersed sheep."

Ezekiel 34:11 "Delivered the captive sheep."

Isaiah 40:11 and Ezekiel 34:13 "Fed the hungry sheep."

b. The Ways of Jesus As The Good Shepherd -
The New Testament reveals Jesus Christ as God incarnate; as such, He is the Good Shepherd of His flock. Jesus' actions are all of those of the Good Shepherd. We see Jesus' life unfold in the New Testament Gospels, just as Jehovah was the Great Shepherd of Israel in the Old Testament. The following scriptures show us Jesus as the Good Shepherd of the New Testament. Meditate with purpose on these verses:

John 10:11-14 "I am the Good Shepherd."

1 Peter 2:25 "Returned unto the Shepherd and Bishop of our souls."

Hebrews 13:20 "Jesus, the Great Shepherd of the sheep.

1 Peter 5:4 "When the Chief Shepherd shall appear."

c. Jesus Is Flesh and Blood, A Real Person -
As we see the heart attitudes of the Lord in the Old Testament, and in the actions of Jesus Christ, the pattern of the shepherd is also evident in the New Testament. These insights are derived from the book of John as discussed below:

John 10:3 "Relates to the sheep."

John 10:1 "...and enter some other way, as thieves and robbers."

John 10:7 "I am the door of the sheep."

John 10:9 "I am the door, by me if any man enter in, he shall be saved."

John 10:11 "Is the Good Shepherd of the sheep."

John 10:18
New King James Version (NKJV)
[18] No one takes it from Me, but I lay it down of Myself. I have power to lay it down, and I have power to take it again. This command I have received from My Father."

d. The Action of a True Shepherd -
The Lord Jesus Christ was a shepherd in the truest sense of the word. During His ministry, He was the perfect model for all the shepherds of God's flock. In our present time, the Body of Christ desperately needs leaders who have a genuine relationship with God and who can guide others who desire to enter into that same kind of relationship with Him. These modern-day spiritual shepherds must be as willing to lay down their lives for their sheep as was Jesus.

Scripture gives us a great number of passages that offer guidance to those of us who would be spiritual shepherds. It is unfortunate and sadly true that in today's Church many of our spiritual leaders are not immersed in the Holy Spirit. Most of them do not seem to be doing the work of true spiritual shepherds, both in their professional and personal lives. Any flock, literally or figuratively speaking, will not last long with shepherds who drink alcohol, are greedy, who are egotistical and materialistic or who are lost in some other sin.

A true shepherd or leader, in the Church or in any secular profession (e.g., business or politics), must be above reproach and as free from the influence of sin as is humanly possible. With the so-called leaders as we have today, the hurt and broken-hearted may very well remain wounded, the Body of Christ will suffer, and Satan will have his evil way. I do hope that the next few lessons will help you to get close to the Holy Spirit.

BRUNO CAPORRIMO; DOMINIC CONTRERAS

LESSON NINE

God Purpose Driven:
Daily Wisdom Key for Today:

GOD IS REAL AND ROYAL

Verse to Remember: Revelation 1:5-6
'And from Jesus Christ, who is the faithful witness,
and the first begotten of the dead, and the prince of
the kings of the earth. Unto him that loved us, and
washed us from our sins in his own blood, and hath
made us kings and priests unto God and his Father, to
him be glory and dominion forever and ever. Amen.'

Question to Meditate On: God made ALL OF US Kings and Priests! For a female, God made you a Princess and Queen. Say it out-loud 3 times:

I AM ROYAL, I AM ROYAL, I AM ROYAL!

LESSON TEN

John 16:7-8
New King James Version (NKJV)
⁷ Nevertheless I tell you the truth. It is to your advantage that I go away; for if I do not go away, the Helper will not come to you; but if I depart, I will send Him to you.

⁸ And when He has come, He will convict the world of sin, and of righteousness, and of judgment:

THE WORKS OF THE HOLY SPIRIT IN THE NEW TESTAMENT

Although the Holy Spirit is seen at work in Old Testament times in creation and in Israel, His operations were not for all mankind. However, the Old Testament prophets clearly foretold a coming day when the Spirit would be poured out upon all flesh, both Israel and Gentile nations. Please see: Joel 2:28-29; Ezekiel 11:19; 36:26,27; Isaiah 44:3; Zechariah 10:1

This could only be fulfilled upon the foundation of the death, burial, resurrection, ascension and glorification of the Lord Jesus Christ. It would be His ministry to receive the fullness of the Spirit as the perfect Man, the Messiah of God and then pour out that same Spirit upon all flesh and upon those who believe on Him unto eternal life. Upon the acceptance of the finished work of the cross, the believer will find available to him the gift of the Holy Spirit and thus come under His gracious ministrations unto glorification. Please review these scriptures:

Matthew 3:11
New King James Version (NKJV)
[11] I indeed baptize you with water unto repentance, but He who is coming after me is mightier than I, whose sandals I am not worthy to carry. He will baptize you with the Holy Spirit and fire.[a]

John 1:30-33
New King James Version (NKJV)
[30] This is He of whom I said, 'After me comes a Man who is preferred before me, for He was before me.'

[31] I did not know Him; but that He should be revealed to Israel, therefore I came baptizing with water."

[32] And John bore witness, saying, "I saw the Spirit descending from heaven like a dove, and He remained upon Him.

[33] I did not know Him, but He who sent me to baptize with water said to me, 'Upon whom you see the Spirit descending, and remaining on Him, this is He who baptizes with the Holy Spirit.'

Romans 8:25-32
New King James Version (NKJV)
[25] But if we hope for what we do not see, we eagerly wait for *it* with perseverance.

[26] Likewise the Spirit also helps in our weaknesses. For we do not know what we should pray for as we ought, but the Spirit Himself makes intercession for us[a] with groanings which cannot be uttered.

[27] Now He who searches the hearts knows what the mind of the Spirit *is,* because He makes intercession for the saints according to *the will of* God.

28 And we know that all things work together
for good to those who love God, to those who
are the called according to *His* purpose.

29 For whom He foreknew, He also predestined *to
be* conformed to the image of His Son, that He
might be the firstborn among many brethren.

30 Moreover whom He predestined, these He also
called; whom He called, these He also justified;
and whom He justified, these He also glorified.

God's Everlasting Love

31 What then shall we say to these things?
If God *is* for us, who *can be* against us?

32 He who did not spare His Own Son, but
delivered Him up for us all, how shall He not
with Him also freely give us all things?

1. He was born of the Spirit (Luke 1:35; Matthew 1:1820).
2. He was filled with the fullness of the Spirit (John 3:34).
3. He was led by the Spirit (Matthew 4:1; Luke 4:1).
4. He was empowered by the Spirit (Luke 4:14).
5. He was anointed by the Spirit (Luke 4:18).
6. He spoke and taught by the Spirit (Luke 4:18).
7. He healed the sick by the Spirit (Luke 4:18).
8. He cast out devils by the power of the Spirit (Matthew 12:28).
9. He was justified (vindicated) by the Spirit (1 Timothy 3:16).
10. He was offered up on Calvary by the eternal Spirit (Hebrews 9:14).
11. He was resurrected by the Spirit (Romans 8:11; 1 Peter 3:18).

12. He gave commandments to the disciples by the Spirit (Acts 1:2).
13. He baptized and empowered the Church by the Spirit (Acts 1:5-8).
14. He directs and governs the Church also by the Spirit (Revelation 2:7,11).

Thus, the whole life of Jesus as the perfect Man was governed by the Spirit. If Jesus depended upon the Holy Spirit in such a manner, how much more should the believer constantly depend upon the Holy Spirit. All that God has for us and wants to do in us will only be done by the operation of the Holy Spirit in our lives. Hence the need for believers individually and the church corporately to open their hearts to seek the fullness of the Spirit working in them.

The Holy Spirit in the life of the Believer:

The life of the believer follows that example of the Lord Jesus.

1. The new birth is brought about by the Spirit (John 3:5-6).
2. The Spirit indwells the believer's spirit (Romans 8:9; 1 Corinthians 3:16; 6:17; 1 John 2:27).
3. The Spirit gives assurance of salvation (Romans 8:16).
4. The Spirit fills the believer with Himself (Acts 2:4; Ephesians 5:18).
5. The Spirit, by the baptism in the Spirit, enables the believer to speak in unknown languages (Acts 2:4; 10:44-46; Mark 16:17; 1 Corinthians 14:2,4,18).

   The expression "baptism in or with the Spirit" is a Scriptural expression and experience (Matthew 3:11; Acts 1:5; 1 Corinthians 12:13; John 1:33; Luke 3:16).

6. The Spirit speaks to the believer (Acts 8:29; 1 Timothy 4:1; Revelation 2:7, 11, 17, 29).
7. The spirit opens the believer's understanding to the things of God (1 Corinthians 2:12).
8. The Spirit teaches the believer, and guides him into all truth (John 16:13; 1 John 2:27).
9. The Spirit imparts life (John 6:63; 2 Corinthians 3:6).
10. The Spirit brings about renewal (Titus 3:5).
11. The Spirit strengthens the believer's inner being (Ephesians 3:16).
12. The Spirit enables the believer to pray (Jude 20; Romans 8:26-28).
13. The Spirit enables the believer to worship in spirit and in truth. (John 4:23-24; Philippians 3:3; 1 Corinthians 14:15).
14. The Spirit leads the believer (Romans 8:14).
15. The Spirit enables the believer to put fleshly deeds to death (Romans 8:13).
16. The Spirit produces Christ-likeness in character and fruit in the believer's life (Galatians 5:22,23).
17. The Spirit gives a calling to the believer for special service (Acts 13:2-4).
18. The Spirit guides believers into their ministry (Acts 8:29; Acts 16:6,7).
19. The Spirit empowers the believer to witness (Acts 1:8).
20. The spirit imparts spiritual gifts to the believers as He wills (1 Corinthians 12:7-11).
21. The Spirit will bring about the resurrection and immortality to the believer's bodies in the last day (Romans 8:11; 1 Corinthians 15:47-51; 1 Thessalonians 4:15-18).

1 Thessalonians 4:15-18
New King James Version (NKJV)

[15] For this we say to you by the word of the Lord, that we who are alive *and* remain until the coming of the Lord will by no means precede those who are asleep. [16] For the Lord Himself will descend from heaven with a shout, with the voice of an archangel, and with the trumpet of God. And the dead in Christ will rise first. [17] Then we who are alive *and* remain shall be caught up together with them in the clouds to meet the Lord in the air. And thus, we shall always be with the Lord. [18] Therefore comfort one another with these words.

LESSON TEN

THE WORKS OF THE HOLY SPIRIT
IN THE NEW TESTAMENT

Verse to Remember: John 16:7-8
'Nevertheless, I tell you the truth; it is expedient
for you that I go away, the Comforter will not come
unto you; but if I depart, I will send him unto you.
And when he is come, he will reprove the world of
sin, and of righteousness, and of judgment:'

Question to Meditate: Do you really have the comfort that is spoken of above?

LESSON ELEVEN

Acts 2:1-4
New King James Version (NKJV)
Coming of the Holy Spirit
2 When the Day of Pentecost had fully come, they were all with one accord[a] in one place. ² And suddenly there came a sound from heaven, as of a rushing mighty wind, and it filled the whole house where they were sitting. ³ Then there appeared to them divided tongues, as of fire, and *one* sat upon each of them. ⁴ And they were all filled with the Holy Spirit and began to speak with other tongues, as the Spirit gave them utterance.

THE HOLY SPIRIT IN THE LIFE OF THE CHURCH

Not only is the work of the Spirit seen in the individual believer but it is also seen in the Church. The coming of the Holy Spirit to form the Church, the many-membered body of Christ, was foreshadowed in Israel under the Feast of Pentecost, even as the work of Christ was foreshadowed under the Feast of Passover (Exodus 12; Leviticus 23; Acts 2:1-4). The Holy Spirit is the executive agent of the Godhead who came to earth to build the Church that the Lord Jesus said He would build (Matthew 16:16-20). The Holy Spirit could not be given until Jesus Christ was glorified after His death, burial, resurrection and ascension.

John 7:38-39
New King James Version (NKJV)
[38] He who believes in Me, as the Scripture has said, out
of his heart will flow rivers of living water." [39] But this
He spoke concerning the Spirit, whom those believing[a]
in Him would receive; for the Holy[b] Spirit was not
yet *given,* because Jesus was not yet glorified.

It is the indwelling work of the Spirit that seems to be the difference between the experiences of Old and New Testament saints. It is the distinguishing feature of the New Covenant times.

This is seen in the baptismal sign, which was given to John the Baptist, concerning the Messiah.

John 1:33
New King James Version (NKJV)
[33] I did not know Him, but He who sent me to
baptize with water said to me, 'Upon whom you
see the Spirit descending, and remaining on Him,
this is He who baptizes with the Holy Spirit.'

This qualified Jesus to be the Baptizer in the Holy Spirit. In the Old Testament, the Spirit descended on special ones equipping and filling them but not remaining or indwelling them continually. Jesus promised His disciples that the Spirit would come and dwell with them and in them and that, as the Comforter, He would abide with them forever. (See also John 14:16-17).

THE MAJOR FEATURES OF THE SPIRIT'S WORK IN THE CHURCH INCLUDES THE FOLLOWING:

1. The Holy Spirit formed the Church on the Day of Pentecost into a corporate structure, the Body of Christ. He baptized the living members into this spiritual body. Pentecost is called the birthday of the Church (Acts 2:1-4; 1 Corinthians 12:12-27 and Ephesians 1:22-23).

2. The Holy Spirit formed the Church to be the new and living temple of God, setting believers into their places as living stones in the New Covenant temple (1 Corinthians 3:16; 6:16; Ephesians 2:20-22).

3. The Holy Spirit brings anointing, illumination and direction to the Church as the New Covenant Priestly Body (2 Corinthians 1:21; Psalms 133:1-2; 1 John 2:20,27; Ephesians 1:17-18; Acts 10:38; 1 Corinthians 12: 12-13).

4. The Holy Spirit brings gifts and graces to the members of the Church (1 Corinthians 12:3-11, 28-31; Romans 12:6-8; Galatians 5:22-23). The gifts of the Spirit are a demonstration in the Church of the Spirit's omnipotence, omniscience, and omnipresence. The fruit of the Spirit is the evidence of the nature and character of the Holy Spirit in the members of the Body of Christ.

5. The Holy Spirit is the Agent of direction and government in the Church. The Lord Jesus is the Head of the church in Heaven and He directs his affairs in His Body by means of the Holy Spirit. It is the Spirit who calls, quickens, energizes and equips the various ministries in the Church and every member of the Body of Christ according to their particular place (Acts 13:1-3; 15:28; 20:28; 1 Corinthians

12:8-11; Ephesians 4:8-12; 1 Peter 1:12; 1 Corinthians 2:1-5; Acts 1:8).

Thus, as Jesus Christ, the Head of the Body was under total control and domination of the Spirit, and the Spirit was able to flow freely in perfect and unhindered operation. This is to be manifested in the Church as the visible and mystical Body of Christ in the earth.

THE HOLY SPIRIT IN THE WORLD

The work of the Holy Spirit is summarized clearly in John 16:9-11. The Holy Spirit has come with a three-fold ministry in relation to the world: to reprove the world of sin, righteousness and judgment.

John 16:9-11
New King James Version (NKJV)
[9] of sin, because they do not believe in Me;
[10] of righteousness, because I go to My Father
and you see Me no more; [11] of judgment,
because the ruler of this world is judged.

1. Of sin: because they believe not on Christ. The damnable sin is that of unbelief. It is the root sin of all others. This area of reproof or conviction especially deals with the sin of man.

2. Of righteousness: because Jesus Christ has gone to the Father and at present we do not see Him. This area of conviction involves the righteousness of Christ, as the Savior of men.

3. Of judgment: because the prince of this world, Satan, was judged at Calvary. This area of conviction involves the

judgment of Satan and his hosts and their defeat at Calvary. The work of the Holy Spirit in relation to the unconverted is to convince, convict and convert. An example of this convicting work is seen in Paul's ministry before Felix, when Felix trembled as Paul reasoned with him of "righteousness, temperance and judgment to come" (Acts 24:25; Acts 1:5-8; 2:37-42; 7:51-59; Genesis 6:3).

SYMBOLS OF THE HOLY SPIRIT

Because of the various operations and manifestations of the Holy Spirit's work and ministry, it has pleased the Father that the Spirit be symbolized. These varied symbols set forth the nature, character and function of the Spirit, even as do the symbols of Jesus Christ, the Son of God.

1. Water

(John 7:38, 39; 4:4; Psalms 72:6; 87:7; Isaiah 44:3; Exodus 17:6 with 1 Corinthians 10:4)

The Spirit symbolized as water speaks of the life-giving flow, which refreshes and satisfies. It also speaks of washing, cleansing and fruitfulness.

2. Fire

(Matthew 3:11; Acts 2:3; Isaiah 4:4; Exodus 19:18; Malachi 3:2-3; Hebrews 13:29)

This symbolizes the holiness of God whereby the Holy Spirit is sent forth in judgment to purge, purify and enliven with zeal.

3. Wind or Breath

(Acts 2:2; John 3:8; Ezekiel 37:9-10; Isaiah 40:7)

These symbolize the life-giving breath of God in its regenerating power. It underscores the fact that the Holy Spirit is invisible as a person, yet the effect of His work can be seen.

4. Dew

(Psalms 133:1-3; Acts 10:38; 1 John 2:20, 27; Psalms 23:5)

Dew only comes in the stillness of the night, bringing refreshing to the mown grass. So, it is with the refreshing work of the Spirit in the Church.

5. Oil

(Luke 4:18; Acts: 10:38; 1 John 2:20, 27; Psalms 23:5; 1 Samuel 1:16)

Oil was distinctly involved in the anointing of the prophets, priest and kings to their offices. It speaks of the consecration and supernatural enablement of the Spirit's anointing grace, the illumination of His teaching, the soothing and healing balm of His presence. It is the Spirit who anoints the members of the Church to their priestly functions.

6. The Dove

(Matthew 3:16; Luke 3:22; Genesis 1:2; Matthew 10:16)

The symbol of the dove is used to represent purity, beauty, gentleness and peace, the nature and character of the Holy Spirit.

7. The Seal

(Ephesians 1:13; 2 Corinthians 1:22; Ephesians 4:30; 2 Timothy 2:19)

A seal is significant of ownership, genuineness and security. This emphasizes the Spirit's activity confirming to us God's ownership of us, His authority over us and our security in Him.

8. The Still Small Voice

(Genesis 3:8; 1 Kings 19:11-13; Acts 8:29)

The Spirit is the voice of God within man bringing a revelation of God's will to him.

9. The Finger of God

(Luke 11:20; Matthew 12:28) The Spirit is the one who points the accusing finger at the sinner, to bring about conviction with a view to the accused accepting Jesus as the advocate.

10. The First Fruits (Romans 8:23)

The first fruits were always symbolic of the full harvest to come, so the Spirit's initial work of regeneration points to the full salvation and glorification of the believer before God.

11. The Earnest

(2 Corinthians 1:22; 5:5; Ephesians 1:13-14)

The earnest was always down payment, a pledge of more to come. So, the Spirit's work in salvation is simply the pledge of full and total redemption to come. This symbol is similar to the first fruits.

12. Enduement

(Luke 24:49 with Judges 6:34; Isaiah 61:10)

The symbol of enduement means the clothing of the spirit upon someone. The baptism of the Holy Spirit is this divine clothing from above. It is the believer's garment for ministry before the Lord.

13. The Number Seven

The number seven is used in relation to the Holy Spirit. It is a number symbolic of fullness, completeness and perfection. It represents the fullness and perfection of the Spirit's operation in the earth.

Three examples show this symbolic truth of the Spirit's work.

a. Seven lamps (Revelation 1:3-4; 4:5; 5:6) These are symbolic of the Spirit's illumination, revelation and inspiration. Lamps must have oil to have light. (Proverbs 20:27)
b. Seven horns (Revelation 5:6) Horns are symbolic of power and defense. Seven horns speak of omnipotence; the Spirit is all-powerful.
c. Seven eyes (Revelation 5:6; Zechariah 3:9; 4:10) Eyes are symbolic of sight, insight, perception, intelligence and discernment. Seven eyes speak of the Spirit's omniscience, fullness and perfection of sight and insight.

LESSON ELEVEN

Bible Purpose Driven:
Daily Wisdom Key for Today:

THE HOLY SPIRIT IN THE LIFE OF THE CHURCH

Verse to Remember: Acts 2:1-4
New King James Version (NKJV)
Coming of the Holy Spirit
2 When the Day of Pentecost had fully come, they were all with one accord[a] in one place. ² And suddenly there came a sound from heaven, as of a rushing mighty wind, and it filled the whole house where they were sitting. ³ Then there appeared to them divided tongues, as of fire, and *one* sat upon each of them. ⁴ And they were all filled with the Holy Spirit and began to speak with other tongues, as the Spirit gave them utterance.

Question to Meditate: Do You want to be a part of the Church to receive all of God's wealth. Then say out-loud 3 times: I DO, I DO, I DO!!

LESSON TWELVE

1 John 5:7
New King James Version (NKJV)
⁷ For there are three that bear witness in heaven: The Father, the Word, and the Holy Spirit; and these three are one.

TITLES OF THE HOLY SPIRIT

Three in one. The word trinity is not found in the bible but is revealed to us by revelation. The greek words to define three in one are 'Trio' and 'manos' meaning - trinity.

Here's an illustration: $1 \times 1 \times 1 = 1$

Again, the above illustration means TRINITY.

Even as there are numerous names and titles of the Father and the Son in Scripture, so there are of the Holy Spirit. These titles set forth different aspects of the Spirit's character, functions and ministrations. Most of these titles refer to some specific work or operation that the Holy Spirit desires to perform in the hearts and lives of the people of God.

TITLES OF HIS DEITY

This group of titles sets forth the deity of the Holy Spirit and shows His distinction from and association with the Father and Son. A number of them set forth the Spirit as representing either the Father or the Son, but all show his divinity. We pray that, now that you are well on your way in this book, that you begin to pray and seek bible purpose with these scriptures, in order to apply them to your own finances. We trust that, as you work with the Holy Spirit on that, that he will also begin to reveal himself to you and lead you in your next business deal or ministry activity.

1. The Spirit (John 3:6-8)
2. The Holy Spirit (Luke 11:13; Isaiah 63:11)
3. The Spirit of God (1 Corinthians 3:16; 2:11)
4. The Spirit of the Lord God (Isaiah 61:1)
5. The Spirit of the Lord (Isaiah 63:14; Luke 4:18)
6. The Spirit of the Living God (2 Corinthians 3:3)
7. The Spirit of the Father (Matthew 10:20; 16:7)
8. The Spirit of Jesus (Acts 16:6-7)
9. The Holy Spirit of God (Ephesians 4:30)
10. The Spirit of Christ (Romans 8:9; 1 Peter 1:11)
11. The Spirit of Jesus Christ (Philippians 1:19)
12. The Spirit of His Son (Galatians 4:6)
13. The Spirit which is of God (1 Corinthians 2:12)

TITLES OF HIS ATTRIBUTES AND MINISTRY

This group of titles sets forth more particularly the essential and moral attributes of the Holy Spirit. Each of these attributes is related to some special need of man. It is the Holy Spirit who brings to us the wisdom, faith and power of God Almighty. All that is in God is brought to us by the Holy Spirit. He is to us all that we need.

1. The Spirit of Wisdom (Isaiah 11:2; Ephesians 1:17)
2. The Spirit of Knowledge (Isaiah 11:2)
3. The Spirit of Counsel and Might (Isaiah 11:2)
4. The Spirit of Grace and Supplications (Zechariah 12:10)

5. The Spirit of Judgment (Isaiah 4:4)
6. The Spirit of Burning (Isaiah 4:4)
7. The Breath of the Almighty (Job 32:8; 33:4)
8. The Spirit of Him who raised Jesus from the dead (Romans 8:11; 1 Peter 3:18)
9. The Power of the Highest (Luke 1:35)
10. The Eternal Spirit (Hebrews 9:14)
11. The Spirit of Holiness (Romans 1:4)
12. The Comforter (John 14:16, 26; 15:26; 16:7)
13. The Spirit of Love (1 Timothy 1:7)
14. The Spirit of Truth (John 14:17; 16:13; 15:26; 1 John 4:6)
15. The Spirit of Life (Romans 8:2; Revelation 11:11)
16. The Spirit of Adoption (Romans 8:15)
17. The Spirit of Faith (2 Corinthians 4:13)
18. The Spirit of Promise (Ephesians 1:13-14)
19. The Spirit of Grace (Zechariah 12:10; Hebrews 10:29)
20. The Spirit of Glory (1 Peter 4:14)
21. The Spirit of Power (2 Timothy 1:7)
22. The Spirit of Wisdom and Revelation (Ephesians 1:17)
23. The Spirit of Prophecy (Revelation 19:10)
24. The Good Spirit (Nehemiah 9:30; Psalms 143:10)
25. The Free Spirit (Psalms 51:12)
26. The Unction from the Holy One (1 John 2:20)
27. The Anointing which teaches us (1 John 2:27)
28. The Voice of the Lord (Ezekiel 1:24; Genesis 3:8; Isaiah 6:8)

In conclusion, we see the work of the Spirit in the New Testament is all that it was in the Old Testament, but more so, for now the Spirit is for all people, all believers out of every kindred, tongue, tribe and nation. The Holy Spirit not only "falls upon," Acts 8:16; 10:44 is "poured out" Acts 10:45 "comes" Acts 19:6 but now He indwells, to remain and abide forever within the heart of the redeemed. This is the promise of the Father to the Son and the promise of the Son to the Believer.

The Holy Spirit as the Spirit of Promise brings all the promises of God to fulfillment in the redeemed community. The Lord Jesus is the Son of God Who is the example of the workings of the Spirit in humanity in an unhindered operation. The believer as a son of God and member of the Church should follow in His steps and come under the same workings of the Holy Spirit. (Review 1 Peter 2:21; Romans 8:29). So, let

Him come in and let Him love you and He will give you great relationship, just like Jesus declared in John 14:16:

John 14:16
New King James Version (NKJV)

[16] And I will pray the Father, and He will give you another Helper, that He may abide with you forever.

So, you see, the difference between the Holy Spirit being a power or a person couldn't be more profound:

1. If the Holy Spirit is a power, we'll want to get hold of it. If the Holy Spirit is a Divine Person, we'll want Him to get hold of us.
2. If the Holy Spirit is a power, we'll want it to accomplish our will and whim. If the Holy Spirit is a Divine Person, we'll want to surrender more to Him in awe and wonder.
3. If the Holy Spirit is a power, we'll be proud that we have it and feel superior to those who do not. If the Holy Spirit is a Divine Person, we'll be humbled that in His great love the very Third Person of the Godhead has chosen to dwell within us.

It is indeed unfortunate that millions of people view the Holy Spirit merely as a heavenly power or influence. They hold Him in the utmost regard and speak of Him with great reverence, but they don't know Him through personal communion and fellowship. This is doubly sad because first, it's absolutely futile to attempt to understand the work of the Holy Spirit without first knowing Him as a person; and second, they fail to take advantage of the marvelous fellowship of the Holy Spirit, one that even extends into our personal lives in the areas of money, job, giving and business and finance. The Holy Spirit wants to be directly involved in all of these areas of your life and mine. He is waiting for us to assign the job to him!

SURRENDER TO THE BLESSED HOLY SPIRIT

There is no greater way to express our love to the Lord than to surrender to His Holy Spirit every day. In fact, it is absolutely essential if you are to know the person of the Holy Spirit intimately and experience His work profoundly and receive your financial breakthroughs with purpose. BUT SURRENDER IS ONLY POSSIBLE THROUGH PRAYER AND BROKENNESS BEFORE THE LORD.

People often ask me, "Can everyone experience the Holy Spirit like you do? Can everyone see the Holy Spirit do the things that you've experienced?" The answer is absolutely yes! There is no special gift involved - only brokenness and surrender. So the question is not, "Do I have the gift?" The question is, "Can I surrender all to Him?" Here's how the process begins. As you get to know the Lord, it is then that He begins to manifest Himself and His love to you. And a fellowship begins that grows and intensifies until you get to the place where you will say, "Lord Jesus, I give You my life, my mind, my heart, my dreams, my emotions, my thoughts; I give them all to You. I surrender spirit, soul, and body. Do with me as You will."

And as you surrender to Him, it is then that the Holy Spirit begins to teach you, not just about yourself, but about all that the Father has for you (read John 14:26). It is then that He imparts to you His strength and His living faith. For as Isaiah declared:

Isaiah 30:15
New King James Version (NKJV)
15 For thus says the Lord God, the Holy One of Israel:
"In returning and rest you shall be saved;
In quietness and confidence shall be your strength."
But you would not,

Everything about the Word of God now becomes stronger, and everything about prayer now becomes richer. A passage of Scripture you have read countless times becomes more powerful than ever because of the presence of the Holy Spirit. Your communion with God is richer than you've ever known, all because of the presence of the Holy Spirit. And a peace will come and tranquility will come into your life, and for the first time you will understand what the Lord Jesus meant when He said, "My peace I give unto you." All of this becomes yours because of the Holy Spirit, a real person whom you must come to know in your daily life and fellowship with throughout your lifelong journey into prosperity and reconstruction provision in this faith walk with the Lord Jesus Christ. Hopefully, this chapter has dispelled some myths and commonly believed "truths" about the nature of God as a real person - in each of the three entities of the Father, the Son, and the Holy Spirit.

1 John 5:5-7
New King James Version (NKJV)
5 Who is he who overcomes the world, but he
who believes that Jesus is the Son of God?

The Certainty of God's Witness[6] This is He who came
by water and blood—Jesus Christ; not only by water,
but by water and blood. And it is the Spirit who bears

witness, because the Spirit is truth. [7] For there are three that bear witness in heaven: The Father, the Word, and the Holy Spirit; and these three are one.

Psalm 71:22
New King James Version (NKJV)
[22] Also with the lute I will praise You—
***And* Your faithfulness, O my God!**
To You I will sing with the harp,
O Holy One of Israel.

The Hebrew Word ISRAEL means three persons in the Godhead Here is the illustration:

'Is' – means CHRIST

'Ra' – means Holy Spirit Comforter

'El' – means God the Father

LESSON TWELVE

God Purpose Driven:
Daily Wisdom Key for Today:

TITLES OF THE HOLY SPIRIT

Verse to Remember: 1 John 5:7
New King James Version (NKJV)
[7] For there are three that bear witness in heaven: The Father, the Word, and the Holy Spirit; and these three are one.

Question to Meditate On:
Illustration for revelation - 1 X 1 X 1 = 1

Again, the above illustration means TRINITY. Shout AMEN if you have the revelation knowledge of WHO GOD is!

LESSON THIRTEEN

Colossians 1:16-17
New King James Version (NKJV)
**16 For by Him all things were created that are in heaven
and that are on earth, visible and invisible, whether
thrones or dominions or principalities or powers. All
things were created through Him and for Him. 17 And
He is before all things, and in Him all things consist.**

CHRIST AND HIS CREATION –
ANGELIC BEINGS

The Bible gives us a clear view of the heavenly and infernal worlds. Scripture contains many revealing passages that tell us all we need to know of the unseen worlds. By the unseen worlds, we mean all the heavens and the underworld of departed spirits and even the invisible things about us on Earth. By the spirit world we mean all the different spirit beings that live in the invisible material worlds. Numerous spirit beings are revealed in Scripture; they are full of the supernatural. There is but a single step from the natural world to the spiritual world. The following is a description of five angelic beings that inhabit the spirit world:

1. SERAPHIM

These beings are mentioned twice in Scripture in Isaiah 6:1-7:

Isaiah 6:1-7
New King James Version (NKJV)
Isaiah Called to Be a Prophet
**6 In the year that King Uzziah died, I saw the Lord sitting
on a throne, high and lifted up, and the train of His** *robe*
filled the temple. ² **Above it stood seraphim; each one
had six wings: with two he covered his face, with two he
covered his feet, and with two he flew.** ³ **And one cried to
another and said: "Holy, holy, holy** *is* **the L**ORD **of hosts;
The whole earth** *is* **full of His glory!"**⁴ **And the posts
of the door were shaken by the voice of him who
cried out, and the house was filled with smoke.**⁵
So I said: "Woe *is* **me, for I am undone!
Because I** *am* **a man of unclean lips,
And I dwell in the midst of a people of unclean lips;**

**For my eyes have seen the King,
The L**ORD **of hosts."**⁶ **Then one of the seraphim flew to
me, having in his hand a live coal** *which* **he had taken
with the tongs from the altar.** ⁷ **And he touched my mouth**
with it, **and said: "Behold, this has touched your lips;
Your iniquity is taken away,
And your sin purged."**

The seraphim function in full obedience to the commands of the Lord:

SERAPHIM STOOD ABOVE THE LORD'S THRONE - EACH HAD SIX WINGS

SERAPHIM STOOD ABOVE THE LORD'S THRONE - EACH HAD SIX WINGS

2. CHERUBIM

Cherubim are mentioned in many passages, so we will give only a brief summary of them. Ezekiel saw visions of God and of cherubim. He described cherubim as looking like men except that each one has four faces, four wings and feet of a calf. Two wings cover their bodies and two are joined at the tips. They have the faces of a man, an ox, an eagle and a lion. They appear like fire and move with the speed of lightning. They are connected to wheels which look like a wheel within a wheel. The wheels are very high and look like beryl and above them there is a throne on which God sits and He has the appearance of a man. Glorious fire and lightning are all about and a rainbow is above the throne of God (read Ezek. 1:5-28, 8:1-4, 10:1-22). Cherubim drove man from Eden and guarded the tree of life (Gen. 3:24).

CHERUBIM HAVE THE FACES OF A MAN,
AN OX, AN EAGLE, AND A LION

CHERUBIM HAVE THE FACES OF A MAN, AN OX, AN EAGLE,
AND A LION

3. ZOA OR LIVING CREATURES

These beings are similar to cherubim, except that they have only one head each and are full of eyes in front and behind. They are like the seraphim in that they have six wings. One has a face like a lion, one like a calf, one like a man, and one like a flying eagle. They cry, 'Holy, holy, holy' to God day and night (read Rev. 4:6-9). In this passage, zoa means living creature. The zoa are shown in Rev. 5:6 as having harps and singing and worshipping God. They are also seen in other parts of Revelation as behaving much as man does (read Rev. 6:1-8, 7:11, 14:3, 9-11, 15:7, 19:4).

4. SPIRIT HORSES AND CHARIOT DRIVERS

Paul explains that there is much of the invisible world that is like the visible world. Romans 1:20 states:

Romans 1:20
New King James Version (NKJV)
20 For since the creation of the world His invisible attributes are clearly seen, being understood by the things that are made, even His eternal power and Godhead, so that they are without excuse,

Paul says that during his vision of the third heaven, he heard unspeakable words, which is not lawful for a man to utter (read 2 Cor. 12:1-4). People could not comprehend all that Paul had seen and would have considered him to be insane. He knew it was best not to tell all he had seen or else they would reject the good news of the Gospel. We cannot limit the number of creatures in scriptures. Elisha gives us this description concerning his father, Elijah:

THERE APPEARED A CHARIOT OF FIRE AND HORSES OF FIRE

2 Kings 2:11-12
New King James Version (NKJV)
**[11] Then it happened, as they continued on and
talked, that suddenly a chariot of fire *appeared*
with horses of fire, and separated the two of them;
and Elijah went up by a whirlwind into heaven.**

**[12] And Elisha saw *it,* and he cried out, "My father,
my father, the chariot of Israel and its horsemen!"
So, he saw him no more. And he took hold of his
own clothes and tore them into two pieces.**

Later, when the Syrian army came to get Elisha, he prayed to God to show his servant who was on his side. God opened the young man's eyes and he could see.

2 Kings 6:14-17
New King James Version (NKJV)
**[14] Therefore he sent horses and chariots and a great army
there, and they came by night and surrounded the city.**

**[15] And when the servant of the man of God arose early
and went out, there was an army, surrounding the
city with horses and chariots. And his servant said
to him, "Alas, my master! What shall we do?"**

**[16] So he answered, "Do not fear, for those who *are*
with us *are* more than those who *are* with them."**

**[17] And Elisha prayed, and said, "Lord, I pray, open his eyes
that he may see." Then the Lord opened the eyes of the
young man, and he saw. And behold, the mountain *was*
full of horses and chariots of fire all around Elisha.**

Zechariah saw red, black, white, and speckled horses. They were called the spirits of the heavens doing scout work for God (read Zech. 1:8-11, 6:1-8). In Revelation 19:11-21, we see the armies of Heaven on white horses following Christ, who also rides a white horse, coming from Heaven to take control of this world and to rule forever.

5. ARCHANGELS

Archangels are found twice in Scripture. First, with Christ coming in the air to take the living and dead saints home (read 1 Thess. 4:16) and second, in Jude 9, where Michael argues with Satan over the body of Moses.

ARCH is defined as CHIEF, and it infers that archangels are a class of beings greater than common angels. In Dan. 10:21, 12:1, Michael is described as: "...the great prince which standeth for the children of thy people."

6. MICHAEL THE ARCHANGEL AND HIS ROLE IN GOD'S KINGDOM

Ancient Talmudic writings refer to Michael as "Michael the Archangel" and as "The Great Prince." The name, Michael means in Hebrew, "Who is like God." His name is formed from three Hebrew words; MI (who), KA (like), EL (God), and it can be transliterated in this manner MI-KA-EL. According to Dan. 10:13, he is "one of the chief princes." He is the archangel who is closest to the

Lord and is His divine messenger and executes His will. Jewish scholars have held for centuries that Michael guarded and lead the Jews during their forty years of wandering in the desert. Michael was appointed by the Lord to be Israel's guiding angel. During their time in the wilderness God prepared His people for their entrance into the Promised Land and His fulfillment of His Covenant with them. God told them in Exodus 23:20-23:

Exodus 23:20-23
New King James Version (NKJV)
The Angel and the Promises
[20] **"Behold, I send an Angel before you to keep you in the way and to bring you into the place which I have prepared.** [21] **Beware of Him and obey His voice; do not provoke Him, for He will not pardon your transgressions; for My name *is* in Him.** [22] **But if you indeed obey His voice and do all that I speak, then I will be an enemy to your enemies and an adversary to your adversaries.** [23] **For My Angel will go before you and bring you in to the Amorites and the Hittites and the Perizzites and the Canaanites and the Hivites and the Jebusites; and I will cut them off.**

Rev. 12:7-9 says that Michael is the commander of the angels of God who will fight against Satan and his demons and will cast them down to the Earth. He is called one of the chief princes of God in Dan. 10:13. Gabriel is an archangel according to Dan. 8:16-19, 9:20-23, 10:8-11 and Luke 1:19-26. In fact, Lucifer and some angels rebelled against God and now follow him as rulers of certain kingdoms of this world.

MICHAEL THE ARCHANGEL

7. COMMON ANGELS

Scripture mentions angel and common angels 294 times. Taken from Hebrew and Greek, ANGEL means "MESSENGER." He is called the angel of God (read Gen. 21:17, 31:11, Ex. 3:2, Judges 6:29, 13:9, Acts 27:23), the angel of the Lord (read Gen. 16:7-11, 22:11-15, Ex. 14:19, Num. 22:22-35, Judges 2:1-4, 6:11-12, 21-22, 13:3-6, 13-21, 2 Kings 1:3-15, 19:35, 1 Chron. 21:12-30, Ps. 34:7, 35:5-6, Isa. 37:36, Zech. 1:9-19, 3:1-6, 12:8, Acts 7:30-38), His angel (read Gen. 24:7-40, Ex. 23:20, 33:2, Num. 20:16, 2 Chron. 32:21, Dan. 3:28, 6:22), the angel (read Gen. 48:16, Eccl. 5:6, Hos. 12:4), mine angel (read Ex. 23:23, 32-34), and the angel of His presence (read Isa. 63:9).

ANGELS HAVE BODIES LIKE HUMANS

8. THE NATURE OF ANGELS

The Bible describes angels in many books and passages. It says that they are intelligent, wise and have great patience (read 2 Sam. 14:20, Matt. 24:25, 2 Peter 2:11, Luke 20:36). They are powerful, mighty and immortal (read 2 Thess. 1:7-10).

9. ANGELS HAVE BODIES LIKE HUMANS, REAL AND TANGIBLE

They have appeared on earth in human-like form and people could not tell the difference. In, Paul says:

Hebrews 13:2
New King James Version (NKJV)
² Do not forget to entertain strangers, for by so *doing* some have unwittingly entertained angels.

ANGELS HAVE BODIES LIKE HUMANS

This and many other parts of Scripture could not be true if angelic beings were not real with physical, tangible bodies. It must certainly follow that the triune God - God the Father, God the Son and God the Holy Spirit - must have spirit bodies and souls.

The speed of light is 186,000 miles per second and the angels fly faster than the speed of light. So, you see, I would like to encourage you to be strong and use wisdom and use your authority in the name of Jesus to command the angels to do combat in spiritual warfare against the enemies of God. Rev. 12:7 declares that Satan and his demons are cast out by Michael and the angels, so we must continue to combat the enemies day and night. Our Lord Jesus Christ gives us the power and authority over all the ability of the enemy and we have the victory.

Here is an illustration: The distance of the earth from one point to the other is about 22,000 miles in distance. So, the angel, in one second, can go around the earth eight times. Hallelujah! This is good news for you and me. My point is, to the body of Christ, that in times of trouble you can call upon the angels in the name of the Lord Jesus Christ to help you.

For instance, when I began to understand this wonderful revelation, I began to pray for other people and calling the name of Jesus and asking the Lord to send the angels, especially Michael, to pull down the stronghold in peoples' lives and I began to intercede and find that the prayer was answered much faster. I believed that the angels are all around us to help us in times of need. (Heb. 1:14)

Also, I have found in the scriptures, in Psalm 91:11, that God sends angels to rescue us, especially since we live in such a demonically-influenced world. In 1991, in Arizona, I was awakened by a thunderstorm and a hurricane that literally destroyed every roof on homes in my area. I was so scared that I got on my knees and began to pray and ask the Lord to send the angels. Immediately I was in the Spirit and the glory of God filled my home. I saw Michael and Gabriel inside the room holding the ceiling and roof up. There was such a peace around me that I felt like I was in heaven. Several hours later I stepped out of the house. The people were on the street looking at my house which was the only house not damaged in the area. The people knew that I was a Christian and a preacher of the Gospel because for over five years I had continued to witness to them. Their lifestyles were drinking and gambling, but now they looked at me and they knew that God's protection was upon my life. Amen!

I hope that you adopt this teaching and put the angels of God to work for you and others because the angels like to stay busy in carrying out assignments. In your 52-lesson map towards God's blessing, let the angels bring the message of prosperity and wealth to you. Whether it is a new job, a promotion, a clean financial slate, a new business or increase in order to bless God's people, I promise you that they can and will deliver the mail to you, for God, and on HIS behalf. There are many Christians that never put the angels to work because they do not have the knowledge of the Spirit. I believe from this day forth when you are engaged in spiritual warfare, particularly when you are asking and receiving from the Lord, you will remember to get the angels involved on your behalf in Jesus' name. Why not? Satan sends his demons to attack us. Why not involve the true angels of God, which are powerful and faithful and obedient in every area of the work of the Gospel?

Please review Hebrews 1:7-14. I hope this illustration is a help to you in building God's armies. By the way, dear reader, the angels are God's police on patrol in the earth to protect man. Read Exodus 23:20-23. Congratulations, this lesson is concluded, I love you in the Lord.

Recording artist, songwriter, Marty Miller put it this way in his song "Shining Suits:"

Each silent home in Dothan lay in enemy hands

Elisha prayed his fearful servant would understand

God showed the brilliance of all those invisible

Guarding every heavenly plan

CHORUS:

Those men in shining suits, they're standing all around

Some are in the trees, some are lying on the ground

Each one's on fire, just ready to explode

You'll never fight alone

As you walk the narrow road

To the kingdom's throne

Through the angel zone

You'll never be alone

It's hard to walk in darkness while on enemy ground

Trusting invisible strength, though you hear dangerous sounds

But never too far away stands a mighty display

Defenders of His heavenly crown

Repeat Chorus

BRIDGE:

Angels were created for His service.......

Slaves to righteous rendezvous, no slacker......

As celestial wings take to flight

The demons slowly fall

Repeat Chorus

Music and Lyrics by Marty Miller ©Marty Miller Music 1999

LESSON THIRTEEN

God Purpose Driven:
Daily Wisdom Key for Today:

CHRIST AND HIS CREATION - ANGELIC BEINGS

Verse to Remember: Colossians 1:16-17
New King James Version (NKJV)
16 For by Him all things were created that are in heaven and that are on earth, visible and invisible, whether thrones or dominions or principalities or powers. All things were created through Him and for Him. 17 And He is before all things, and in Him all things consist.

Question to Meditate: Am I giving God glory for the times, over and over, in which he has rescued me, especially when I was unaware. If your answer is yes, shout 3 times:

HALLELUJAH, HALLELUJAH, HALLELUJAH!

LESSON FOURTEEN

Luke 4:18
Amplified Bible (AMP)
¹⁸ The Spirit of the Lord [is] upon Me, because He has anointed Me [the Anointed One, the Messiah] to preach the good news (the Gospel) to the poor; He has sent Me to announce release to the captives and recovery of sight to the blind, to send forth as delivered those who are oppressed [who are downtrodden, bruised, crushed, and broken down by calamity],

GOD CAN AND DID SUPERNATURALLY CANCEL YOUR DEBT

<u>God cancelled your greatest debt on Calvary!</u> Wow, the Lord's first message covers it all. The Lord can also cancel your financial debt. It doesn't matter what situation you are in, now you belong to Him and if you don't faint or quit and you learn to follow through with all of these lessons in this book, you will not and cannot fail. The bible declares in I Kings 4:1-7:

2 Kings 4:1-7
Amplified Bible (AMP)
4 Now the wife of a son of the prophets cried to Elisha, your servant my husband is dead, and you know that your servant feared the Lord. But the creditor has come to take my two sons to be his slaves.

² Elisha said to her, What shall I do for you? Tell me, what have you [of sale value] in the house? She said, Your handmaid has nothing in the house except a jar of oil.

³ Then he said, go around and borrow vessels from all your neighbors, empty vessels—and not a few.

⁴ And when you come in, shut the door upon you and your sons. Then pour out [the oil you have] into all those vessels, setting aside each one when it is full.

⁵ So she went from him and shut the door upon herself and her sons, who brought to her the vessels as she poured the oil.

⁶ When the vessels were all full, she said to her son, Bring me another vessel. And he said to her, There is not a one left. Then the oil stopped multiplying.

⁷ Then she came and told the man of God. He said, Go, sell the oil and pay your debt, and you and your sons live on the rest.

Right now, you may be buried deeply in debt, feeling overwhelmed without hope. God does not want you living a life of servitude and slavery to financial difficulties. You can live a wealthy, debt free lifestyle. Borrowing should not be a way of life. I want to make this clear, the bible does not declare or say specifically that it is wrong to borrow money. The richest man who ever lived is King Solomon. He clearly points out that the wealthy have control over the persons they lend money to – and the borrower is at the mercy of the lender. We read in Proverbs 22:7:

Proverbs 22:7
Amplified Bible (AMP)
⁷ The rich rule over the poor, and the borrower is servant to the lender.

The bible does not forbid to borrow money, it is permissible when you have the ability to pay back by having assets such as property, gold, stocks, bonds, oil, etc. It is then permissible for your home, business, transportation and so on. However, you must be cautious not to allow debt to become a habit or pattern of life for you or your family.

God warns us and does not want you under the control of a vicious lifestyle of debt. For instance, let's look at America and the final result of the beginning of 2013. The national debt to other nations is over 16 trillion in debt. Without a doubt, divine judgment is inevitable unless there is a serious revival and recommitment of the people to cry to the Lord in repentance and to cry out loud because America has broken the laws of God concerning reckless debt. In the United States, the economy has been driven by the deception of the political leaders making the wrongs decision which are not based on political concepts that our forefathers gave us by the Constitution which made America strong and united by the Spirit of the Lord.

It is obvious that the US economy is driven by consumer debt. We have gone from an industrial nation that once made things and created and built a strong nation with great value in family, in business and education and culture to buying things – replacing our factories with shopping malls. Statistically 2/3 of our gross domestic product (GDP) is generated by consumers spending billions and billions of dollars. The credit industry has discovered through careful research that consumers will spend more than 50% on credit cards instead of using hard cash. America has shifted more than 60% of its companies overseas and they have created clever marketing and scientific commercials that strongly reinforce the subconscious mind and associate success and happiness with credit card living lifestyles. The bible is very clear that an honest day brings an honest pay.

By keeping this in mind, we need to go back to the foundation and do it God's way.

DEBT IS A DEMONIC SPIRIT AND CAN STEAL YOUR HOPE

You have an enemy. There is a demonic spirit that wants to destroy everything that God has meant for you to have and possess. It is a sprit called DEBT that strips you of your covenant rights and blessings outlined in Deuteronomy 28. Read what the bible tells us about this phenomenal spirit that causes warfare in your life.

Ephesians 6:12
Amplified Bible (AMP)
¹² For we are not wrestling with flesh and blood [contending only with physical opponents], but against the despotisms, against the powers, against [the master spirits who are] the world rulers of this present darkness, against the spirit forces of wickedness in the heavenly (supernatural) sphere.

You can be free. As a child of God, you have been given spiritual authority to break the spirit of DEBT! You must exercise this authority as a believer and rebuke and cast out this spirit from controlling your life. II Kings 4:1-7 outlines the biblical basis for agreeing with God that HE will do this for YOU. It is a wonderful story to see the supernatural debt cancellation of this widowed woman. The account begins to unfold when the prophet Elisha was approached, one day, by a widow in desperate financial need.

Unspeakable tragedy happened to this woman's life. Her husband died and now she found herself alone and buried deeply in debt. She had no money and no dependable income and she was unable to pay her debtors. Can you imagine how desperate this woman was, to the point of debt? To make things worse, her creditors were threatening to take her 2 sons as bondsman and throw them into prison until what she owed was paid. The Jewish law gave right to claim the children of the debtors. The spirit of debt left her family without hope and nowhere to turn to but GOD. She cried out hard to the Lord!

GOD LOOKED DOWN FROM HEAVEN AND SENT A RESCUER – ELISHA

God heard the woman's desperate appeal and responded immediately by sending the man of God to her house. You need to know that when a believer is faithful in God's ways and when trials, tribulations and problems come to him, he can go to the source and cry to the Lord and ask God, anytime, for a miracle and HE will send a person to your life. This is called a divine connection. The almighty spoke to the prophet Elisha and commissioned him to go to this particular house. When he arrived, basically, he did not focus on the widow's bleak situation – instead he asked her a surprising question. This is where the miracle story unfolds through inquiry asked by Elisha. What do you presently have left in your house?

EVERYONE HAS A SEED FOR DEBT CANCELLATION

Everything is a seed and everyone has a seed. From the very beginning there hasn't been a single human being in the earth that doesn't possess something to sow. This principle found in Genesis can really change your life forever. It is written in the bible and is known by many as the law of seedtime and harvest. We read in Genesis 8:22:

Genesis 8:22
New King James Version (NKJV)
22 "While the earth remains,
Seedtime and harvest,
Cold and heat,
Winter and summer, and day and night
Shall not cease."

She only had a small pot of oil but it was enough to become a seed. This is why we must inventory our seed bank, searching diligently for any seed you currently possess for your future. What do you have available around you? Your seed may be small now and it might be insufficient to meet your present needs but, remember, your seed is alive and contains invisible instructions and will multiply and become more and more and much more. Remember, every seed brings harvest but God will always require something that you possess. Your seed will bring deliverance so it is very important to inventory your total possessions. Stop dwelling on what you do not have and see what you do have within this very moment, within your reach.

When you sow in good faith it will create supernatural debt cancellation and you will have enough now, not tomorrow or next week or even next year, but NOW you will have enough. We see our forefathers, through the bible, from Able through all the prophets always by faith sowed seeds. Finally, God sowed the greatest seed of all, His only begotten Son. Through Jesus Christ now He has a family which is the church, the body of Christ. By the way, seed faith is not a one-time event. It is a lifestyle. What seed faith is is sowing something you have got for something you have not. It is sowing what you possess for what you want from God.

GOD'S GUARANTEE IS TO SUPPLY A SEED TO YOU

2 Corinthians 9:10
New King James Version (NKJV)
[10] Now may[a] He who supplies seed to the sower, and bread for food, supply and multiply the seed you have *sown* and increase the fruits of your righteousness,

What is a seed? Anything you sow that has the potential to increase, multiply and become more. The seed is what you sow. The harvest is what you keep. You have many seeds that you can sow. For example;

1. Your very being can be given to the Lord
2. Love is a seed
3. Words are seeds
4. Money is a seed
5. Serving others is seed
6. Your time can be sown as seed
7. Material things like clothing and furniture can be sown
8. Giving food away is sowing seed
9. Engaging to help other people without expecting anything is a seed
10. Spending time in praise and worship to the Lord
11. Reading the bible
12. Recognize and dedicate all that you own to God
13. Land, property and buildings as investment
14. Oil, livestock and commodities

Whatever you have available in your possession right now is the catalyst to blessings, increase, favor & prosperity. Every farmer understands the power hidden in a tiny seed. Yes, it is true that every seed has a unique and hidden DNA. It has instruction to reproduce after its kind. You cannot see it because it is too small to see with the natural eye but it is there.

1. You sow grape seeds you reap grapes
2. You sow apple seed you reap apples
3. You sow tomato seed you reap tomatoes
4. You sow banana seed to reap bananas
5. And so on and on......

Once you release your seed from your hand into good soil, God see's it and multiplies it 30, 60 and 100-fold. The 100-fold meaning in Hebrew means unlimited amount. Wow, don't you want that. Then do it God's way and you'll stay to eat the fruit of the land. If you disobey you hit the highway.

GOD WAS AND STILL IS THE FIRST FARMER

The bible is crystal clear that God is the first farmer. Let's read Genesis 2:8:

Genesis 2:8
New King James Version (NKJV)
Life in God's Garden
⁸ The LORD God planted a garden eastward in Eden, and there He put the man whom He had formed.

God established this principle in Genesis from the beginning, then you and I should accept that this is God's method to provide for us. In fact, you must know that whether you accept this principle or not, it operates in your life every single day. God is continuously sowing seed. You cannot stop sowing! The only influence you have is whether you sow good or bad seed. Have you ever heard the following statements;

1. What goes around comes around!

2. You will get what is coming to you.
3. You're going the wrong way.
4. You have made the wrong decisions.
5. You're going to reap what you sow.

Galatians 6:7
Amplified Bible (AMP)
[7] Do not be deceived *and* deluded *and* misled; God will not allow Himself to be sneered at (scorned, disdained, or mocked [a]by mere pretensions or professions, or by His precepts being set aside.) [He inevitably deludes himself who attempts to delude God.] For whatever a man sows, that *and*[b]that only is what he will reap.

Proverbs 18:21
Amplified Bible (AMP)
[21] Death and life are in the power of the tongue, and they who indulge in it shall eat the fruit of it [for death or life].

The words you speak and the confession that you make have the creative force and the power to change the climate of your life whether you are in the room, elevator, outdoors or on the telephone! If you really desire your circumstances to be transformed into God's highest moral law which is the best good for all mankind. Then, boldly speak the word of God out loud. Speak and shout and command that mountain of unpaid bills to go.

Please remember that supernatural and supercharged power is the power of God AND available only when you believe what you are saying will actually come to pass.

Mark 11:23-24
Amplified Bible (AMP)
[23] Truly I tell you, whoever says to this mountain, be lifted up and thrown into the sea! and does not doubt at all in his heart but believes that what he says will take place, it will be done for him.

[24] For this reason I am telling you, whatever you ask for in prayer, believe (trust and be confident) that it is granted to you, and you will [get it].

James 1:6
Amplified Bible (AMP)
[6] Only it must be in faith that he asks with no wavering (no hesitating, no doubting). For the one who wavers (hesitates, doubts) is like the billowing surge out at sea that is blown hither *and* thither and tossed by the wind.

Matthew 12:34
Amplified Bible (AMP)
[34] You offspring of vipers! How can you speak good things when you are evil (wicked)? For out of the fullness (the overflow, the [a] superabundance) of the heart the mouth speaks.

Look at this closely with me. Jesus said, "Whosoever can have whatsoever he desires, if he'll speak and believe in his heart." Surrender to the voice of faith. Every mountain of debt in your life must succumb to the verbal seed that you sow when you believe what you are saying. Believe – then speak the word of God over your debt or over every mountain that is trying to stop you in fulfilling your goals.

LESSON FOURTEEN

Bible Purpose Driven
Daily Wisdom Key for Today:

GOD CAN AND DID SUPERNATURALLY CANCEL YOUR DEBT

God cancelled your greatest debt on Calvary!

Verse to Remember: Luke 4:18
Amplified Bible (AMP)
18 The Spirit of the Lord [is] upon Me, because He has anointed Me [the Anointed One, the Messiah] to preach the good news (the Gospel) to the poor; He has sent Me to announce release to the captives and recovery of sight to the blind, to send forth as delivered those who are oppressed [who are downtrodden, bruised, crushed, and broken down by calamity],

Question to Meditate On: Begin to meditate on these words:

I AM DOING IT GOD'S WAY AND MY FINANCIAL FREEDOM IS ON THE WAY!

LESSON FIFTEEN

Proverbs 14:12
Amplified Bible (AMP)
¹² There is a way which seems right to a man *and* appears straight before him, but at the end of it is the way of death.

TEN POINTS TO HELP YOU TO NOT FALL INTO SIN

Have you been encumbered by the daily responsibilities of life such as mortgage, car, student loan and so on? Has the burden of debt overwhelmed and weighed you down making relief seem impossible because of your ignorance or greed or because you have been misled by the devil and are living in a fantasy island? You have tried and searched for ways to dig yourself out of the interest rate mess you have gotten yourself in, but with very little success, because the interest rate in your existing accounts have escalated from 5% to 18%.

Now you find yourself juggling from one bank to another and one company to another because the bank and loan company has promised you a better opportunity and a better life., they prove to be only a marketing illusion to draw you into their purpose and get you to sign your name to get more credit cards. Hopelessness and despair are the emotions you are feeling now as you watch the American dream move beyond your reach. Then you talk to your partners or wife and ask, "How did this happen to me? How did I get into this mess?"

20 years ago, you promised yourself that this wouldn't happen to you the way it happened to your mom and dad. It's easy to make excuses for being in debt. You say to yourself over and over, everyday and every week, "I will dig myself out of this hole, one of these days." But the years go by and every year you make a new resolution to make a new excuse.

THERE IS HOPE FOR YOU TODAY AS YOU VENTURE TO GET YOURSELF OUT OF DEBT

How? By identifying specific habits and attitudes which in reality are behind your spending patterns. These subconscious threats are controlling your money. Once you acknowledge you will be empowered with information to change.

1. Confess all of your wrong doing and your wrong ways to God. Confession is good for the soul. As you do you will be liberated from the chains that have entangled you.
2. Make God your partner in every move and affair of your life and expect and let him lead you in every way and in every move that you make by seeking Him in prayer and by waiting for His wisdom to make a new approach.

Psalms 37:23
'The steps of a righteous man are ordered by the Lord, even though he stumbles, the Lord will pick him up.'

3. Do not be impulsive in buying things that you do not need. Remember, often you return home from a shopping trip to find you spent more than you planned to. Just because something is on sale at a good price don't buy it if you don't need it. For the majority of people this is a minor problem, however, for some it is a tremendous struggle and a trap which takes them

deeper into debt. What causes impulsive behavior and causes you to fall? Avoid pitfalls which eventually lead you into the bottomless pit of spending.

4. Avoid places that entice you to spend like flea markets, swap meets, grand opening malls. This will take up your time and cause you to spend more money. Remember the saying 'out of sight, out of mind.' I will make a confession towards my wife – 20 years ago when I began to date her, we went camping and her dress got ripped. I took her to a Goodwill store and she said, "I don't want to wear second-hand clothing, who do you think I am?" I smiled at her and persuaded her and she found a beautiful dress for $2.00. Well, she was so excited, for the next 15 years she shopped at the Goodwill store in every city that we went to when we traveled and did Ministry and she bargained and got good deals on clothing, shoes, gifts and flowers, etc. I would say, "Lydia, we don't need this." I finally realized that she became impulsive and addicted and she would reply to me, "Honey, I want these as gifts to give to other people." I also found myself carrying 4 suitcases of gifts from Taiwan to America and other countries to satisfy her hobby. My purpose in travelling the nations was to do Mission work yet I was still a slave to her spending. This went on from 1991 to 2012. In July 2012, we moved the operation from Arizona to Los Angeles and over $20,000 in items, which filled a large room, were given away to people in need and to the Goodwill because we didn't have enough room in the truck to carry it all. When she found out she was very upset and finally, after 3 months she confessed and she broke the addiction and thank God she got healed. Now I love to carry my books from books from country to country because they are inspired by God to empower other

people to a way of living for God and they also bring me a financial income. Another factor is not recognizing that there is a problem and refusing to deal with it when it is recognized. Here are some suggestions: avoid impulsive spending behaviors and instead incorporate them into your life slowly so that you have a balance in your life.

5. Take control of your future by changing your present spending patterns. Do not be too quick to run out. Sit down and write down the things that you need then pray over it and find out if you really need it.

6. Get rid of all your credit cards except one. Sit down and burn and cut your credit cards and make sure that before you use the one, that you have money in it so you will pay no interest rate because the credit card does not belong to you, it belongs to the bank. When you use it and you cannot afford it, you are breaking the law of prosperity and you will fall behind again, into a ditch. SPEND CASH MONEY AND NOT PLASTIC. Adopt this habit and your life will become easier. Be firm and make a commitment for the next 6 months that all of your spending will be cash money and try to avoid where they do not take cash. Non-cash spending is created by the credit card companies to increase their interest revenue. The goal is to brainwash the new generation to believe that we are headed toward a cashless society.

7. You must not avoid your obligations and responsibility. America and other nations in society and our politicians, sad to say, have adopted an attitude of always blaming the other guy for their wrong doing. They always point the finger and people say, "It is there fault that I am in trouble." You must take responsibility for your action in every area of your life and stop blaming everyone else for your spending mistakes. Admit when you are

wrong. "I am wrong, I am sorry, I repent to the Lord and swallow my pride and acknowledge and hope for a better change." These sentences are rather small but they are highly significant. The road to financial recovery begins today, NOW. Today is the best day your life, to start improving your personal finances. Tackle these disturbing habits and attitudes one at a time. You can do it. John 15:7 says:

John 15:7
New King James Version (NKJV)
⁷ If you abide in Me, and My words abide in you, you will[a] ask what you desire, and it shall be done for you.

8. Continue to organize your life and establish it. Take inventory of the things that you have around you. If you have 3 cars, sell two of them and keep one. Most Americans have a 2-3 car garage full of junk which is treasure to others and valuable. Begin, in the weekend on your free time, to have an estate sale or garage sale. You will be surprised that people will pay a high price for the things that you have accumulated.

9. Eliminate spending by eating out and ordering food to be delivered. Take the time to eat home-cooked meals with your family. You can save more than 50% of your disposable income by eating at the house or cooking in the office and you will spare yourself the pain of becoming a victim of these modern-day chefs and their recipes which are full of chemical, preservative and sodium, because everything today on the market is not fresh but the enemy has tainted it.

10. These are some suggestions and an outline of what you can do to help you to maintain and repair your credit if the level of action is already against you: you will

determine what steps are necessary but one things is for sure, doing nothing will yield negative results:

a. Talk with your creditors and keep an open line of conversation. Motivate them to help you because they want to be re-paid. They want to retain you as their customer. This will tend to work in your favor. Legally, as soon as you default on debt, the creditor has a right to ask you to pay the debt immediately and in full. This rarely happens because the lender is interested in keeping you as their customer to give you more loans.

b. Call them and set up a new payment method. If you expect to be late, pick up the phone before the due date and call them and let them know you are running late. They can expect a payment. Most lenders already have established payment plans for people who have difficulty in paying.

c. Get a second or third job for you or your wife or your children. If a person lives long enough, hard times will eventually hit. Sometimes they are caused by foolish financial decisions, while other times they are beyond the realm of your ability to manage. One thing is certain, they will arrive, however, how you deal with them is in your control. Remember, pray, think right and do right. One of the best ways to get out of a financial pit is to earn extra income by getting a second or third job. Sure, it will require effort, time and sacrifice but it may be the only alternative to keep your good credit in tact. Remember, an honest day and an honest pay. THIS IS THE GOLDEN RULE! You can create!

Philippians 4:13
New King James Version (NKJV)
[13] **I can do all things through Christ[a] who strengthens me.**

You must prioritize your spending. Focus on achieving your goal of becoming debt free. It is based and contingent upon whether you are willing to alter, change and adopt different spending habits. Spend to make money and not to lose it.

LESSON FIFTEEN

TEN POINTS TO HELP YOU
TO NOT FALL INTO SIN

Verse to Remember: Proverbs 14:12
Amplified Bible (AMP)
12There is a way which seems right to a man *and* appears straight before him, but at the end of it is the way of death.

Question to Meditate On: The Gospel is GOOD NEWS! Begin to say out loud, "I am debt free and all my needs are met and I am out of debt and there is much more coming to me because my help comes from the Lord." Psalms 1:21.

LESSON SIXTEEN

John 3:16
New King James Version (NKJV)
16 For God so loved the world that He gave His only begotten Son, that whoever believes in Him should not perish but have everlasting life.

GIVING TO OTHERS

It is crystal clear that God gave the best for eternity for all of us. Only through Him we can have love, joy, peace, happiness, success, prosperity. and everlasting eternal life. We hope and pray that these chapters will help you, as they are designed to help the reader to overcome every obstacle that you have encountered in your life. These chapters are designed specifically so that you will obtain from God every benefit that God has already abundantly provided for. Remember, that everything in life happens according to God's cycles and seasons. The Key to success is in understanding God's timing and his seasons. The bible declares through Solomon in:

Ecclesiastes 3:1-8
New King James Version (NKJV)
Everything Has Its Time
3 To everything *there is* a season,
A time for every purpose under heaven:

² A time to be born,
And a time to die;
A time to plant,
And a time to pluck *what is* planted;

³ A time to kill, And a time to heal;
A time to break down,
And a time to build up;

⁴ A time to weep,
And a time to laugh;
A time to mourn,
And a time to dance;

⁵ A time to cast away stones,
And a time to gather stones;
A time to embrace,
And a time to refrain from embracing;

⁶ A time to gain,
And a time to lose;
A time to keep,
And a time to throw away;

⁷ A time to tear,
And a time to sew;
A time to keep silence,
And a time to speak;

⁸ A time to love,
And a time to hate;
A time of war,
And a time of peace.

Generally, as people go through life they always want to know what they are going to get out of everything that is done. Often people fail and lose what they already have. They might lose friends or even become an outcast from society. No one then wants to be around these types of individuals and they go through life alone. We say that If one would start out with the idea of giving instead of getting they will succeed and not fail. Give service to men in your business and you will prosper. Bless men and seek God and His righteousness in life and all the blessings you need in life will be added to you. If there is one thing that you can succeed in life doing, it is GIVING. One can always give, and if he will do this he will have, to give. This is a law that never fails. Jesus said,

Luke 6:38
New King James Version (NKJV)
[38] Give, and it will be given to you: good measure, pressed down, shaken together, and running over will be put into your bosom. For with the same measure that you use, it will be measured back to you."

People may temporarily hinder you in making money, but they cannot hinder you from giving. No one wants to hinder you in this phase of life. YOU BECOME A HERO WHEN YOU GIVE. You are a wonderful person to everybody as long as you have things to give and as long as you are generous to others. Something wonderful happens when you start to give. Start by giving yourself to God and to others to serve them.

Romans 12:1-2
New King James Version (NKJV)
Living Sacrifices to God
12 I beseech you therefore, brethren, by the mercies of God, that you present your bodies a living sacrifice, holy, acceptable to God, *which is* your reasonable service.
[2] And do not be conformed to this world, but be transformed by the renewing of your mind, that you may prove what *is* that good and acceptable and perfect will of God.

Give your good will, your wishes, your time, your talents, your life, and your all; and you will begin receiving from both God and men whom you bless. Once in a while you may find one who will not give you in return, but for one who does not, there are many who will give back to you in appreciation for what you are giving them. You should give your all to the service of God and man, not because you expect something in return, but because you know it is right and because it is your nature and the giving back to you will be a natural result.

You will have many friends who will be pulling for you to succeed in anything you undertake. They will put forth every effort to help you succeed. One will show you how to make more money. Another will cause an open door of blessings here and one there. Others will give you this and that in life that will help you in the time of need. As you are prospered materially and spiritually, give out to help others, and your supply will never be exhausted. "Give and it shall be given you" is not only a divine law, but it is also a divine promise. The Christian thus will prosper, and as he does, he should give himself to hospitality, remembering that "Love worketh no ill to his neighbor: therefore, love is the fulfilling of the law" (Rom 12:13; 13:10). Paul said,

2 Corinthians 9:6-12
New King James Version (NKJV)
The Cheerful Giver
⁶ But this *I say:* He who sows sparingly will also reap sparingly, and he who sows bountifully will also reap bountifully. ⁷ *So let* each one *give* as he purposes in his heart, not grudgingly or of necessity; for God loves a cheerful giver. ⁸ And God *is* able to make all grace abound toward you, that you, always having all sufficiency in all *things*, may have an abundance for every good work. ⁹ As it is written:

**"He has dispersed abroad,
He has given to the poor;
His righteousness endures forever."[a][10] Now may[b] He who
supplies seed to the sower, and bread for food, supply
and multiply the seed you have *sown* and increase the
fruits of your righteousness, [11] while *you are* enriched in
everything for all liberality, which causes thanksgiving
through us to God. [12] For the administration of this
service not only supplies the needs of the saints, but
also is abounding through many thanksgivings to God**

As we come to the end of the chapter we remind ourselves to
thank the Lord for HIS wonderful word that cannot fail! When
you and I or anyone, wherever they may be around the world,
Africa, South America, England or China or anywhere else on
the globe, submit to the teaching of the gospel and obey HIS
word then we are bound to WIN AND CANNOT FAIL.

LESSON SIXTEEN

God Purpose Driven:
Daily Wisdom Key for Today:

GIVING TO OTHERS

Verse to Remember: John 3:16
New King James Version (NKJV)
16 For God so loved the world that He gave His
only begotten Son, that whoever believes in Him
should not perish but have everlasting life.

Question to Meditate On: To be faithful in obedience is the only way to go.

LESSON SEVENTEEN

Proverbs 3:8-9
New King James Version (NKJV)
[8] It will be health to your flesh,[a]
And strength[b] to your bones.
[9] Honor the LORD with your possessions,
And with the first fruits of all your increase;

FIRSTFRUITS

If we do this we have the promise: "So shall thy barns be filled with plenty, and thy presses shall burst out with new wine." We also have the promise in Malachi 3:10-11:

Malachi 3:10-11
New King James Version (NKJV)
[10] Bring all the tithes into the storehouse,
That there may be food in My house,
And try Me now in this,"
Says the LORD of hosts,

"If I will not open for you the windows of heaven
And pour out for you *such* blessing
That *there will* not *be room* enough *to receive it.*

[11] "And I will rebuke the devourer for your sakes,
So that he will not destroy the fruit of your ground,
Nor shall the vine fail to bear fruit for you in the field,"
Says the LORD of hosts;

In this passage found in Malachi, we have an accusation by God that He was being robbed; we have a command to bring all the tithes into the storehouse; and we have a challenge by God to prove Him and see if He would not cause prosperity. If one will pay the tithes or ten percent of all his income, wages, increase or profit to the Lord and keep books, so that there will be no mistakes, God is under obligation to meet His challenge.

The next four chapters have been blended in with some of brother Billy Burke's message and a teaching, on this scripture, he gave in 2004 in Westminster, California. We believe that it is very appropriate and inspired by God to include this chapter in, Bible Financial Purpose Driven to help you with some 'do's and dont's' in the elimination process and in correcting some areas in your life. By reading this content from brother Burke and thereby understanding the character of God, which he conveys very well, we believe that this will be essential and important teaching to help you obtain your financial freedom. We believe and hope that you will be blessed as I was blessed. All of the staff of Everlasting CHIP Ministry are grateful to Billy Burke Ministries for allowing us to use this material:

~

"Malachi Chapter 3, it says this in verse 9. It's often the part of this we don't look carefully at. Say it with me, "You are cursed with a curse, for you have robbed me more than a whole nation. Bring all of your tithes into the storehouse that there may be meat in Mine house and prove Me now if I will not pour upon you, open up the windows of heaven and pour upon you a blessing, that there shall be not room enough to receive it." Verse number 9, say it, "You are cursed with a curse because you're robbing Me with tithes and offerings." Very elementary, very ABC, I'm not going to spend a lot of time on this but you need to hear it because some of you are in violation. God said that He demands that a tenth, a minimum of a tenth of what you have is owed to Him. It's not optional. He said when you don't give Me a tenth, now this is not three percent, this is not eight percent, it's not what you feel like, it's a tenth of any kind of money you have coming into your house. Social Security check, alimony check, child support check, coal miner's black lung, whatever you have coming into your home, whatever level of revenue, God said ten percent of that you owe Me. It's not your choice, it's not your luxury, it's not up to you whether you should give that or not, God is saying like you owe on your house, on your car, on your credit card, you owe Me, I demand a tenth of that to come towards Me. Now God says, whenever you refuse that, later on into this book, He says if you refuse that, you will be cursed with a curse.

Now, we're talking about a money curse here. The Bible is filled with many different kinds of curses.

You know about the curse of the law. Come on, say "the curse of the law." Then we know about the curse that comes with fornication. We know about the curse that comes with idolatry. Certain things carry with them certain curses. But there is a curse that deals strictly with your money or the issues of money. What does that mean? It means, the harder you work, the more money that you make, it slips through your hands. It's like you never get the information that you need to get the best deal you can. All the things I just mentioned, you never get connected with the right people that can help you. You don't get the best car insurance, you think you have until you meet somebody else at church and find out they have a way better deal than you do. It just seems that the harder you work, the less benefit and favor you have and you never seem to get connected, you never seem to have enough, and you can't figure it out, working, working, working, you're making it but where does it go?

Curse on your money. A curse is something that you can't necessarily put your finger on. You feel the impact of it. It's like you're banging against this brick wall. The windows aren't opened. They're closed and they're locked. When you don't give God ten percent on a regular basis with every amount of money you have, then everything that you have in place of that is stolen merchandise. If I'm not tithing, this suit is stolen. If I'm not tithing, the car I drive in Florida is a stolen car. If I'm not tithing, then any money that I spend that I consider to be my own is stolen stuff. And today we have churches where people go to church and in the parking lot is a stolen car, they're wearing stolen clothes, beautiful glasses they got, they didn't have them last week, nice new frames, they're stolen frames, because they got those frames, they drive that car, they wear that dress and that nice new belt that has rhinestones on it, but they're robbing God and they're cursed with a curse. I hope you like that belt because that's about the best it's going to get for you in this life and you begin to adopt the curse that begins to bottleneck, come on, say that word, "bottleneck".

Bottleneck is when something is rushing and gushing and all of a sudden it becomes tight and stream like. It comes up the neck of the bottle. You see, God is never going to let you do without because you're His son, you're His daughter. He's always going to provide for you, but whenever you're robbing Him, what's going to happen is everything in the name of finance will be bottlenecked. Well I know people that's not doing that and – yeah but they have sorrow in their life. The Bible says God makes a man rich and adds no sorrow. Meaning what? You get money, you keep your health. You get money, you keep your marriage. You get money, you keep your morals. You get money, your kids turn out right. You see, a lot of people are making money, but they're losing their kids to get it. A lot of people are getting more money, but they lose their faith getting it. That's why a lot of people get a lot of money and then they're corrupted. They take different women and different men and they begin to drink and do drugs, they begin to do this and they become a law unto themselves. And that's not God prospering them. When

God prospers a man or a woman, He blesses you and there's no, nada, zero, nein, there's no sorrow in it. It's clean.

It's pure and it's without mixture. Come on, somebody give God praise! Hurry!

The ten percent of the tithe is not money that you choose to give to God, it's money that you owe. I'm going to say that: It's money that you owe God and He counts very well. He has a recording angel. When Jesus was here, He said – weren't there then of you that were healed, one, two three, four-ten. How many know, if you don't think God counts, in the book of the Old Testament, there's a book called Numbers. Come on, somebody. He counts. He's very aware of every detail of your finances, and whenever you aren't giving the tithes, you begin the process of financial curse. Now, don't believe that because I said it tonight, that's why I wanted to start the evening off with that verse.

As simple as that verse is, before we go any further tonight with some other issues, and there's other issues tonight that I can help you with. Before we get there, this here is a simple hurdle. We have people that come to meetings and they come to this church. There's people in this church that do this and that is they will tithe when they are here, but if they miss a week, they won't make up. Well, did you get a paycheck that week? Yeah, we understand you can't get to church every week. Something is going to come up in the course of a year, a vacation, or you need to sleep in one day to catch up on some rest, or your family's in town, or your daughters at a soccer match, and God bless you, we're praying for you. But if you're a member of that church and you got a paycheck that week, either you send that tithe into the church or you bring it with you next week when you come. You don't take a Sunday off and then not pay God, then you're robbing Him, because that tenth, listen to me, that tenth that is in your pocket is going to be spent somewhere else. Do you hear me? The Bible says when you do that, when you keep the sacred portion in your pocket, in the Bible, Book of Malachi, it says that a flying scroll will be released in your home.

That flying scroll and the Scripture says will come into your house and hide in the walls of your house because you've kept My sacred portion. And it says it's not until you get, what? The sacred portion back into the house of God, back into the place where He's commanded you to put it, will the flying scroll be removed from your home. What does the flying scroll do to your house? It turns the walls green. It means what? Anything that's in the realm of negativity begins to be unleashed in your household. So, if you can imagine a scroll with wings in it that flies into your home and just sits and just hides in your house until you get this thing right. I know you have dreams, I know you have desires, and I know you think it doesn't make any sense after you work hard and pay taxes to take a tenth off of the top of that, and just go, you know.

One lady came to me and she said "Billy", she says, you know, "I can't give much now," but she said, "I tell you someday, someday, I'm going to have me so much money," I said "Look at me, if you can't give me ten bucks out of a hundred, how are you ever going to write a million dollar check out of ten million. You're kidding yourself. If you can't give ten percent out of what you have now, what makes you think you're going to be able to write out ten percent out of what you think you're going to have." When you have a hundred bucks and that's all you have; ten bucks is a lot. And you lose ten bucks in your mind, you only have ninety left. But you don't know that ten bucks is going into the hands of God. Come on now, say "God's hand is bigger than my hand." And when you release what's within your hand, then God's able to release what is within His hand. And His hand is so much bigger than your hand. Come on, somebody put it together for God.

You say, "Yeah, but all I have is a paper route." Doesn't matter. "I clean houses." Doesn't matter. Yeah, but I'm a lawyer, and I never know when my check's coming in. "Well, we'll wait for it. "But I'm not on a regular pay scale." We're patient. We'll wait. When it hits, then ten percent off of that. And God's watching you. He's watching you. You know, He's watching you. And if you're here and you're making big deals, and maybe you make a lot of money, maybe you're making –maybe you put a deal together and you sell something, maybe you're some kind of a broker, you're brokering yachts or homes or property. There are a lot of real estate people that are millionaires. A lot of consultants and they go to church somewhere. A lot of these professional athletes. A lot of the people you see on TBN, making millions and they go to church somewhere.

Dion Sanders goes to church somewhere. Goes to T.D. Jake's church. Writes checks out for a hundred thousand. Emmet Smith for the Dallas Cowboys writes checks out for a million and you go, "Oh my God!" Well, you got to show God that you would do the same. How? By giving a tenth out of what you have now and that becomes what? That becomes one of your defenses against keeping that curse off of your money. You may be healthy tonight. You may have a good marriage tonight. You may live in a house and you may have a car but your money is crippled. Keep that in mind tonight. We're talking about your money. We're not necessarily talking directly about you. Separate it because it would be so easy for you to sit back there tonight and what you might do tonight is throw up a defense at me and say, "Well, money isn't everything."

Well, then quit worrying about it. Money isn't everything huh? Well then just quit worrying about it and quit being afraid and just be happy with what you have. But if you're not happy with what you have, maybe you need to listen to me tonight. I may not have all the answers for you, but there may be something God says through me tonight, just one little nugget that you could tweak your life with and say, "Not that – I'm going to begin to do that." Come on put your hands together for God and say Amen!

So, principle number one to get the curse off your money, is make sure you tithe. Make sure you tithe ten percent on a regular basis according to your pay, no matter how much is in the house of God, or tithe to the work of God somewhere, however God is leading you to tithe. In your church, to a missionary, a ministry organization, but it should be somewhere where you're receiving your spiritual food because He said what? When you give that tenth, there's meat and drink in the house. That means what? God keeps the anointing in our midst. He keeps the music anointed, the Word anointed, and it feeds you and strengthens you. So, principle number one, come on and say it, "Keep the tithe going regular in the work of God." Come on, give God a big hand clap tonight.

∼

We hope that you have enjoyed the teaching above. But, hang on, there's more to come……………...

LESSON SEVENTEEN

God Purpose Driven:
Daily Wisdom Key for Today:

FIRSTFRUITS

Verse to Remember: Proverbs 3:8-9
New King James Version (NKJV)
[8] It will be health to your flesh,[a]
And strength[b] to your bones.

[9] Honor the LORD with your possessions,
And with the first fruits of all your increase;

Question to Meditate On: I want to go to a new level mentally, spiritually and financially, therefore, I will obey and honor the Lord. Say it 3 times:

HALLELUJAH, HALLELUJAH, HALLELUJAH.

LESSON EIGHTEEN

Matthew 13:24
New King James Version (NKJV)
The Parable of the Wheat and the Tares
**24 Another parable He put forth to them, saying: "The kingdom
of heaven is like a man who sowed good seed in his field;**

GIVING LOVE GIFTS

Principle number two. Every time you give to help someone, whether it is $1 or $10 or whatever, you are sowing good seeds. Jesus said it is good, good, good to do. Okay, now follow with me because this one's really going to rock you. If you couldn't handle the tithe, I feel bad for you right now, Okay, you gave God ten percent, you gave him ten bucks out of a hundred and now you got ninety bucks left and of course that ninety bucks is yours, or is it? No. But we act like that. There's where the curse comes. You see, the Bible says you were bought and paid for with the purchased blood:

1 Corinthians 6:20
Amplified Bible (AMP)
**20 You were bought with a price [purchased with a [a]
preciousness and paid for, [b]made His own]. So then,
honor God *and* bring glory to Him in your body.**

You, me. I'm owned, I am not my own. Come on say it, "If I'm owned, then everything I have is owned. "You see, we are owners of nothing. Stewards of everything. The Bible calls us stewards, not owners. The house you own, you don't. The bank does. Come somebody. We really own very little here. But, in God's eyes, we own nothing, we are pilgrims passing through. But we are managers. We are stewards of everything God entrusts us with. He puts things into your hands and then He says, "No, you don't own this, I gave it to you, you don't own it. I'm going to trust you with this, to be a steward of this, to manage this," You know the parables of the Gospel. He gave one two, one three, one four, He said "Okay now you don't own this, but go do something with this, I'll return and see how you managed what I gave you."

It's God that gives you increase. So, the ten you owe God. The other ninety, you're a manager of it for God. Now, if the ten you owe, what's the other ninety? That's your seed. Paul said what? "Bread for food, seed for sowing." Say it, "Bread for food, seed for sowing." What God said there is in that ninety percent, do the bread for food. Make sure you realize that bread for food, _spend that money however you see fit that could bless you_. You want that dress, you want to take that trip, you want to get clothes for your children for school? That's bread for food. That's for your self-serving ways, however you can benefit. But you don't forget also _in that ninety percent is seed for sowing_. Come on say it, "Seed for sowing."

The secret to you getting overflow money isn't in the ten percent you owe God. You owe Him that. _It's in the ninety percent He trust's you with_. That ninety percent cycle, therein lays the secret. "But I gave God ten bucks out of a hundred. This other ninety – "No, it's not yours, you're a manager of it. And the Holy Ghost is going to show you how to best spend it. But in that ninety percent that you have left over, that ninety bucks, if you'll take some of that ninety bucks, whether it's five, whether it's one, whether it's fifteen and you'll consider that as seed money. You gave ten you owed, but now here's some seed.

Matthew 13:24
Amplified Bible (AMP)
²⁴ Another parable He set forth before them,
saying, the kingdom of heaven is like a man
who sowed good seed in his field.

Seed doesn't mean the whole thing. How many know how big a seed is? Come on, say "Seed isn't the farm, isn't the silo, it's all the tractors, the chickens. The seed is just a tiny seed." See sometimes we think "I gave God a tithe and now

I've got to sow seed and dear God He wants me to sell the farm." Well He would receive it and bless you farm for farm, but He's asking you for seed. That's whenever you begin to handle that ninety percent, how you handle that ninety percent. Now, that ninety percent oftentimes is money you have designated for something else, right? How you handle that is so precious.

Now hear my voice tonight, about the story of the widow in 1 Kings 17. She told the prophet, "I have a handful and this is for me and my son." I have a handful and that's for my trip to the Holy land. I have a handful and that's for a down payment for my college tuition. All I have is – I have seed, all I have is a handful and the prophet looked at her and here's what he said: "Give me some drink." When he said that, if you read the story, she turned and began to walk back to the house. It was no big deal to get him some water. As she's walking, the prophet yells at her and says, "And bring me also a little bit of bread." What? See, the water she didn't mind giving. But the bread, she reacted and she said, "What? You want – hey water, I can understand water, but don't you know that this if for me and my son and it's been set aside for our last supper and I can't part with this." And he basically said, "Lady, if you eat that seed, it will be your last supper.

But if you'll take that seed that you have set apart for something else, as precious as it is, and you give it to the work of God." Say it, "That's against the way I think." Come on, say it. Then the curse of death, not only the curse from your seed, but the curse of death will come off of you and off of your whole family. <u>The secret to breaking the curse besides giving the tenth is seeing that other ninety percent not as yours, but you are a manager of that</u> and God freely says, "Buy clothes with it, I don't care, it's bread for food." "Oh, but I like this Mustang, I can get a great buy." Go ahead, it's fine. "Oh, I'm getting my nails done, pedicure, manicure." Go ahead, praise God, go ahead. <u>But God's saying don't forget in that ninety percent now, bread for food, seed for sowing. Sow some of that seed God's way.</u>

Give it away from yourself. Do you hear me? Now, when you give to your children, that's not giving away from yourself. That's expected of you. That's duty. "I put three kids through college." Well, you're supposed to. 'Well, I tell you what, it takes a whole lot to take care of four kids." Well, you had them. You had fun making them. Come on somebody. "Well, I'll tell you, when you have a family of six, it takes a whole lot, brother Billy." Well, that's you know – see, no pity from me to you. That's just duty.

When you go beyond the bloodline, you get into sacrifice. The Bible said no man yet hated his own flesh. So, whenever you give up, anything you've given to the bloodline, you can't say it's sacrifice. Because what? They're bone of your bone, flesh of your flesh and it's expected of you. Jesus said, "No man will be rewarded for that in heaven." For Jesus said, "I'll turn to you and say isn't it thy duty?" There's no reward from heaven." We think we're going to get rewarded for not getting divorced. "Wait until I get there, man, I really had some rough times and I held it together." Well, you're in for a shock of your life. If you don't start sowing seed, come on, you're going to be on the last row of heaven. Come on somebody. You're going to be way down there. You're not even going to get a *waterfront condo on the sea of glass. Come on. How many want to get a water front condo on the sea of glass? Come on.*

So, we have the ten percent you owe God, but then in that ninety percent, so we gave a tenth, praise God that keeps the curse off of me, but now I've got this ninety. I've got to begin to see that ninety is not mine. I'm a manager of that. And if I manage it wisely, I'm allowed to spend as much of that on me as I want. But if I spend it all on me. If I get in my checkbook, and it's me, me, my family, my kids, me, them, me and no work of God, hair, hair, clothes, belt, shoes, food but no God, then I have eaten my own seed and when you eat your own seed, there will be no harvest. Do you hear me? So, number one, say it, "I pay the tithe because I owe it." Number two, "I manage the ninety percent. That means money for me. But I got to manage the seed to sow some to the work of God." Come on, put your hands together give God praise, hurry! Come on, put your hands together,

Number three, when you speak against something, you can never have what you speak against. Don't speak against prosperity. You cannot have what you talk against. If you talk against – now you see what happens is you fall into Proverbs 6:2, you're ensnared by the words of your mouth, and Matthew 12, you become a kingdom divided against yourself. When you become a kingdom divided and begin to talk about those preachers on TV, all they talk about is money, all they talk about is money. Maybe God has raised them up to be an Apostle of money and maybe what's bothering you about them is your lack. When you have what they're talking about, it doesn't bother you. But when you don't have what they're talking about, it gets to you.

Why? Because it's reminding you that you are a person of – you were created to have a whole lot more than what you do. You say, "Well, help me get it" I'm trying! You'd be surprised of the attitude of a whole lot of people in church, inside their mind they have anger, hostility, they don't think the Bible mentions this. They haven't read their Bible. They've only read a few pages of their

Bible. There's a whole lot they haven't read. Jesus wore one of the most expensive pieces of clothing that was ever made. The seamless garment. It had no seams in it. It was pure silk and that's why they cast lots for it. It was worth thousands and thousands of dollars on the open market. And it was white. So, if you want to get mad at me for wearing a white suit tonight, well my friend right over here, because he always outdoes me, I tell you, right over here. I thought, "I'm going to be sharp tonight" and I walk in tonight and he's got the sharpest thing on here! <u>My point is this, you've got to be very careful about your attitude and what comes out of your mouth about other people who are being blessed.</u> This is because, if you search their background, many times you will find that at one time they too were at a poor level. Step by step, by being obedient, God brought them to the level of faith that they operate at now." ....

~

<u>This very book is designed to get you out of debt and poverty and into God's wealth</u>. WE must do it God's way or we won't get the HIGH-WAY! You might say, "But we don't have anything. How many years is it going to take me to be wealthy and prosperous?" It will begin right now as you apply these principles in every area of your life! For example, look at King David's life. Over and over he declares in the Psalms how he came from a poor family and God turned him around and made him a super-rich multi-billionaire.

Psalm 119:10-14
Amplified Bible (AMP)
[10] With my whole heart have I sought You, inquiring for *and* of You *and* yearning for You; Oh, let me not wander *or* step aside [either in ignorance or willfully] from Your commandments.

**¹¹ Your word have I laid up in my heart,
that I might not sin against You.**

¹² Blessed are You, O Lord; teach me Your statutes.

**¹³ With my lips have I declared *and* recounted
all the ordinances of Your mouth.**

**¹⁴ I have rejoiced in the way of Your
testimonies as much as in all riches.**

The Jewish Rabbi teaches us that David was about 50 years old when he wrote this Psalm. He declared that he loved God more than all of the wealth that was set before him. David put it all on the line to build God's Kingdom. We can see that he had a clear view of the sowing and reaping of his financial management. We can see, crystal clearly, from the scripture that it did not happen to him overnight. The very purpose of David's life is obedience! Now let's get back to Billy..............

~

"Cain should not have killed Abel. He was so stupid and foolish. He should have just stepped back and said, "You know what? I'm working hard to grow fruit and vegetables, but it looks like to me like God's accepting bloody animals. Well, I am just going to ask my brother for one of those animals. I'm going to draw from what's working." But instead he killed him. And today in the church instead of trying to find out what successful people are doing, we criticize them. We get jealous of them. You know, we have to cop this attitude to justify our own lack so we say, "Money isn't everything. I'd rather have what I have then what they have because I know they're not happy, they're miserable. They're not happily married. Look at their kids. Let me tell you something. Do you want to know the truth? A lot of people on TV that you say aren't happy, are. A

*lot people you say, "Well, they may have money, but they're empty."
A lot of them aren't. Hello!*

*But see we have to trick our own mind to justify our lack and that
makes us feel good. "Well, I'll tell you what, I may not have money
but I got Jesus." And somehow, somehow that makes you feel good.
Well, you ought to be happy you have Jesus but go get Jesus to pay
for your lunch, come on somebody. Come on! Somebody better
shout here! That's why Paul said in first Corinthians 15, first the
natural then the spiritual. You're born of water before you're born
of the Spirit. They filled the pots with water before it turned to
wine. They went fishing for a real fish before supernatural money
came. You see, God wants you to cover the natural base, as you
know how to cover it, before His Spirit will breathe and give you the
supernatural results you want, come on church! Don't talk against
prosperity because, if you do, you can't have what you talk against.
It's real simple. Take a step back and realize what? There's enough
for everybody. The wealth that God has put on the earth in creation
has not jumped off the earth yet! It is still here.*

*What did God say to Cain? "Wouldn't I have accepted your sacrifice
too if you had done the right thing?" Just humble yourself. Take a
step back, and you may be a hardworking man, a hard-working
lady, maybe you've had different circumstances than somebody
else, but this works in Africa, this works in Ethiopia, this will work
anywhere. Why? It's the Word of God. Don't speak against it.
Instead of attacking somebody that has three cars to your one, just
say, "You know what, in His time, Hallelujah. I'll tell you what, I
know I'm growing in faith and bless God, it's only a matter of time,
it's coming my way too." Get a right attitude. Be happy for them.
"Well, I would be happy for them, but it's just the way they...."
Leave it go, leave it go. "I mean she walks in here with her yellow
shoes, yellow dress, black hat, it's like 'look at me!'"*

No, you're bothered by something else. You're not bothered by her, you're bothered she has it. No, it's not everything, but it's something and if it didn't bother you – I mean, if you didn't want it, it wouldn't bother you. The fact that it bothers you tells you there's something in you that's desiring for more than you're destined for. I mean, how many would like a car that starts every morning? Come on somebody. It's true! I'm getting tired of those Fonzy cars. You know, you got to kick them to get them going, come on. You kick 'em and hit 'em then it will start. God wants to bless you. He doesn't want you to stand in front of your wardrobe in your closet thinking, "How am I going to – well, wore that last week to church. Well, that's the same skirt I wore two weeks in a row to church. Maybe if I change blouses no one in the church will know. Maybe if I wear a red scarf with it and different beads, they'll think it's a whole new outfit."

It's sad how you have to struggle and rob and pull and stretch because in you. Why? Because in you, you know that you were destined for more. And if it weren't for the lack of education or what happened to you or who taught you or the wrong Gospel you sat under for years, if it weren't for that, you'd be saying, "Well, okay, we can't go back, but we can go forward, and we can send the blessing ahead.' Come on, somebody give God praise! Now watch this. There's going to be a lot of people who handle God's resources inappropriately. Don't confuse that with the will of God to bless. I'm going to say that again. A lot of people are going to get money, sometimes ahead of where they are in, of where they are in God and they're not going to handle it right. Well, don't let that put a distaste in your mouth for the actual fact that God wants to bless you.

What does HE say I wish above all things? That's pretty strong people. It's pretty hard for anybody that's against prosperity to get around III John 2. How do you get around it? How do you just kind of - what do you do to make that disappear? But I wish above all things – that's strong. I mean that's like smelling a bottle of alcohol. Come on, that is strong. I wish above all things that you would be *in health and prosper. It's right there! So, yes, somebody is going to mishandle it, somebody's going to carry it wrong, we're people, not everybody knows how to do that the right away. So, take a step back and say, "Boy, God, you're good. You blessed him, he don't know how to handle it, he's got some growing up to do" But I tell you what, don't cut it off. Don't throw the baby out with the bath water. How many see what I'm talking about? Say, "Man, God gave him all that and he's acting like that. He ought to be ashamed of himself. I tell you God You're amazing..."*

Let God amaze you and let yourself know the only reason he has that is because of God and the mercy of God and don't talk against the prosperous message. Amen? Come on, put your hand over your mouth and say, "I'm not going to be ensnared by the words of my mouth. I'm not going to be a divided kingdom. I see it in the Bible. God wants His children to prosper above and beyond. They may handle it wrong. They may not use it right. It doesn't change the truth that God became poor that we can be made rich." Come on, somebody give God praise! Come on, come on".

LESSON EIGHTEEN

God Purpose Driven:
Daily Wisdom Key for Today:

GIVING LOVE GIFTS

Verse to Remember: Matthew 13:24
New King James Version (NKJV)
The Parable of the Wheat and the Tares
24 Another parable He put forth to them, saying: "The kingdom of heaven is like a man who sowed good seed in his field;

Question to Meditate On: I will continue and look, with all of my heart, to BLESS OTHERS FOR THE RIGHT PURPOSE.! I will be a GIVER not just a taker.

LESSON NINETEEN

2 Corinthians 6:14-18
Amplified Bible (AMP)
¹⁴ Do not be unequally yoked with unbelievers [do not make mismated alliances with them or come under a different yoke with them, inconsistent with your faith]. For what partnership have right living *and* right standing with God with iniquity *and* lawlessness? Or how can light have fellowship with darkness?

¹⁵ What harmony can there be between Christ and Belial [the devil]? Or what has a believer in common with an unbeliever?

¹⁶ What agreement [can there be between] a temple of God and idols? For we are the temple of the living God; even as God said, I will dwell in *and* with *and* among them and will walk in *and* with *and* among them, and I will be their God, and they shall be My people.

¹⁷ So, come out from among [unbelievers], and separate (sever) yourselves from them, says the Lord, and touch not [any] unclean thing; then I will receive you kindly *and* treat you with favor,

¹⁸ And I will be a Father to you, and you shall be My sons and daughters, says the Lord Almighty.

PRINCIPLE OF PROSPERITY

Principle number 4 - Don't put your money towards unclean things. Don't touch the unclean thing. Make sure that your money – if you want to keep the curse off it-see, because you can do all this, you can tithe, you can sow seed, you can say, "Man, I believe in prosperity", but then it can get you another way. When you begin to put your money towards things that are not clean like pornography, nicotine, alcohol, drugs, even when you invest in the stock market, you know the company you're investing in is a proponent of abortion, or a proponent of using fetal tissue to make cosmetics and makeup. There's a lot of stocks out there that people are putting their money in just to get money but the stocks they have their money in are unclean because it's at the expense of aborted babies. It's at the expense of other issues. I mean, pornography is a multi-billion-dollar business and these wicked people have learned how to hide their stock and not come out-you don't even know you're investing in Hustler or Penthouse or some of these other filthy magazines or some of the rag magazines, some of the tabloids.

See, it's your job to be a wise investor, to be a good steward, and if you're going to put money into a stock or into a mutual market fund or into some of these it's good for you to know where all of this money goes. Don't let a broker tell you "Well, we're building malls and we're building doctors' buildings", and when something goes into social improvement of the neighborhood, "What is that? Where is that money going?" Because when you put your money towards something that is unclean, nicotine has been proven to kill you. "Remember the Marlboro man?" Handsome, mustache, rope, picture of health. He died at eighty plus years old with both lungs coal black, charred with cancer because of Marlboros. I have yet to see a billboard that has him up there before and after, why? Because no one would buy Marlboro. But they picked a handsome man out on the range with a rope, great cowboy, come on somebody, man, lady's look up there and see a cigarette hanging out of his mouth, "I'm the Marlboro man."

Hollywood has marketed nicotine for years. Back in the days of the 'Rat Pack' with Sinatra and Sammy Davis Jr. and Dean Martin. You couldn't see Dean Martin... you did not see Dean Martin his last few days, did you? You know why? Because he was filled with that disease that ate away his throat and his lungs. He found out that he was a mere mortal man and a lot of these people died lonely deaths with no stage presence and maybe one or two people in their room and the fan clubs didn't even know and actually don't even care. Nicotine is not clean. Pornography's not clean. Any place out there – even you find information about some of the food you're eating, it's not clean, it's defiling you. You can't sin against the light, and you continue to put your money into things that aren't clean, there's a curse that comes on your money.

Keep your money out of unclean things. You might go out there and buy a Playboy and no one in the church ever finds out about it, but God sees it and the devil sees it and the devil goes day and night before the throne saying to God, "Hey, you're going to bless him? You're going to prosper him? He's buying Penthouse. He's buying nicotine. He's drinking a fifth of Jack Daniels every day. He's doing this and he's doing that." God is a just God and Satan plays on the just side of God because Satan just says to God, "You kicked me out. You kicked me out of heaven. Come on, what are you going to do to them? He makes accusations up there. He lets God know what he sees going on in you and God has to work with that and that's why curse can come on your money whenever you put it on unclean things. Gambling. What do you think gambling is? Do you think gambling is God's way to prosperity? Anytime wrong choices are made we pay a price. The bibles declares in I John 5:17:

1 John 5:17
Amplified Bible (AMP)
¹⁷ **All wrongdoing is sin, and there is sin which does not [involve] death [that may be repented of and forgiven].**

<u>Note from the Author</u>: Everytime we make a wrong choice we end up going the wrong way. Many times, with all of my heart, I begin to do something thinking that it is the right choice but along the way I find out that it is the wrong choice. This is why the bible declares that all wrong is sin. Every time we do stupid things and make the wrong investments we always lose something. Then I have to pick myself up and start over again. Could this maybe be you today? It's not too late to turn it around.............

~

"But I feel the Lord showing me that the dice are going to come up boxcars! God's going to show me what the winning number is this week!" There are Christians that have won the lottery. There are Christians that have done wonderful things with the money that they've won. But it's proven in the lottery system, I don't have the papers with me tonight, its proven that over 80 percent that have won the lottery are either dead, divorced or in the nuthouse. You know, where they make good peanuts! Come on, somebody, you know why? Because it was money that came ahead of their growth. It was money that came that added sorrow to their life. It wasn't clean. Betting on the horses. Money today buys people. Money today buys loyalty. It's unclean. It's not clean money. Don't put your money where it's not clean. Keep the curse off your money. Come on, somebody give God praise.

Hallelujah, hallelujah! How many's glad to be in church on Wednesday night? How many feel a little tired from being in all these meetings? Come on, you've been in meetings for about a month now, I hear. Your body – I believe your body ought to feel the sacrifice of being in the presence of God. Do you hear me? If you go home from church and you've been in meetings, you say, "Man, those meetings all night long and I'm tired and that's a lot of meetings." That's a good sign. I mean we give Caesar our body all week long. We give the gym, hello? We give the restaurants, I know we give the restaurants, I know it. We give our body and we feel the effects of it and somehow, we think that the church is the day of rest. No. It's the day of rest where you quit working for the world. It's the day you come here and labor for

God. Man, you ought to – come on, your arms ought to feel it, from lifting up my arms, from singing so long, from shouting so loud! I mean your eyes ought to be a little blurry from turning so many verses through the night and you do that a couple of nights for a few weeks out of every month and I'll tell you what, your body will begin to be a living sacrifice for God. Amen!

Put your hands up all over the place. Great to be with you tonight. Oh, God's going to do some great things here tonight. There's going to be some curses come off of your money tonight. There's some promotion coming your way. Oh, hallelujah! Holy Ghost, tonight we say thank you for all of the healings this week. We say thank you for all the seeds of righteousness that have been planted this week. We say thank you for the completion, for the fulfillment of prophecies this week. We're reminded that we are so feeble in ourselves. So, incapable of helping, really anybody, in and of ourselves. It's not by might nor by power. We are very aware it's by Your Holy Spirit, breathe on us tonight in this room. Let us feel You, sense You, put thoughts in our mind, let us have

Your voice arise in us tonight and cause us to choose right choices, cause us to walk out of darkness tonight. Cause us to reach for the hem of Your garment tonight. Cause us to want and desire more of You in our life than ever, ever before. Cause us to get on the winning team tonight. *Mighty Jesus, Mighty Jesus, anoint this service tonight with healing and with increase, I pray tonight that everyone who has ears to hear, will know that increase is coming to their finances.*

Everyone that has ears to hear! Come on, say it, "Holy Ghost, I have ears to hear. Bring it on. Let the wind blow, not form the east, not from the west, but from the Lord." Come on give Him praise! Hey! Whew! Bam! See, "You know I'm not too young to be a millionaire." Just say it. Say "I'm not too white to be a millionaire." Now, if you're black, don't say that okay? "I'm not too black to be a millionaire. I'm just right. The target of the Holy Ghost has been painted on me. He's aiming for me tonight." Come on, give God praise! Whew! Somebody better shout. I want to say this. I want to say a couple of things before we move into the evening because you know what? I don't exactly know where this thing is going to go tonight. I'm going to do my best to deliver what God's put into my heart and this thing could end up, who knows? But I want to say this before I get carried away or God carries this meeting away: If you're here tonight and you don't have a home church, listen to me, if you're visiting or maybe you're visiting tonight and you're in between churches, or you're in a church but not fully happy with the one you're in, I just want you to know that I really recommend this church. You need to try it. I really believe in Pastor Jim and Penney. I think they are a great dynamic couple. Jim's working at it. Penney's there, come on. They're dynamic and I tell you what, they're real, and I can see where they've been through some storms and that's ok. How many want to identify with people that have been somewhere, come on, and always remember this, always remember this, Jesus heals us out of His wounds.

That's who God raises up is wounded healers. The healing that you receive through this vessel, you don't know me, you don't know what I've been through or where I come from. I don't tell that story, but the wounds healing pours through wounds, not through brilliance, not through the educated, not through the high and the mighty and not through people that look like they haven't made any mistakes. The wounds of the Gospel pour through people that have been through some stuff. I just like the fact that these guys have been through some heavy stuff. They're still here, they still carry the torch, they still love people. They could have given up years ago. So, if you're looking for a church and you're not quite sure, even you're not sure about this one, try it here at Crossroads Church for a few Sundays. Come out Sunday morning, 10:00 am, 6:00 pm on Sunday night and even though we leave after tonight Pastor Jim is here sharing the Word and other ministries and Pastor Charlie is here. Come on, I mean, somebody give God praise!

Everybody here needs a shepherd. You all need to be under spiritual authority. You need to be in a house. You need to have someone that knows you by name that can help you like that, or help your children, that can teach you the Bible, that can get you on the right track. You know what I mean?

They can speak into your life. You really, really need that. You got to quit living by the law of AAA. you know what I mean? You get in a ditch and you call for help. You know what I mean? Get out of that. Get out of the crisis mentality. Get in somewhere, learn the Bible. Learn the approach of Christianity. It becomes all consuming and worth everyday that you wake up. I've got another day with Jesus. What are you going to do with me today? Come on, Amen. Hug somebody tonight and say, "I think there's enough for everybody here." Come on. Hallelujah! How many do we have visiting here tonight? How many people are visiting? Stand to your feet. Wow, the house is full of guests tonight. Come on church, give them a big God bless you!

LESSON NINETEEN

God Purpose Driven:
Daily Wisdom Key for Today:

PRINCIPLE OF PROSPERITY

Verse to Remember: 2 Corinthians 6:14-18
Amplified Bible (AMP)
¹⁴ Do not be unequally yoked with unbelievers [do not make mismated alliances with them or come under a different yoke with them, inconsistent with your faith]. For what partnership have right living *and* right standing with God with iniquity *and* lawlessness? Or how can light have fellowship with darkness?

¹⁵ What harmony can there be between Christ and Belial [the devil]? Or what has a believer in common with an unbeliever?

¹⁶ What agreement [can there be between] a temple of God and idols? For we are the temple of the living God; even as God said, I will dwell in *and* with *and* among them and will walk in *and* with *and* among them, and I will be their God, and they shall be My people.

¹⁷ So, come out from among [unbelievers], and separate (sever) yourselves from them, says the Lord, and touch not [any] unclean thing; then I will receive you kindly *and* treat you with favor,

¹⁸ And I will be a Father to you, and you shall be My sons and daughters, says the Lord Almighty.

Question to Meditate On: I will not have a part with any wrong doing that may cause shipwreck in my life.

LESSON TWENTY

Luke 4:18-19
Amplified Bible (AMP)
[18] The Spirit of the Lord [is] upon Me, because He has anointed Me [the Anointed One, the Messiah] to preach the good news (the Gospel) to the poor; He has sent Me to announce release to the captives and recovery of sight to the blind, to send forth as delivered those who are oppressed [who are downtrodden, bruised, crushed, and broken down by calamity],

[19] To proclaim the accepted *and* acceptable year of the Lord [the day [a]when salvation and the free favors of God profusely abound].

HEALTH, HEALING AND THE MONEY CONNECTION

God has anointed and gifted me to flow under the anointing with a 5-Fold Ministry which includes a financial anointing and to bring healing to people, for a long time and for all kinds of diseases, terminal diseases, crippling diseases. I've prayed for a lot of dead people, we've seen a lot of dead people raised and we've seen limbs grow. We've seen a lot of wonderful things. I've been privileged to see some amazing things. But you may ask tonight, "Okay, healing, I understand that, but why are you talking about money tonight? "It's because you'd be shocked to know how money and your health is connected. Let me say it another way. How the lack of money and your health are connected. It's amazing that the lack of money in your hand —let's just say one area is just to meet the needs of your family and your own needs in one area, but the lack of money to do the will of God for you. God does not want everybody to have the same amount of money so get out of that. Your money that God wants you to have is connected to your purpose.

How many know Pat Robertson, 700 Club? He needs some serious change. Come on somebody. He needs a whole lot of quarters. He needs multi-millions, why? Because it's connected to the reason why he was born. Now, you may not need that much in a life time. Some of you here if you had one million, it would last you forever. Come on, you'd be talking about it in New Jerusalem. You'd be still spending it in New Jerusalem. You'd be buying Elijah a Coke, come on. Well, their budget, just Oral Roberts' budget, I mean, many, many years ago, his budget was something like sixteen million a day and that was years ago. My point is this, the amount of money that God wants you to have in your lifetime is strongly connected to the reason for which you were born. When you are deprived of that because of whatever reason, let's just pick on the devil, let's pick on poor choices, let's pick on your parents didn't teach you the right things, let's pick on a nasty divorce, a bankruptcy, born on the wrong side of the tracks. Take any one of these issues. When you are deprived of your potential, it effects the way you think, if effects the cells of your body.

A lot of depression comes from lack. A lot of when the doctor comes out and says, "I don't know what's wrong, we can't find nothing wrong." And there you are, exhausted, depleted, messed up, confused, angry. A lot of it is because, listen to me, you lack the amount of resources you need. I haven't seen too many ladies yet when given the money to get a brand-new dress, come on somebody, you would think you gave them the whole mall. It's amazing how your day can be turned around, come on. Just from a birthday card with twenty bucks in it. That twenty bucks is, "Oh my God, that's my nails and my toes right there!" It's like, 'Man!' When that happens, see, what's released through you is joy. What's released in your system is a merry heart, enzymes, chromosomes, chemicals from your brain and from your body are released because of that and what does that do? It builds up your immune system. What does your immune system do? It fights off all of the disease, it fights off all the wrong things that we are and the way we abuse ourselves. It fights all that stuff off and sends it back to where it came from. Now, that's why money and your health is connected, or the lack of money. Now I don't know which one you are tonight. You may be sitting here and you may have too much money. Well, you can share it will all of us tonight. Or you may be sitting here saying I don't have nearly enough. I'm way behind the eight ball. Or you could be sitting here tonight saying, "You know what? I'm thanking God for what I do have, but I know there's more." Whichever category you're in tonight, I want you just to pay attention. I don't want you to think this is just some way or some means wherewith to get more of your money. You will have an opportunity later tonight to sow seed into what we're doing. You'll have that opportunity. I hope after you hear what you're going to hear, you'll want to. That you'll value the information because knowledge is one of the top four resources you need to make it in life. Come on say it, "There's only one source. That's God. But many resources. One source, many resources." See, God is the only way. Jesus said in John 10:9:

John 10:9
Amplified Bible (AMP)
⁹ I am the Door; anyone who enters in through Me will be saved (will live). He will come in and he will go out [freely], and will find pasture.

"I'm the door. If you're going to get love, you better get it through Me. If you get healing, you better get it through Me. If you get money, you better get it in a righteous way. There's no sorrow with it. If you're going to build friendships, you got to go through the right door or

they're going to end up hurting you. There's one source, but many resources. Now, we get these confused. People are a great resource. But so often we see people as the source. So often if somebody gives you some money, we begin to see them as a source for our money. No, no, no. God will remove that. God will break up friendships and break up great people that hang out together because we begin to replace source with resource. People that were never meant to be your source. Now, when you're a little kid, how many of you know? Jesus is your mother and your dad?

Come on somebody. Well that's pretty understandable. But as you grow up, you begin to understand, wow, they work and God provides. They work by the sweat of their brow and it's the Lord that gives the increase. But people are a great resource. Money is a resource. Money is never the means to get everything. Money does answer all things, but yet it can't get everything. It can't buy your health and it can't buy your happiness. The Beatles used to sing a song "Can't buy me love, no, no, no". Thought I'd just throw that little part in there for all you Beatles fans. So, we see people are a great resource, money is great resource. Knowledge is number three. Say "Knowledge, Information" Today, information, Pastor Jim is what separates the highly successful from the marginally successful. See, God don't want you to be marginally successful. A lot of people that are marginally successful are so thrilled because they are no longer failures. Better seems better so much, you know than-but "better" becomes the enemy of "best" and "some" becomes the enemy of 'all".

You were never intended just to have some. You were intended to have all. All that you can contain spiritually, all that you can contain emotionally, all that you can contain physically. You are a triune being and God intended you to be, not full, God intended you to be overflow. My cup runneth over. Come on say, "Off the cup, on the saucer, on the floor, out the door." That's the way God intended it. God intended to where you wouldn't have to wrestle with giving money because everything in the cup belongs to you and the overflow belongs to whoever God leads you to help. But it's whenever you don't have anything in the cup and you're in survival, you're now deprived of being a blessing to anybody you want to be a blessing to. You can't even respond to God. You can't even hear God. Even the pastor says, or the man of God says, or the lady of God says, "Give an offering." You can't even think. "I can't give nothing, I have food, I have bills, I have this." And you're all crunched up in fear, crippled and little. Sitting in lack and you want to, your heart's right, but you don't know how to get there from here.

Were you ever going down the California freeway, you know California freeways, how many know California freeways? You see the top of the building you're trying to get to and you watch yourself passing it right by and it's so frustrating because you think, "Well, did I get here to get to there?" How do I get there from here? Tonight, I'm going to show you how to get where you are, hopefully, to where you're still trying to get. What do you mean hopefully? Because some people give up. They have tried for so long. They've accepted that this is just for a few that He kind of shines His face on. It's for a few of the fortunate Christians that are out there that have struck it rich and you're even wondering saying, "I don't know how they did it." You believe It's for the few and somehow you no longer see the potential for yourself to really soar with the eagles and to walk on the high places of the earth, to get money more than what you're capable of earning. Now, this may sound like a pitch tonight to some infomercial. I want to tell you something. Jesus talked more about money than He did any other subject of the Bible.

If you're studying the red letter of Jesus, he was talking more about money – Why? Because, say this with me, "I live in a house, I wear clothes, I eat food, I drive a car, I pay taxes." See, that's real life. Real life isn't sitting in church. Real life isn't singing in the choir. Real life is, I live in a house or maybe a condo or an apartment. You know what I mean, shelter. "I wear clothes, I eat food, I pay taxes,

I drive a car." You know, and if you live in Southern California, its ditto, twice that. So that's reality and for so long, in the church, we sing all these songs and get all spiritual and we love the Lord and we get all pumped up and we come down and we get prayer for our needs, but somehow this money issue has evaded us.

Well let me tell you, when Jesus saved you and became Lord of your life, He didn't come into your life to just kind of make sure you're going to heaven, make sure you have some marginal happiness. He came in to make you a testimony to everybody that knows you, that says, "Look what I can do with someone that fully gives themselves to me, I can change not just this part or that part, but I change every single part of your life." Now, he did it to Job. He gave Job four times what he originally had. Job had to go through some tough places. How many have been through some tough places? How many thought you've been "Joab" or "Job" or whatever you call him? Come on somebody. He gave Jacob, He gave Joseph, He gave Abraham. I mean, you say, "What about the apostle Paul?" Well, Apostle Paul chose by his own convictions. He chose to work on the side making tents and receive offerings, but if you'll look in the Book of Philippians, you'll see that he celebrated them as the most giving church in his ministry. He said "You know what? Nobody else was supporting me but man you did and the only reason I received your gifts was so that God may add fruit to your account."

Come on say, "I have an account here and I have and account there and when I put it in there, it comes out here." Come on, give God praise! Come on somebody shout!

So tonight, as we do this, and we will be praying for the sick tonight and it goes together. We have no trouble making a bridge between what we're going to be talking about. I believe, if you'll have ears to hear tonight and listen intently, take some notes, get this tape and study this tape for the next couple of days, you're going to hear something tonight that you're going to really like. You're going to really like some of the things that God is going to say to you. Now, you're going to her some other things that's going to just pin you against the wall, because it's going to show how you're violating some principals that's letting the curse remain on your money, and it's not how much money you make, it's how much you keep. Somebody says, "I'm making a hundred and fifty thousand." Well, why are you driving the same car for twenty years? Your wife hasn't bought a new dress for how long? You haven't even taken a vacation. "Well, I mean, you know the government takes it." Don't blame it on the government. The government is not the devil. That tax money, that's a blessing. That money they take out of there, I know it seems rough, but that money there goes in and pays for roads and lights and things that you benefit from.

I'd rather them do that than me have to go do that. Come on, I don't want to be looking for light bulbs for the streetlights on my street. Come on somebody. I have enough busy stuff to do in my life. So, I don't mind paying my share to make things better. Now, do they misspend that, do they misappropriate that? I'm sure they do. I'm sure that's all somewhere out there in the midst. But I'll say, you know, I live in this neighborhood here, I'll be happy to pay my portion. Whatever you do with that, hey you do with that.

I got to focus on the more weightier matters of life. Come on, can you give God praise here today? Boy, this is exciting tonight! I believe that the spirit of entrepreneurship later on this evening is going to fall on this crowd! I believe coming out of this audience tonight is going to be people starting their own businesses. I believe there's going to be some people closing their business they have and starting another business. I believe there are some people handing in their pink slip this week and they are getting rid of the old wine and replacing it with the new wine.

As we have come to the end of the sermon, let the choir come forth. Every one of you lift your hands up and totally forget who you are, whether you are a Pastor, business man, lawyer, doctor, policeman or doorkeeper and surrender 100 % tonight to the Holy Spirit. Jesus declares in Matthew 5 that you must forgive everyone or God will not forgive you. Forgive everyone tonight and forgive yourself and let the Holy Spirit bring divine healing to you, mentally, physically and financially. Now put your hands together and give God a big God bless you because the spirit of discernment has shown me that the healing power is in this house and God is taking away all of your burdens and releasing a fresh anointing into your life tonight. Receive it, all of you, in the name of Jesus and take this fresh anointing with you into your home, to your family and into your business and work. Somebody shout, Hallelujah and put your hands together and give God some praise."

Now ladies and gentlemen, please stand up and repeat this prayer after me:

'Dear Lord Jesus, please birth this teaching into my heart and into my soul and do not let it fall to the ground. So, it will be a part of my life forever. I choose to believe you Lord, that I will live a moral life and be debt free, in Jesus' name I pray, amen.'

~

(As we conclude this third chapter of Billy Burke we hope that you have been inspired by his teaching and hope that the next one will bring you to a new level.........................)

LESSON TWENTY

God Purpose Driven:
Daily Wisdom Key for Today:

HEALTH, HEALING AND THE MONEY CONNECTION

Verse to Remember: Luke 4:18-19
Amplified Bible (AMP)

[18] The Spirit of the Lord [is] upon Me, because He has anointed Me [the Anointed One, the Messiah] to preach the good news (the Gospel) to the poor; He has sent Me to announce release to the captives and recovery of sight to the blind, to send forth as delivered those who are oppressed [who are downtrodden, bruised, crushed, and broken down by calamity],

[19] To proclaim the accepted and acceptable year of the Lord [the day [a]when salvation and the free favors of God profusely abound].

Question to Meditate On: In my obedience, I will receive FINANCIAL HEALING AND DIVINE HEALING.

Mark 11:23-24
Amplified Bible (AMP)
²³ **Truly I tell you, whoever says to this mountain, be lifted up and thrown into the sea! and does not doubt at all in his heart but believes that what he says will take place, it will be done for him.**

²⁴ **For this reason I am telling you, whatever you ask for in prayer, believe (trust and be confident) that it is granted to you, and you will [get it].**

GROW TO ADOPT A GOOD CONFESSION

Speak to your mountain of financial obligations. God gave you a mouth to conquer your mind. WHY? Because our mind has a sin nature and stinks. It cannot be trusted. But our NEW BIRTH, that is in Christ Jesus gives us HIS mind and wisdom that cannot fail. Your words are creating your world. What you say and the confession you make matters. Words are a creative force and have the power to change the climate of your financial life. If you want to supercharge your mindset then speak to your circumstances. Boldly begin to say, "Abundance is provided for me by God's word." Declare, "I will not have a mentality or lifestyle of debt." Words matter. What you say is important, but how you say them is just as significant. Here is what King Solomon declared about being careful of what you say;

Proverbs 18:21
New King James Version (NKJV)
21 Death and life *are* in the power of the tongue,
And those who love it will eat its fruit.

Another ingredient to supercharge is necessary. Your words are your faith. In fact, faith is a voice activated. Remember, power comes only when you believe the things that you are saying will actually come to pass. The bible teaches us that the words that we speak and believe are powerful.

Hebrews 11:1-6
Amplified Bible (AMP)
11 Now faith is the assurance (the confirmation, [a]the title deed) of the things [we] hope for, being the proof of things [we] do not see *and* the conviction of their reality [faith perceiving as real fact what is not revealed to the senses].

2 For by [faith—[b]trust and holy fervor born of faith] the men of old had divine testimony borne to them *and* obtained a good report.

3 By faith we understand that the worlds [during the successive ages] were framed (fashioned, put in order, and equipped for their intended purpose) by the word of God, so that what we see was not made out of things which are visible.

4 [Prompted, actuated] by faith Abel brought God a better and more acceptable sacrifice than Cain, because of which it was testified of him that he was righteous [that he was upright and in right standing with God], and God bore witness by accepting *and* acknowledging his gifts. And though he died, yet [through the incident] he is still speaking.

5 Because of faith Enoch was caught up *and* transferred to heaven, so that he did not have a glimpse of death; and he was not found, because God had translated him. For even

before he was taken to heaven, he received testimony [still on record] that he had pleased *and* been satisfactory to God.

⁶ But without faith it is impossible to please *and* be satisfactory to Him. For whoever would come near to God must [necessarily] believe that God exists and that He is the rewarder of those who earnestly *and* diligently seek Him [out].

FAITH FILLED WORDS HAVE THE ABILITY TO CHANGE YOUR IMPOSSIBLE CIRCUMSTANCES INTO MIRACLE SOLUTIONS

Remember, we possess limitless power by our faith-filled spoken words. When you are double-minded your words become powerless. You must think with your mind, feel with your heart and listen to the inner man which is the Holy Spirit in you. Some people call this going with your instinct or listening to your gut feeling. The bible is filled with more than 6,000 promises and they are the same today, tomorrow and forever.

If you obey you cannot fail. Do not be double-minded. When you become double-minded you will say one thing with your mouth and believe something else with your heart or vice versa.

James 1:5-8
Amplified Bible (AMP)
⁵ If any of you is deficient in wisdom, let him ask of [a]the giving God [Who gives] to everyone liberally *and* ungrudgingly, without reproaching *or* faultfinding, and it will be given him.

⁶ Only it must be in faith that he asks with no wavering (no hesitating, no doubting). For the one who wavers (hesitates, doubts) is like the billowing surge out at sea that is blown hither *and* thither and tossed by the wind.

⁷ For truly, let not such a person imagine that he will receive anything [he asks for] from the Lord,

⁸ [For being as he is] a man of two minds (hesitating, dubious, irresolute), [he is] unstable *and* unreliable *and* uncertain about everything [he thinks, feels, decides].

Your confession should line up with what is in your heart. In fact, the bible teaches that your heart will tell on you.

Matthew 12:34
'For out of the abundance of the heart the mouth speaketh.'

When you surrender your thoughts for His thoughts and your ways for His ways, your spoken words will be consistent with His desire for your life to succeed. You will not be double minded but God minded! Your personal testimony and past victories are the miracles and the powerful weapon to use against your debt and any lack in your life. Carefully document all of your progress on paper of every battle you have fought and won. Take time to journal every supernatural victory that God has given you because you are a overcomer and you cannot fail. Step by step, link by link and day after day you are coming out with great miracle testimony.

Revelation 12:11
'And they overcame him the devil by the word of their testimony'

YOU ARE A STEWARD OF WHAT THE LORD GAVE YOU TO MANAGE AND GOD WILL EMPOWER YOU TO SUCCEED

Deuteronomy 8:18
KJV
Remember the Lord thy God for it is He that giveth thee power to get wealth, that He may establish His covenant with you.'

In these lessons, we are making this simple and clear to you that wealth is not only a money word, it is also a supply word. God wants to supply you with a happy home, abundant health, a successful marriage and yes, financial resources too. The bible is crystal clear that God will give you concepts, ideas and insight to create wealth. The purpose of wealth is for God to establish His covenant on the earth.

Your responsibility is to oversee and multiply what He has entrusted to your care. He provides the power; you provide the vessel and through Him will come all wealth. As you continue to be a steward you must sow seeds for the next harvest. Your seed is the connection to serve between you, others and the providence of God's purpose.

Malachi 3:8-10
Amplified Bible (AMP)
8 Will a man rob *or* defraud God? Yet you rob *and* defraud Me. But you say, in what way do we rob *or* defraud You? [You have withheld your] tithes and offerings.

9 You are cursed with the curse, for you are robbing Me, even this whole nation.

¹⁰ Bring all the tithes (the whole tenth of your income) into the storehouse, that there may be food in My house, and prove Me now by it, says the Lord of hosts, if I will not open the windows of heaven for you and pour you out a blessing, that there shall not be room enough to receive it.

WE DO WANT THE WINDOWS OF HEAVEN OPEN AND ALL THE DAYS OF OUR LIVES

My seeds are my faith to MOVE MOUNTAINS of starvation, poverty and blockage and my seeds will open doors to bring the gospel to all the nations. I will declare to be BIBLE PURPOSE DRIVEN moving!

LESSON TWENTY-ONE

God Purpose Driven:
Daily Wisdom Key for Today:

GROW TO ADOPT A GOOD CONFESSION

Verse to Remember: Mark 11:23-24
Amplified Bible (AMP)
23 Truly I tell you, whoever says to this mountain,
be lifted up and thrown into the sea! and does not
doubt at all in his heart but believes that what he
says will take place, it will be done for him.

24 For this reason I am telling you, whatever you
ask for in prayer, believe (trust and be confident)
that it is granted to you, and you will [get it].

Question to Meditate On: I want to be in God's center for every purpose that come's my way.

LESSON TWENTY-TWO

2 Corinthians 5:17
Amplified Bible (AMP)
¹⁷ Therefore if any person is [ingrafted] in Christ (the Messiah) he is a new creation (a new creature altogether); the old [previous moral and spiritual condition] has passed away. Behold, the fresh *and* new has come!

NOW THAT YOU ARE IN CHRIST

1. WE MUST MAKE A COMPLETE CONFESSION OF VISIBLE AND INVISIBLE SINS DAILY

When we confess our sinful state, we are acknowledging that Jesus died for our sins and His sacrifice on the cross atoned for all the sins of man for all time. Our confession identifies us with Christ Jesus, His incarnation in the flesh, His ministry and His ultimate sacrifice at Calvary. This supreme, selfless act of love for us is the blood sacrifice of God's perfect Son so that we, as imperfect sinners, may enter into the presence of the Almighty Lord of the Universe and remain in everlasting communion with Him. We are cleansed of our sins. We read 1 John 1:9:

1 John 1:9
Amplified Bible (AMP)
⁹ If we [freely] admit that we have sinned *and* confess our sins, He is faithful and just (true to His own nature and promises) and will forgive our sins [dismiss our lawlessness] and [continuously] cleanse us from

**all unrighteousness [everything not in conformity
to His will in purpose, thought, and action].**

When we confess visible and invisible sins that occur along the
way of your journey God is faithful to intervene, on your behalf,
and He releases a fresh anointing into your daily life so that you
can become victorious mentally, physically and financially. To
confirm this statement read the passage in I John 2:1:

**1 John 2
Amplified Bible (AMP)
2 My little children, I write you these things so that
you may not violate God's law *and* sin. But if anyone
should sin, we have an Advocate (One Who will
intercede for us) with the Father— [it is] Jesus Christ
[the all] righteous [upright, just, who conforms to the
Father's will in every purpose, thought, and action].**

2. WE MUST CRUCIFY THE OLD MAN

Prior to our being saved, Satan lived through us and he worked
his will in our lives. Satan is constantly at work to re-establish his
control and dominion over us AFTER we are saved. Therefore,
we are to be vigilant and never give Satan a chance to get his
foot in the door of our lives (read Eph. 4:27, 5:10-18, James 4:7,
1 Pet. 5:8-9). We may be tempted to give into Satan's traps,
but that does not mean that we have reactivated the old man in
ourselves, or that we are in league with Satan. It is only when we
give into sin again that we are in harmony with the devil. The
crucifixion of the old man means simply that we have thrown
him off and we are no longer in obedience to him in any way.
He is finished, never to return. Paul says in Rom. 6: 6-14:

Romans 6:6-14
Amplified Bible (AMP)

[6] We know that our old (unrenewed) self was nailed to the cross with Him in order that [our] body [which is the instrument] of sin might be made ineffective *and* inactive for evil, that we might no longer be the slaves of sin.

[7] For when a man dies, he is freed (loosed, delivered) from [the power of] sin [among men].

[8] Now if we have died with Christ, we believe that we shall also live with Him,

[9] Because we know that Christ (the Anointed One), being once raised from the dead, will never die again; death no longer has power over Him.

[10] For by the death He died, He died to sin [ending His relation to it] once for all; and the life that He lives, He is living to God [in unbroken fellowship with Him].

[11] Even so consider yourselves also dead to sin *and* your relation to it broken, but alive to God [living in unbroken fellowship with Him] in Christ Jesus.

[12] Let not sin therefore rule as king in your mortal (short-lived, perishable) bodies, to make you yield to its cravings *and* be subject to its lusts *and* evil passions.

[13] Do not continue offering or yielding your bodily members [and [a]faculties] to sin as instruments (tools) of wickedness. But offer *and* yield yourselves to God as though you have been raised from the dead to [perpetual] life, and your bodily members [and [b]faculties] to God, presenting them as implements of righteousness.

¹⁴ For sin shall not [any longer] exert dominion over you, since now you are not under Law [as slaves], but under grace [as subjects of God's favor and mercy].

We must declare ourselves to be no longer open to sin but open and alive to God. We are to see sin as habits of the past and now as non-existent in our lives. We are to recognize that God is everything and He is the only thing that truly matters in our lives. As believers, we must completely give up sin and all of its manifestations and tell God and our brethren that sin will never again have a place in our hearts. Just as a parent disinherits an incorrigible and sinful child, we must cast out sin in all of its forms.

This can be accomplished by declaring our faith in Christ and by giving ourselves wholly to the service of God and to a life of holiness in Christ Jesus. Your old self, your sins and all the ways in which Satan functions in our lives must be renounced and rejected once and for all. Our old selves, or "our old man" which is another description of Satan's operation in our lives, must be done away with completely and forever. We recognize that we are new creatures in Christ, our old selves are dead and we no longer live in sin. Our old lives are in the past and the new life is in us. Satan has no more influence on us so that, in effect, to us he is dead. I John 5:18 states:

1 John 5:18
Amplified Bible (AMP)
¹⁸ We know [absolutely] that anyone born of God does not [deliberately and knowingly] practice committing sin, but the One Who was begotten of God carefully watches over *and* protects him [Christ's divine presence within him preserves him against the evil], and the wicked one does not lay hold (get a grip) on him *or* touch [him].

Our old sinful life is gone and is dead in us. We come alive to God and all that is Godly. He is now our Master and not Satan. Our old life, with its sins, our old man and the sinful things of the past exist in the world, but as far as we are concerned they are not real, because we no longer entertain them. When we were slaves of sin we were dead to God and as far as we were concerned He was not in existence. When we turn our hearts and minds to God and come alive to Him we become dead to sin and to Satan's lies. We can't possibly live in both worlds. We must choose which master we will serve, God the Father and eternal life or Satan and eternal damnation.

3. WE MUST HAVE FAITH IN CHRIST JESUS

1. This includes faith in His Name (read Acts 3:16, 4:12),
2. faith in His Blood (read Rom. 3:24-25),
3. faith in His Word (read John 15:7, 2 Cor. 1:20),
4. AND faith in His death, burial, and resurrection (read Rom. 6:1-8, 1 Cor. 15:1-19).

We must believe that what Christ died for is ours the moment we accept it. We identify ourselves with Him by faith in all His work and we then receive the benefits for which He died.

4. BY WALKING IN THE LIGHT

John 1:7-9
Amplified Bible (AMP)
⁷ This man came to witness, that he might testify of the Light, that all men might believe in it [adhere to it, trust it, and rely upon it] through him.

⁸ He was not the Light himself, but came that he might bear witness regarding the Light.

⁹ There it was—the true Light [was then] coming into the world [the genuine, perfect, steadfast Light] that illumines every person.

This means as we get to know truth, we accept it and obey it and it makes us free (read John 8:31-32). This is the process of growing in grace and in the knowledge of God (read 2 Pet. 1:4-10, 3:18).

5. BY TAKING UP OUR CROSS DAILY TO FOLLOW CHRIST

This means forsaking all that the Gospel requires one to give up and loving the Lord with all our hearts and souls (read Luke 14:25-27, 33, Matt. 19:27-30). As one learns about the truth he must conform to it daily. Whatever the cross may be that we are called upon to bear we must carry it in conformity to the Will of God. All selfishness in obeying truth must be denied and the Gospel must be obeyed, regardless of our personal interests (read Mark 8:34-38, 10:23-31).

6. BY WALKING AND LIVING IN THE SPIRIT

This means that we seek to know the will of God by the Holy Spirit and the Word of God and that we shall always follow the leading of the Spirit and reject anything in our lives that would be contrary to the Word of God and our best spiritual interests. We must put to death all the works of the flesh and cultivate the fruit of the Spirit (read Rom. 8:116, Gal. 5:16-26, Col. 3:5-17, Jude 20:24, 1 Pet. 1:3-9).

7. BY CONSTANT PRAYER AND STUDY OF THE WORD OF GOD

We have need of prayer and how to get answers to our prayers. Along with praying, we should be in constant meditation in the Word of God and be of cheerful obedience to it. It is by meditation and study that we get to know the fine points of truth and of the spiritual leading of God. Men are required to study (read 2 Tim. 2:15), search (read John 5:39), continue in, and know the truth (read John 8:31-36), obey it (read John 14:23-24, Acts 5:32, Rom. 1:5), and meditate in it day and night (read Ps. 1, Josh. 1:7-8). It is by prayer, study and obedience to the Word that faith is increased (read Rom. 10:17). We are promised that if the

Word abides in us and we abide in Christ we can ask what we will and it shall be done (read John 15:7). It is by this that we learn in what ways to identify ourselves with Christ and how to do it.

8. BY FAITHFUL WORK FOR GOD AND CONSECRATION TO HELP OTHERS

We should realize our responsibility and that we are saved in order for us to serve. We should find the most spiritual church in our community, not necessarily the most popular one, for this latter kind is not always the most spiritual one. We should choose a church that holds up a genuine standard of Christianity and clean holy living according to the Gospel. We should go to a church that demands of its members that they live free from sin and the bad habits that will damn the soul. It will pay us great dividends here and hereafter to choose wisely the church that will help develop our faith and encourage us in following the whole Bible.

9. OUR DUTY FOR THE COMMUNITY AND THE NATIONS

We must be sure we cooperate with the pastor and the program of the LOCAL CHURCH in the winning of souls. The Bible says in Hebrews 10:25:

Hebrews 10:25
Amplified Bible (AMP)
25 Not forsaking *or* neglecting to assemble together [as believers], as is the habit of some people, but admonishing (warning, urging, and encouraging) one another, and all the more faithfully as you see the day approaching.

We should back our pastor in prayer and be the kind of members that he can depend upon. We should get busy for God and use every opportunity we get to be a witness for Jesus either in public or private. Never turn down an opportunity to lead prayer meetings, visit the sick, help the needy or to do religious social work in the community.

10. HOW TO OVERCOME

If you will study the Bible, believe its promises, and follow the simple instructions that we give you, it will be impossible to fail or to not get from God the wonderful benefits He has promised. Believe in the reality of sin, sickness, Satan, demons and God. Learn that the true source of help in life comes from God. Learn how to pray and what to pray for. Do not be satisfied to live like the lukewarm Christians around you. Step ahead of the crowd and be an example to others and never stumble over anything. If one hypocrite causes you to stumble and fall, then he is ahead of you or else you would not have stumbled over him in the first place.

Practice constantly the presence of God in order to overcome sin and bad habits. Believe that you can have healing and health and all the things promised by God. Seek God daily to attain these benefits and your life will be blessed beyond anything that you now realize. The Lord commands all Christians (His "Saints") to put on the full armor of God (read Eph. 6:11-18). As such, we are to prepare for battle with the enemy and carry out the duties of His service, which requires us to:

1. Know the devices of Satan (2 Cor. 2:11).
2. Give Satan no place (Eph. 4:27).
3. Resist him (James 4:7, 1 Pet. 5:8-9).
4. Be sober and vigilant in waging war against him (1 Pet. 5:8-9).
5. Overcome Satan by the Word of God (Matt. 4:1-11, 1 John 2:14).
6. Overcome him by the blood of Christ and your testimony (Rev. 12:11).
7. Overcome him by Christ and His name (Eph. 1:19-22, 2:6, 2 Cor. 2:15).
8. Overcome him by the Holy Spirit (Rom. 8:1-13, Gal. 5:16-26).

LESSON TWENTY-TWO

GOD PURPOSE DRIVEN:
Daily Wisdom Key for Today:

NOW THAT YOU ARE IN CHRIST

Verse to Remember: 2 Corinthians 5:17
Amplified Bible (AMP)
¹⁷ Therefore if any person is [ingrafted] in Christ (the Messiah) he is a new creation (a new creature altogether); the old [previous moral and spiritual condition] has passed away. Behold, the fresh *and* new has come!

Question to Meditate On: I AM FORGIVEN I AM CHOSEN AND I AM A OVERCOMER!

LESSON TWENTY-THREE

1 Timothy 2:1
Amplified Bible (AMP)
2 First of all, then, I admonish *and* urge
that petitions, prayers, intercessions, and
thanksgivings be offered on behalf of all men,

INTERCESSORY PRAYER: THE INVISIBLE WAR

Daniel's first line of defense in the invisible war of the spirit realm was always PRAYER. This is illustrated in Daniel 6:1 and 9:3, as well as here in our commentary scripture which best illustrates the warfare of intercessory prayer. In these passages, we discover that Daniel's supplications to God were heard by Him from the very first day that Daniel set his heart to purity of purpose and uttered his prayers. But then the invisible war was set in motion. The "prince of the kingdom of Persia," who is the devil or Satan, held back God's emissary who was sent to deliver the answer. For 21 days, a great struggle took place in the heavenlies between the forces of God and the forces of Satan before Daniel saw his ultimate victory.

In the New Testament, the greatest example of a life of dedicated, effective prayer and intercession was Jesus. Our Lord Jesus Christ was the greatest BREAKTHROUGH WARRIOR - the greatest Intercessor Who ever lived. Just hours before He offered Himself up to be betrayed, denied, mocked, beaten, tortured and crucified, He won...through intercessory prayer...

breakthroughs that would protect, shape and solidify His Church forever! As a soldier in God's Army, you now know that there are no victories without battles. This especially holds true for the consecrated Christian and his/her finances. Anyone who is sold out for the Lord and intends to use his/her money and finance to subsidize and sponsor the gospel and God's people, already know, that they will immediately be under attack from Satan. Yet, who can fully imagine the extent of Satan's brutal attack on Jesus, as the fiercest powers and principalities of the evil realm converged to try and prevent HIS intercession from going forth?

Which one of us can truly comprehend the intensity of this invisible war as Jesus stood in the gap, winning great 'victories for us by praying: John 17:9-25 reads:

John 17:9-25
Amplified Bible (AMP)
9 I am praying for them. I am not praying (requesting) for the world, but for those You have given Me, for they belong to You.

10 All [things that are] Mine are Yours, and all [things that are] Yours belong to Me; and I am glorified in (through) them. [They have done Me honor; in them My glory is achieved.]

11 And [now] I am no more in the world, but these are [still] in the world, and I am coming to You. Holy Father, keep in Your Name [[a]in the knowledge of Yourself] those whom You have given Me, that they may be one as We [are one].

12 While I was with them, I kept *and* preserved them in Your Name [[b]in the knowledge and worship of You]. Those You have given Me I guarded *and* protected, and not one of them has perished *or* is lost except the son of perdition [Judas Iscariot—the one who is now doomed to destruction, destined to be lost], that the Scripture might be fulfilled.

¹³ And now I am coming to You; I say these things while I am still in the world, so that My joy may be made full *and* complete *and* perfect in them [that they may experience My delight fulfilled in them, that My enjoyment may be perfected in their own souls, that they may have My gladness within them, filling their hearts].

¹⁴ I have given *and* delivered to them Your word (message) and the world has hated them, because they are not of the world [do not belong to the world], just as I am not of the world.

¹⁵ I do not ask that You will take them out of the world, but that You will keep *and* protect them from the evil one.

¹⁶ They are not of the world (worldly, belonging to the world), [just] as I am not of the world.

¹⁷ Sanctify them [purify, consecrate, separate them for Yourself, make them holy] by the Truth; Your Word is Truth.

¹⁸ Just as You sent Me into the world, I also have sent them into the world.

¹⁹ And so for their sake *and* on their behalf, I sanctify (dedicate, consecrate) Myself, that they also may be sanctified (dedicated, consecrated, made holy) in the Truth.

²⁰ Neither for these alone do I pray [it is not for their sake only that I make this request], but also for all those who will ever come to believe in (trust in, cling to, rely on) Me through their word *and* teaching,

²¹ That they all may be one, [just] as You, Father, are in Me and I in You, that they also may be one in Us, so that the world may believe *and* be convinced that You have sent Me.

22 I have given to them the glory *and* honor which You have given Me, that they may be one [even] as We are one:

23 I in them and You in Me, in order that they may become one *and* perfectly united, that the world may know *and* [] recognize that You sent Me and that You have loved them [even] as You have loved Me.

24 Father, I desire that they also whom You have entrusted to Me [as Your gift to Me] may be with Me where I am, so that they may see My glory, which You have given Me [Your love gift to Me]; for You loved Me before the foundation of the world.

25 O just *and* righteous Father, although the world has not known You *and* has failed to recognize You *and* has never acknowledged You, I have known You [continually]; and these men understand *and* know that You have sent Me.

I remember 28 years ago, after crying to the Lord, God baptized me and filled me with the Holy Spirit. Even though I was transformed, I still did not know how to pray or how to do intercession prayer. God sent someone to rent a room in the apartment above my garage. This man was Spirit filled and a bible teacher and a great intercessor. He committed to me for 30 days and we began to pray for 1 hour every morning. There I experienced the unlimited anointing of GOD FLOWING through our lives. So, I adopted this custom and made a habit out of praying 1 hour and reading the bible every morning.

THE TRUTH TRANSFORMS US

Spiritual growth is the process of replacing lies with truth. Jesus asked Peter why he could not pray for even one hour. Intercession and prayer is essential and unavoidable for the child of God. Matthew 4 states:

Matthew 4:4
Amplified Bible (AMP)
⁴But He replied, it has been written, Man shall not live *and* be upheld *and* sustained by bread alone, but by every word that comes forth from the mouth of God.

Acts 20:32
Amplified Bible (AMP)
³²And now [brethren], I commit you to God [I deposit you in His charge, entrusting you to His protection and care]. And I commend you to the Word of His grace [to the commands and counsels and promises of His unmerited favor]. It is able to build you up and to give you [your rightful] inheritance among all God's set-apart ones (those consecrated, purified, and transformed of soul).

Intercession and sanctification requires revelation. The Spirit of God uses the word of God to make us like the Son of God. To become like Jesus, we must fill our lives with His word. The bible says that through the word we are put together and shaped up for the task that God has for us. When you and I get involved in spiritual warfare, our faith is being released and strongholds are broken over your life and the life of others. The enemy is pushed back and God releases the anointing into your life and in the life of others. We encourage everyone that reads this, Bible Purpose Driven book to find a balanced church that knows how to do spiritual warfare so that you too can be trained and be equipped just like I was equipped 28 years ago. You can also go on-line and get our best-selling book, The Invisible War: Equipping God's Army for Spiritual Battle.

In the next two lessons that follow, they will prepare you to equip you and make you stronger in living a victorious life. Then, in the other chapters that follow, we will be discussing the principles, step by step, until your faith is built up so that you can come to a new level. We will bring you through the bible, back and forth and we will touch every issue, tithing, giving, first fruits, love offerings as we have already built the foundation in the first lessons of this manual of your life reconstruction provisions through Christ Jesus. We are excited for you because we know that you will come to a place of supernatural miracles and living by faith and a VICTORIOUS life! If you stay saved and continue to be saved and do not doubt, you will see God's promises come to pass. Remember, it took many years to get to the position that you are at now. You must be patient and allow God to do His work in your life. Matthew 7:7 reminds us:

Matthew 7:7
Amplified Bible (AMP)
7 [a]**Keep on asking and it will be given you;** [b] **keep on seeking and you will find;** [c]**keep on knocking [reverently] and [the door] will be opened to you.**

YOU MUST POSSESS VIOLENT FAITH THAT CANNOT BE DENIED

If you are in need of healing, financing, or another area of your life needs breakthrough then you are on the right path to success.

LESSON TWENTY-THREE

God Purpose Driven:
Daily Wisdom Key for Today:

INTERCESSORY PRAYER: THE INVISIBLE WAR

Verse to Remember: 1 Timothy 2:1
Amplified Bible (AMP)
2 First of all, then, I admonish *and* urge
that petitions, prayers, intercessions, and
thanksgivings be offered on behalf of all men,

Question to Meditate On: Prayer TRANSFORMS every situation of my needs here on the earth.

LESSON TWENTY-FOUR

Joshua 1:8
Amplified Bible (AMP)
⁸ This Book of the Law shall not depart out of your mouth, but you shall meditate on it day and night, that you may observe *and* do according to all that is written in it. For then you shall make your way prosperous, and then you shall deal wisely *and* have good [a]success.

VICTORIOUS LIVING

As you continue to read the book of Joshua, we see that Joshua entered the promised land and God was with him step by step and he also inherited the wealth of the land. How much more will God give you and I through His Son Jesus Christ?

Here are some of the benefits of victorious living which are available for the believer and are the primary consideration of this chapter. Ephesians 1:7 says (referring to Jesus):

Ephesians 1:7
Amplified Bible (AMP)
⁷ In Him we have redemption (deliverance and salvation) through His blood, the remission (forgiveness) of our offenses (shortcomings and trespasses), in accordance with the riches *and* the generosity of His gracious favor,

And in Psalms 107:2, we read:

Psalm 107:2
Amplified Bible (AMP)
²Let the redeemed of the Lord say so, whom He
has delivered from the hand of the adversary,

Therefore, I can say: THROUGH THE BLOOD OF JESUS I AM REDEEMED OUT OF THE HANDS OF THE DEVIL. THROUGH THE BLOOD OF JESUS ALL MY SINS ARE FORGIVEN AND I AM DEBT FREE. AMEN!

Romans 5:9
Amplified Bible (AMP)
⁹Therefore, since we are now justified ([a]acquitted, made righteous, and brought into right relationship with God) by Christ's blood, how much more [certain is it that] we shall be saved by Him from the indignation *and* wrath of God.

Let us now look at all of the benefits of the shed blood of Jesus Christ. The shedding of Jesus' blood brought the following to us:

1. Redemption. (Eph. 1:7, Col. 1:14, Heb. 9:12, 1 Pet. 1:18-19, Rev. 5:9)
2. Sanctification. (Hebrews 10:29, Hebrews 13:12)
3. Eternal Inheritance. (Hebrews 9:12-15)
4. Forgiveness. (Ephesians 7, Colossians 1:14, Hebrews 9:22)
5. Cleansing. (Hebrews 9:14, John 1:7)
6. Justification. (Romans 5:9)
7. Peace. (Colossians 1:20)
8. Boldness to enter in before God's presence. (Hebrews 10:19, Ephesians 2:13)
9. Healing. (Isaiah 53:4-5, 1 Peter 2:24, Matthew 8:17)
10. Reconciliation. (Romans 3:25, Colossians 1:20)

11. Purging. (Hebrews 9:14)
12. Overcoming. (Revelation 12:11)
13. Prosperity. (John 3:2)

HOW TO WIN IN COMBAT OVER SATAN WITH THE BLOOD OF JESUS CHRIST

A simple formula defines the victory of Christians over Satan:

Redemption + Sanctification + Forgiveness + Justification + Cleansing + Peace + Boldness + Healing + Reconciliation = AN OVERCOMER!

ASKING AND RECEIVING FROM GOD

The subject of this lesson is one of the most vital to human existence, in both this life and the eternal life to come. Without a precise and correct understanding of this subject we miss much of the blessings that our Lord wants so dearly to bestow on us. By faithfully applying the principles presented here the believer will not experience the confusion and disappointment of seemingly "unanswered prayers."

IF WE FOLLOW GOD'S INSTRUCTIONS AND LIVE BY HIS HOLY WILL FOR OUR LIVES, WE CAN LITERALLY GET ANYTHING WE WANT.

We, as believers, have been given a mandate and an absolute assurance by God of receiving in an abundance that is greater than we can hold, all that we rightly desire:

Luke 6:38
Amplified Bible (AMP)
[38] **Give, and [gifts] will be given to you; good measure, pressed down, shaken together, and running over, will they pour [a]into [the pouch formed by] the bosom [of your robe and used as a bag]. For with the measure you deal out [with the measure you use when you confer benefits on others], it will be measured back to you.**

GIVE LAVISHLY! LIVE ABUNDANTLY!

The more you give, the more you get,

The more you laugh, the less you fret,

The more you do unselfishly,

The more you live abundantly,

The more of everything you share,

The more you'll always have to spare.

The more you love, the more you'll find

That life is good and friends are kind,

For only what we give away

Enriches us from day to day.

-Helen Steiner Rice

The following points are about how to pray in a Biblically correct and effective manner. Learn and practice them diligently until your asking of the Lord and receiving His blessings are the norm and not the exception.

1. WHAT IS THE NATURE OF PRAYER?

The proper attitude of prayer is our coming before the Lord, in humility, obedience and loving confidence that His promises to us are genuine and His will for us is for our good and ultimate glory. We come before the throne of the Almighty God, Creator of the Universe in worship and gratitude to plead our cause. True prayer is seeking His perfect will in matters that are often not within our human understanding. This is our personal petition to a real and personal God. Just as our Lord Jesus did, we come not to impose our will, but to receive the Will of the Father and to cooperate unfailingly with it.

2. WHAT THE BIBLE SAYS ABOUT PRAYER

  a. Scripture Commands Us to Pray Throughout the Word of God, we are instructed (in fact, commanded) to pray (read Heb. 4:16, 1 Thess. 5:17-18, 1 Chron. 16:11, 2 Chron. 7:14, Ps. 105:4, Isa. 55:6, Phil. 4:6, Matt. 7:7-11 and Eph. 6:18).

     Paul tells us in 1 Thess. 5:17-18, Verse 17, "Pray without ceasing."

     Verse 18, "In everything give thanks: for this is the will of God in Christ Jesus concerning you."

  b. Postures and Attitudes in Prayer Lying down (read 2 Sam. 12:16-20), standing (read Luke 18:13), sitting (read Acts 1:14, 2:2 and Luke 10:13), kneeling (read Ps. 95:6, Luke 22:41, Dan. 6:10 and Acts 9:40, 20:36, 21:5), meditating (read Ps. 5:1), weeping (read Ezra 10:1, 1 Sam. 1:10), talking (read Gen. 18:23-33), and in the Spirit (read Eph. 6:18, Jude 20).

c. The Times to Pray In the morning (read Ps. 5:3: 88:13, 143:8), twice per day (read Ps. 88:1), three times per day (read Ps. 55:17, Dan. 6:10), without ceasing (read 1 Thess. 5:17), in the evening (read Mark 1:35, Luke 6:12), and night and day (read Luke 2:37).

d. Places to Pray In a prayer closet (read Matt. 6:6), on a mountain (read Matt 14:23), in the home, temple and everywhere. (read 1 Tim. 2:8, Acts 1:13-14, 2:46, 3:1, 12:12)

e. Improper Prayer in Matt. 6:5-8, Christ Jesus warns us, Verse 5: "And when thou prayest, thou shalt not be as the hypocrites are, for they love to pray standing in the synagogues and in the corners of the streets, that they may be seen of men. Verily, I say unto you, they have their reward."

Verse 6: "But thou, when thou prayest, enter into thy closet, and when thou hast shut thy door, pray to thy Father which is in secret; and thy Father which seeth in secret shall reward thee openly."

Verse 7: "But when ye pray, use not vain repetitions, as the heathen do, for they think that they shall be heard for their much speaking."

Verse 8: "Be not ye therefore like unto them; for your Father knoweth what things ye have need of, before ye ask Him."

f. The Purpose of Praying The ultimate purpose of all prayer is to GLORIFY THE LORD GOD as is indeed the ultimate reason for our very existence. Jesus instructs us in John 14:13 that,

"And whatsoever ye shall ask in my name, that I will do, that the Father may be glorified in the Son."

g. The Basis for Petition and Answered Prayer The only true basis for prayer, and our Lord's response to it, is to be born again in the Holy Spirit and to live in right relationship with Him. The unsaved, who live in rebellion against God's Will and who refuse to submit, have no right of petition before Him. God, in His infinite wisdom and mercy, hears our cries for help but He is only obligated to come to the aid of those who obey His Perfect Law. God loves us and yearns to have us in communion with Him. He simply desires our obedience, our love and our unwavering faith in Him. John 15:7 states the concept very concisely and beautifully:

"If ye abide in me, and my words abide in you, ye shall ask what ye will, and it shall be done unto you."

And in Psalms 66:18, David states the above point from a different perspective. Let's read it together:

"If I regard iniquity in my heart, the Lord will not hear me."

We see from above that David knew the secret to be connected and not miss the mark and we have no choice. We must have faith in HIM, violent faith that cannot not be denied.

LESSON TWENTY-FOUR

God Purpose Driven:
Daily Wisdom Key for Today:

VICTORIOUS LIVING

Verse to Remember: Joshua 1:8
Amplified Bible (AMP)
[8] **This Book of the Law shall not depart out of your mouth, but you shall meditate on it day and night, that you may observe *and* do according to all that is written in it. For then you shall make your way prosperous, and then you shall deal wisely *and* have good [a]success.**

Question to Meditate On: I can get it all and do it all and give it all away. If you agree then say 3 times:

HALLELUJAH HALLELUJAH HALLEJUAH!

LESSON TWENTY-FIVE

Hebrews 11:1
Amplified Bible (AMP)
11 Now faith is the assurance (the confirmation, [a]the title deed) of the things [we] hope for, being the proof of things [we] do not see *and* the conviction of their reality [faith perceiving as real fact what is not revealed to the senses].

FAITH – THE CORNERSTONE OF PRAYER

Scripture makes very simple and clear for us, the secret of answered prayer. It's no great mystery, we have all heard it many times... "HAVE FAITH IN GOD." It is so profound, yet so simple, it should be shouted from the rooftops! As Americans like to say, "You don't have to be a rocket scientist to understand it." So, "HAVE FAITH IN GOD!" Many passages in the Bible, especially in the New Testament make this point concerning faith again and again. For example, Mark 11:22-25 states:

Mark 11:22-25
Amplified Bible (AMP)
22 And Jesus, replying, said to them,
Have faith in God [constantly].

23 Truly I tell you, whoever says to this mountain, be lifted up and thrown into the sea! and does not doubt at all in his heart but believes that what he says will take place, it will be done for him.

²⁴ For this reason I am telling you, whatever you ask for in prayer, believe (trust and be confident) that it is granted to you, and you will [get it].

²⁵ And whenever you stand praying, if you have anything against anyone, forgive him and[a]let it drop (leave it, let it go), in order that your Father Who is in heaven may also forgive you your [own] failings and shortcomings and let them drop. And when ye stand praying, FORGIVE, if ye have ought against any: that your Father also which is in heaven may forgive you your trespasses."

Many other passages refer to the absolute necessity of faith. Faith must precede all else in your prayer life. Faith is the wings of your prayers, without which they cannot fly to the ears of the Lord (read Heb. 11:6, James 1:5-9, Rom. 4:1122). Simple and Solid Faith Requires Fasting and Prayer. Fasting is a powerful tool when used in conjunction with prayer. Faith cannot grow without prayer and our prayer life is greatly enriched by fasting. These two aspects work "hand-in-glove." One without the other is incomplete and therefore discordant, but in concert they form the sweet music that our Lord loves to hear. Fasting humbles us before God (read Ps. 35:13). It lets Him know that we are earnest in our love for Him, and we love Him above all else.

In modern medical terms, fasting allows the digestive tract a rest and rids the body of toxins. It demonstrates that we have mastered our appetites and desires. Jesus demonstrated the vital need for fasting in Matt. 4:1-11. After Jesus had fasted in the desert for forty days and nights, Satan tempted Him repeatedly. The Lord Jesus responded to Satan, with the power of God and the purity of a fast in Matt. 4-10:

Matthew 4:10
Amplified Bible (AMP)
[10] Then Jesus said to him, be gone, Satan! For it has been written, You shall worship the Lord your God, and Him alone shall you serve.

Scripture does not give us definite rules concerning how long or how often we should fast - it simply puts fasting forward as an integral part of a sound spiritual life. The Bible makes thirty-five references to fasting. The following is only a partial list of various biblical figures and how fasting was a part of their walk:

In 1 Kings 21:27-29, Ahab was spared from judgment. Let's read it below:

1 Kings 21:27-29
'And it came to pass when Ahab heard those words, that he rent his clothes, and put sackcloth upon his flesh, and fasted, and lay in sackcloth, and went softly. And the word of the Lord came to Elijah the Tishbite, saying, Seest thou how Ahab humbleth himself before me? because he humbleth himself before me, I will not bring the evil in his days: but in his son's days will I bring the evil upon his house.

Judah was delivered from his enemies in Ezra 8:21-23. Let's read it below:

Ezra 8:21-23
'Then I proclaimed a fast there, at the river of Ahava, that we might afflict ourselves before our God, to seek of him a right way for us, and for our little ones, and for all our substance. For I was ashamed to require of the king a band of soldiers and horsemen to help us against the enemy in the way: because we had spoken unto the king, saying, The hand of our God is upon all them for good that seek him; but his power and his wrath

is against all then that forsake him. So, we fasted and besought our God for this: and he was intreated of us.'

Ninevah was spared from destruction in Jonah 3.

Cornelius received a revelation in Acts 10.

David fasted "until weak" and was delivered from his enemies in Psalms 35:13, 69:10, 109:24:

Psalm 35:13
Amplified Bible (AMP)
¹³ But as for me, when they were sick, my clothing was sackcloth; I afflicted myself with fasting, and I prayed with head bowed on my breast.

Psalm 69:10
Amplified Bible (AMP)
¹⁰ When I wept *and* humbled myself with fasting, I was jeered at *and* humiliated;

Psalm 109:24
Amplified Bible (AMP)
²⁴ My knees are weak *and* totter from fasting; and my body is gaunt *and* has no fatness.

Various lengths of fasting are recorded, ranging from 1, 3, 7, 14, to 21 and even 40 days.

Paul and 276 men were delivered from death after having fasted for 14 days in Acts 27:33-34:

Acts 27:33-34
Amplified Bible (AMP)
³³ While they waited until it should become day, Paul entreated them all to take some food, saying, this is the

fourteenth day that you have been continually in suspense *and* on the alert without food, having eaten nothing.

³⁴ So I urge (warn, exhort, encourage, advise) you to take some food [for your safety]—it will give you strength; for not a hair is to perish from the head of any one of you.

Elijah received a revelation in 1 Kings 19:7-18:

1 Kings 19:7-18
Amplified Bible (AMP)
⁷ The angel of the Lord came the second time
and touched him and said, Arise and eat,
for the journey is too great for you.

⁸ So he arose and ate and drank, and went in the strength of that food forty days and nights to Horeb, the mount of God.

⁹ There he came to a cave and lodged in it; and
behold, the word of the Lord came to him, and He
said to him, what are you doing here, Elijah?

¹⁰ He replied, I have been very jealous for the Lord God of hosts; for the Israelites have forsaken Your covenant, thrown down Your altars, and killed Your prophets with the sword. And I, I only, am left; and they seek my life, to take it away.

¹¹ And He said, go out and stand on the mount before the Lord. And behold, the Lord passed by, and a great and strong wind rent the mountains and broke in pieces the rocks before the Lord, but the Lord was not in the wind; and after the wind an earthquake, but the Lord was not in the earthquake;

¹² And after the earthquake a fire, but the Lord
was not in the fire; and after the fire [a sound of
gentle stillness and] a still, small voice.

¹³ When Elijah heard the voice, he wrapped his face in his mantle and went out and stood in the entrance of the cave. And behold, there came a voice to him and said, what are you doing here, Elijah?

¹⁴ He said, I have been very jealous for the Lord God of hosts, because the Israelites have forsaken Your covenant, thrown down Your altars, and slain Your prophets with the sword. And I, I only, am left, and they seek my life, to destroy it.

¹⁵ And the Lord said to him, Go, return on your way to the Wilderness of Damascus; and when you arrive, anoint Hazael to be king over Syria.

¹⁶ And anoint Jehu son of Nimshi to be king over Israel, and anoint Elisha son of Shaphat of Abel-meholah to be prophet in your place.

¹⁷ And him who escapes from the sword of [a] Hazael Jehu shall slay, and him who escapes the sword of Jehu Elisha shall slay.

¹⁸ Yet I will leave Myself 7,000 in Israel, all the knees that have not bowed to Baal and every mouth that has not kissed him.

Christ Himself received power after His forty days of fasting in the desert in Matthew 4:1-11:

Matthew 4:1-11
Amplified Bible (AMP)
4 Then Jesus was led (guided) by the [Holy] Spirit into the wilderness (desert) to be tempted (tested and tried) by the devil.

² And He went without food for forty days and forty nights, and later He was hungry.

³ And the tempter came and said to Him, If You are God's Son, command these stones to be made [ᵃloaves of] bread.

⁴ But He replied, it has been written, Man shall not live *and* be upheld *and* sustained by bread alone, but by every word that comes forth from the mouth of God.

⁵ Then the devil took Him into the holy city and placed Him on ᵇa turret (pinnacle, ᶜgable) of the temple ᵈsanctuary.

⁶ And he said to Him, If You are the Son of God, throw Yourself down; for it is written, He will give His angels charge over you, and they will bear you up on their hands, lest you strike your foot against a stone.

⁷ Jesus said to him, ᵉOn the other hand, it is written also, You shall not tempt, ᶠtest thoroughly, or ᵍtry exceedingly the Lord your God.

⁸ Again, the devil took Him up on a very high mountain and showed Him all the kingdoms of the world and the glory (the splendor, magnificence, preeminence, and excellence) of them.

⁹ And he said to Him, these things, all taken together, I will give You, if You will prostrate Yourself before me and do homage *and* worship me.

¹⁰ Then Jesus said to him, be gone, Satan! For it has been written, you shall worship the Lord your God, and Him alone shall you serve.

¹¹ Then the devil departed from Him, and behold, angels came and ministered to Him.

We have no greater endorsement for any particular spiritual practice than what is given in Scripture for fasting. Since fasting and prayer are featured so often and prominently in the Bible, it behooves us as believers to adopt the practice ourselves in order to bring victory over Satan and to draw us closer to the Lord in every area of our life and to live a long and healthy life and to occupy our lives until He comes to take us home.

Plant these scriptures in your heart and use them as your navigator towards your financial victory over every plot and ploy of the enemy designed to steal your seed and rob you of your blessings! Take the teachings of this lesson and be the bearer of great fruit by sharing with others and with the generations to come. Be bold, equip yourself properly, and be prepared to fight the Invisible War. You will certainly be blessed as a result with the rewards of a truly victorious life that is birthed, based, measured and purposed by God's holy scripture!

LESSON TWENTY-FIVE

God Purpose Driven:
Daily Wisdom Key for Today:

FAITH- THE CORNERSTONE OF PRAYER

Verse to Remember: Hebrews 11:1
Amplified Bible (AMP)
11 Now faith is the assurance (the confirmation, [a]the title deed) of the things [we] hope for, being the proof of things [we] do not see *and* the conviction of their reality [faith perceiving as real fact what is not revealed to the senses].

Question to Meditate On: I will walk by FAITH and not by sight. All my needs are met and there is much more in my Father's storehouse.

CONTINUE TO MEDITATE ON THIS STATEMENT
UNTIL IT BECOMES A PART OF YOUR DAILY WALK.
This is pleasing to God. This kind of faith cannot be denied.

LESSON TWENTY-SIX

Proverbs 3:5-10
Amplified Bible (AMP)
⁵ **Lean on, trust in, *and* be confident in the Lord**
with all your heart *and* mind and do not rely
on your own insight *or* understanding.

⁶ **In all your ways know, recognize, *and* acknowledge Him,**
and He will direct *and* make straight *and* plain your paths.

⁷ **Be not wise in your own eyes; reverently fear *and***
worship the Lord and turn [entirely] away from evil.

⁸ **It shall be health to your nerves *and* sinews,**
and marrow *and* moistening to your bones.

⁹ **Honor the Lord with your capital *and* sufficiency [from**
righteous labors] and with the first fruits of all your income;

¹⁰ **So shall your storage places be filled with plenty,**
and your vats shall be overflowing with new wine.

HONORING AND TRUSTING GOD

These are just a few of the testimonies of how people found the way of success. We hope that this will build up your faith so that you can take ACTION to make some adjustments in your personal life. Keep in mind that in this book we will go over and over the lessons until you will be transformed. The bible is crystal clear about how millions and millions of people prospered when they obeyed God's decrees and laws:

Mr. Kerr of the Kerr-Mason fruit jar fame started out tithing when he was in debt, had a mortgage on his home and was worried and distressed. Within three months after he began to tithe, unexpected and unforeseen blessing came to him in the form of a fruit jar patent and as he so aptly put it "God opened my eyes to see His love and faithfulness to His promises." That same year with $100 and a strong faith in God's tithing promises contained in Malachi 3:10, he organized a corporation which has grown beyond bounds.

I have never seen nor heard of a man that has not been blessed when he has been faithful in tithing with faith in God's promises and with faith that God will meet His own obligation to bless in material things. There are no testimonies, as far as I know, of rich men commencing to tithe, but there are many testimonies of men who began to tithe when they were poor and they are now rich. A few more may be enumerated as follows:

Mary Kay, a woman with a God-given vision to build a cosmetic company to bless many women around the world.

Dr. Robert Schuller of Garden Grove, California built Crystal Cathedral on 48-acres of land and has a high-powered Christian network to reach the nations of the world, which started out with him, his wife, an organ player, an old car and a $500 seed that he sowed when he came out west. He now is one of the largest and most well-known Ministries around the world. He has inspired millions and millions of people through his 'Hour of Power' television program and he has raised up champions with his teaching of positive thinking and financial economics to the lows and to the highs and he has had many, many testimonies of how people have had a breakthrough in their financing.

Dr. Benny Hinn who heads an International Miracle Healing Crusade team began walking in the ministry at the age of 18.

His family was poor and he had no money. Now, at the age of 58, he has a ministry with a revenue of over $200 million a year because he was obedient to God's law of sowing and reaping, as he applied God's principle to his life.

Dr. Creflo A. Dollar, a well-known African-American motivational preacher and teacher who pastors a large congregation of over 30 thousand members located in Georgia and several satellite churches throughout the nation. He was once poverty-stricken but has overcome the snare of the devil. God has given him a ministry to teach and spread the gospel to people all around the world who have obtained economic and financial freedom by sowing and reaping by faith. His Ministry has inspired millions of people globally and his books are best-sellers and he is an entrepreneur and teacher of sound biblically based 'faith-in-Christ-Jesus' teachings.

Wrigley's, a faithful young man who gave up to 90 percent of his revenue to God. When he was a young man, God gave him a vision and a dream on how to create chewing gum and how to promote it worldwide. As you well-know chewing gum is a very popular item around the world. This man tried to out-give God with his finances. Could this be you too?

Colonel Sanders, twice went nationwide with his chicken franchise and went bankrupt. Then, in his latter days he cried out to the Lord and he heard the gospel and was born again and applied God's financial principles and now in 2012 he is worldwide and especially successful in Asia.

In the early 1900's, one man built a company and dedicated it to the Lord. This man's name was Henry Ford and the Company was Ford Motor Company. The company, in a short time became a world-wide manufacturer and distributor of cars and God blessed him. Recently, during the recession of 2008 up to this time 2012, Ford motor was on the verge of being bankrupt but all of the partners cried out to the Lord and re-committed themselves to God, and God answered their prayers and raised up the American government to bail them out and once again Ford cars are going full throttle.........and there are scores of other companies in America and around the world such as the Campbell's soup co., Colgate-Palmolive Co., Chick-Filet, In-n-Out burger, Carls. Jr. restaurant, who have understood and practiced the simple law of sowing and reaping. We hope and pray that you will be the next one!

MORAL LAW AND THE LORD JESUS

MAN'S SUPPLY IS SOMETIMES CUT SHORT BECAUSE HE DOES NOT UNDERSTAND HIS MORAL OBLIGATION & BECAUSE HE DOES NOT PUT FORTH EVERY EFFORT TO LIVE UP TO IT. MAN IS SUBJECT TO MORAL LAW AND MORAL GOVERNMENT AND HE IS UNDER MORAL OBLIGATION TO LIVE UP TO THE LAW OF MORAL GOVERNMENT. MORAL LAW IS SIMPLY THE RULE OF ACTON FOR

MORAL AGENTS BY RECOGNIZED AUTHORITY TO ENFORCE JUSTICE AND PRESCRIBE DUTY TO THOSE UNDER THEM.

The basis of justice is the intention to act and to choose for the best good of being. Even civil governments judge under the basis of intent to do good or evil. The bible respects the intentions more than the results or outward action.

2 Corinthians 8:12
New King James Version (NKJV)
[12] For if there is first a willing mind, *it is* accepted according to what one has, *and* not according to what he does not have.

James 1:13-15
New King James Version (NKJV)
[13] Let no one say when he is tempted, "I am tempted by God"; for God cannot be tempted by evil, nor does He Himself tempt anyone. [14] But each one is tempted when he is drawn away by his own desires and enticed. [15] Then, when desire has conceived, it gives birth to sin; and sin, when it is full-grown, brings forth death.

All vice and virtue are considered as coming from the heart. Where the heart is right, all is considered right; when the heart is evil all is considered evil. Even sinners do some things outwardly that are required by God, but the heart is not right. The intentions are generally selfish and the good acts do not change the heart. As we have seen, the foundation of moral obligation is the highest good of all. Because this is true, then the entire consecration of free wills is secure. This end constitutes obedience to moral laws. Obedience must be whole and entire. One cannot choose the best good of others and at the same time choose self-gratification. God cannot tolerate half-heartedness in choice or in service

Revelation 3:15-16
New King James Version (NKJV)
[15] "I know your works, that you are neither cold nor hot. I could wish you were cold or hot. [16] So then, because you are lukewarm, and neither cold nor hot,[a] I will vomit you out of My mouth.

If a person is always coming short of full obedience to known duty then there is not a moment that is not under the curse of broken law. God cannot disperse with the execution until repentance, forgiveness and full obedience are realized.

If obedience to moral law consists of the entire consecration to secure the best good of all according to the light received, sin and disobedience consist of the entire consecration of free choice and life to secure self-gratification, regardless of the right of others. It is a commitment of the will to serve Satan and the senses instead of God and the moral law of intelligence and seeking to be governed by impulses and passions instead of intelligent reason. Those men who we mentioned above as examples of obedience in sowing and reaping couldn't practice these laws of prosperity unless they truly gave themselves to God and others, to be a blessing to them in business, otherwise they couldn't reap the rich rewards promised in the laws of prosperity.

If you want to prosper, set your own house in order and follow faithfully the laws stated above and soon God will lead you into blessing that you never thought was possible for you. Apply yourself to a strict observance of these laws and principles and watch things happen that will bless you even more than you are blessing others.

LESSON TWENTY-SIX

Bible Purpose Driven:
Daily Wisdom Key for Today:

HONORING AND TRUSTING GOD

Verse to Remember: Proverbs 3:5-10
Amplified Bible (AMP)
[5] **Lean on, trust in, *and* be confident in the Lord**
with all your heart *and* mind and do not rely
on your own insight *or* understanding.

[6] **In all your ways know, recognize, *and* acknowledge Him,**
and He will direct *and* make straight *and* plain your paths.

[7] **Be not wise in your own eyes; reverently fear *and***
worship the Lord and turn [entirely] away from evil.

[8] **It shall be health to your nerves *and* sinews,**
and marrow *and* moistening to your bones.

[9] **Honor the Lord with your capital *and* sufficiency [from**
righteous labors] and with the first fruits of all your income;

[10] **So shall your storage places be filled with plenty,**
and your vats shall be overflowing with new wine.

Question to Meditate On: I will do my part with a JOYFUL heart and expect INCREASE in my daily life.

LESSON TWENTY-SEVEN

Luke 6:38
Amplified Bible (AMP)
[38] Give, and [gifts] will be given to you; good measure,
pressed down, shaken together, and running over, will
they pour [a]into [the pouch formed by] the bosom [of
your robe and used as a bag]. For with the measure you
deal out [with the measure you use when you confer
benefits on others], it will be measured back to you.

THE LAW OF MULTIPLICATION

The economics of stewardship is governed by the mathematics of the supernatural. George Muller hadn't faced a situation quite like it: before him were 120 orphans, expectantly seated at long dinner tables, but something at this mealtime tested the mettle of Muller's heart. On the dinner plates at that table was nothing but crusts of bread. Eager faces looked toward him, as if to say, "What's for dinner?" But they didn't know that the cupboard was bare and the icebox was empty.

There was no milk, and no money to buy food or drink.

What was George to do? It didn't take long for him to decide. He would do what he had done every other mealtime. He would instruct the children to bow their heads and join him in thanking God for the meal they were about to eat. He would praise God for the faithfulness of His provision, and so he did. Muller prayed simply, directly and with a heart filled with faith.

When the "amen" was pronounced, the plates still had nothing but bread crusts, but as the eyes of those 120 youngsters turned again to the head table, a knock sounded at the door. One of the boys was sent to answer. A moment later, he called out, "Mr. Muller, it's the vegetable man! He's got a lot of stuff for us!" Coincidently, there were many vegetables that would spoil if he didn't do something with them. While the vegetables were being unloaded, another person came to the door- the butcher! He had run out of ice at the end of a hot day and faced the prospect of awful, rotting meat. Could the orphanage use it?

No sooner had he spoken the words than another amazing "coincidence" occurred. The milkman's wagon pulled up, overloaded with milk and dairy products and needing desperately to do something with them! Needless to say, it was quite a banquet that night and it was the finest lesson in faith those orphans ever received. They had just seen the evidence of a spiritual law at work- the Law of Miraculous Multiplication. God had transformed their measly bread crusts into the best meal they had ever enjoyed. He had honored their simple faith with a supernatural supply.

Would the same thing have happened had Muller not prayed, believing God for His provision ahead of time for it? We don't know, but we do know that Jesus said we have not because we ask not and we know that His will for us is to walk by faith, not by sight. This raises several crucial questions: In the realm of stewardship, what does it mean to walk by faith? How can we believe God above and beyond our ability, our resources and our strength? In what ways can we trust Him to provide supernaturally on our behalf? It's clear from Scripture that the faith-driven life is the life God intends for us. In fact, "without faith it is impossible to please God." Trusting Him explicitly, He provides for us absolutely and we mustn't be limited by what we see because His ways transcend human understanding. As the prophet Isaiah explained, His thoughts are above our thoughts, and His ways are above our ways.

FOCUSING ON YOUR DESTINATION RATHER THAN A ROAD OF DESTRUCTION

The more clearly, we define our goals, the more skillful we can be in making wise decisions.

Philippians 3:14
Amplified Bible (AMP)
[14] I press on toward the goal to win the
[supreme and heavenly] prize to which God
in Christ Jesus is calling us upward.

Isaiah 55:8
Amplified Bible (AMP)
[8] For My thoughts are not your thoughts, neither
are your ways My ways, says the Lord.

LESSON TWENTY- SEVEN

Bible Purpose Driven:
Daily Wisdom Key for Today:

THE LAW OF MULTIPLICATION

Verse to Remember. Luke 6:38
Give, and it will be given to you: good measure,
pressed down, shaken together, and running over will
be put into your bosom. For with the same measure
that you use it, it will be measured back to you.'

Question to Meditate On: I will look to JESUS and HIS anointing that gives me all that I need and not my greed.

LESSON TWENTY-EIGHT

John 15:7
'If you abide in Me, and My words abide in you, you will ask what you desire, and it shall be done for you.'

LIVING THE LAWS

WHAT A BLESSING TO KNOW THAT GOD IS WITH YOU and that by faith in Him you can do all things and can get what you want. Your enemies cannot triumph. Your problems cannot defeat you.

THE LAW OF FAITH

The minute that you are tempted and worry and fret about some problem, turn it over to God because He can see farther than you can. He can workout things that are invisible to you. Go to the Cross and nail your worries away and become reckless in faith and confidence in God and accept what comes with peace and thankfulness. This is the victory that overcometh the world, even our FAITH.

1 John 5:1-4
Contemporary English Version (CEV)
Victory over the World
5 If we believe that Jesus is truly Christ, we are God's children. Everyone who loves the Father will also love his children. ² If we love and obey God, we know that we will

love his children. ³ We show our love for God by obeying his commandments, and they are not hard to follow.

⁴ Every child of God can defeat the world, and our faith is what gives us this victory.

Living the Law of Miraculous Multiplication requires confidence, obedience and courage: When faced with a major need, express confidence in the 'need meeter'. This applies especially when you don't comprehend God's purposes at work. Like Abraham of old, who put his own son on an altar as a sacrifice to God, we must rely on the One who is eminently able. We may wonder, what could we possibly have in common with Abraham? The truth is, many things! As God called Abraham to a life of obedience, He also calls us. As God tested Abraham, He tests us. As God called Abraham to a life of faith, so He calls you and me.

When faced with a major need, follow the directions. In order to tap the endless resources of God, the believer must exercise faith by acting in obedience to God's Word. As the Apostle Paul explained to the Romans, "faith comes by hearing, and hearing by the Word of God." When one is prompted by the Word of God or by the leadership of the Spirit, obedience to that prompting is an expression of faith. Such a response enables one to enter into partnership with God and gives the assurance of success even though the end may not be in sight.

When faced with a major need, brace for a great adventure. The life of faith- filled stewardship is anything but boring. Look at the amazing experiences of those in the "Hall of Faith" of Hebrews 11. Noah for example, had never experienced a flood nor had he even seen rain, yet he obeyed with regard only for the Lord. Since the command of God came without a specific schedule, Noah had to believe and act accordingly because faith has no time limit. Faith was the only reasonable response for Noah, as it is for us as stewards today.

SCRIPTURE REFERENCES TO MEDITATE ON:

Hebrews 11:6
Contemporary English Version (CEV)
**[6] But without faith no one can please God.
We must believe that God is real and that he
rewards everyone who searches for him.**

Romans 10:17
Contemporary English Version (CEV)
**[17] No one can have faith without hearing
the message about Christ.**

LESSON TWENTY-EIGHT

God Purpose Driven:
Daily Wisdom Key for Today:

LIVING THE LAWS

Verse to Remember; John 15:7
'If you abide in Me, and My words abide in you, you will
ask what you desire, and it shall be done for you.'

Question to Meditate On: I am connected and I will stay connected. This is my faith in HIM! Though rains and storms may come I will not be denied.

LESSON TWENTY-NINE

I Corinthians 6:19
: "Or do you not know that your body is the temple
of the Holy Spirit who is in you, whom you have
from God, and you are not your own?"

WHAT DOES IT MEAN
TO BE A STEWARD?

God has called us to be Stewards over our life and everything in and around it, and first of all our very own bodies, which belong to the Lord. We read that in the beginning God gave Adam the garden and he was told to cultivate and tend it. But glory to God, God through Christ has given us the unlimited anointing to restore and repair, rebuild and heal every situation.

Our time: "So teach us to number our days, that we may gain a heart of wisdom." Psalms 90:12

Our talents and abilities "…one and the same Spirit works all these things, distributing to each one individually as He wills." I Corinthians 12:11

Our possessions: "Do not lay up for yourselves treasures on earth, where moth and rust destroy and where thieves break in and steal; but lay up for yourselves treasures in heaven, where neither moth nor rust destroys and where thieves do not break in and steal. For where your treasure is, there your heart will be also." Matthew 6:19-21.

Our finances: "Command those who are rich in this present age not to be haughty, nor to trust in uncertain riches but in the living God, who gives us richly all things to enjoy. Let them do good, that they be rich in good works, ready to give, willing to share, storing up for themselves a good foundation for the time to come, that they may lay hold on eternal life." I Timothy6: 17-19

The Gospel: "Let a man so consider us, as servants of Christ and stewards of the mysteries of God." I Corinthians4:1

We should be willing Stewards: "For if I do this willingly, I have a reward; but if against my will, I have been entrusted with a stewardship."

Stewards are Accountable: Moreover it is required in stewards that one be found faithful." I Corinthians 4:2

THE PRAYER OF COMMITMENT

Ephesians 6:18
Contemporary English Version (CEV)
[18] Never stop praying, especially for others.
Always pray by the power of the Spirit. Stay
alert and keep praying for God's people.

Another translation says, "All manner of prayer." (KH) We need all kinds of prayer- not just one kind. The Bible contains several kinds of prayer. One is "the prayer of commitment," or casting your cares upon the Lord. Our main text on this is-

1 Peter 5:7
"Casting all your care upon him; for He careth for you."

My favorite translation of this particular verse is from The Amplified Bible:

"Casting the whole of your care- all your anxieties, all your worries, all your concerns, once and for all- on Him; for He cares for you affectionately, and cares about you watchfully."

Philippians 4:6 contains instructions concerning prayer given by the Spirit of God through the Apostle Paul. The King James Version reads,

Philippians 4:6
KJV
"Be careful for nothing: but in everything by prayer and supplication with thanksgiving let your requests be made known unto God."

That phrase "Be careful for nothing" is unclear to us in the 21st century. A modern translation, which I like better, says,

"Do not fret or have any anxiety about anything, but in everything by prayer and supplication with thanksgiving let your requests be made known unto God."

Now let's look at:

Matthew 6:25;32-34
Therefore, I say unto you, take no thought for your life, what ye shall eat, or what ye shall drink; nor yet for your body, what ye shall put on. Is not the life more than meat, and the body than raiment? For after all these things do the Gentiles seek for your heavenly Father knows that ye have need of all these things. But seek ye first the kingdom of God, and His righteousness; and all these things shall be added unto you. Take therefore no thought for the morrow for the morrow shall take thought for the things of itself. Sufficient unto the day is the evil thereof.

A GOOD STEWARD INTERCEDES FOR THE NEEDS OF HIMSELF & OTHERS

In I Chronicles and II Chronicles the bible declares that there were 21 Kings over Israel who descended after David's rule. Out of these 21 Kings, only 2 had a long life and they prospered. The rest did evil by turning the Israelites to idols and by worshipping demons but there was one king who inspired me the most whom I am delighted to share with you. That King was Jehoiada. The bible declares that this King lived to be 130 years old. Wow, because he was faithful and a good steward in his long rule.

II Chronicles 24:15-16
KJV
'But Jehoiada waxed old, and was full of days when he died; a hundred and thirty years old was he when he died. And they buried him in the city of David among the kings, because he had done good in Israel, both toward God, and toward his house.'

We want to focus on 3 points of view of his STEWARDSHIP

1. Because he did good for Israel
2. He had total faith and obedience to God
3. Was a good steward in obeying the law

By giving people the gospel, the good news, God gave him a long life and he prospered. Hallelujah!

LESSON TWENTY- NINE

Bible Purpose Driven:
Daily Wisdom Key for Today:

WHAT DOES IT MEAN TO BE A STEWARD?

Verse to Remember: I Corinthians 6:19
"Or do you not know that your body is the temple
of the Holy Spirit who is in you, whom you have
from God, and you are not your own?"

Question to Meditate On: I will release my faith to God and receive HIS GRACE AND RIGHTEOUSNESS. Through his righteousness I can be a great STEWARD and live a long life.

LESSON THIRTY

Exodus 20:1-5
KJV
'And God spake all these words, saying, I am the Lord thy God, which have brought thee out of the land of Egypt, out of the house of bondage. Thou shalt have no other gods before me. Thou shalt not make unto thee any graven image, or any likeness of anything that is in heaven above, or that is in the earth beneath, or that is in the water under the earth: Thou shalt not bow down thyself to them, nor serve them: for I the Lord thy God am a jealous God, visiting the iniquity of the fathers upon the children unto the third and fourth generation of them that hate me;'

CLEANING YOUR HOUSE & BRINGING IT TO GOD'S ORDER

Faith without works is dead. On my fifteenth Mission to Taiwan the Lord continued to expand the Ministry all over the island. In doing so, we encountered people in many different situations and many of them had an incredible and tremendous need spiritually, financially and some were in need of healing and some were seeking freedom from the oppression of Satan and through the wrong teaching that came unto them from occultic traditions and the ways of their culture. 95 percent of the 26 million people that live in Taiwan worship idols through their tradition and religion of Buddhism and only 5 percent are redeemed Christians. We are so grateful to the Lord Jesus for the next few pages that will be unveiled to you about how the

Lord anointed us with the Holy Spirit and fire to bring freedom to many, many people who were oppressed by the devil.

Acts 10:38
'How God anointed Jesus of Nazareth with the Holy Ghost and with power: who went about doing good, and healing all that were oppressed of the devil; for God was with him.'

One night we conducted a 10-day crusade. Just after the worship service we were praying for the people when a lady stood up and yelled, "I need help, I have a financial problem." I remember saying to her, "Tomorrow we will have lunch with you and I will give you a financial consultation in the Lord." The very next day at 11:30 am, she picked us up and brought us to her private home in one of the wealthiest buildings in the city. She made us the most wonderful Chinese meal.

As we began to speak, she stated that she had owned three companies for over 20 years. She was now at a crossroad and needed 5 million N.T. (Taiwan dollars), which equals about 150,000 U.S. Dollars. She explained she had only 3 days to pay the bank or the bank would confiscate everything. The first thing that came to my mind was that she hadn't been paying her tithes. This means she had not given God His 10%. She replied, "I have been a Christian for a long time and I do pay tithes." I said, "Are you sure?" She paused for a moment, and then said, "Let me call my bookkeeper and let me check my books." After 20 minutes with her bookkeeper, she came to find out she had not been faithful in giving her tithes the past three years.

She asked, "What should I do?" I replied, "Dear sister Joyce, you must repent, make a commitment and be obedient and God will never fail you." When I mentioned to her to be obedient with her tithes and offerings, the sweet lady took a red envelope and handed it to me. She said, "I had already prepared this, before you got here." I replied to her, I am not here to take an offering from you. I am here to help you, God sent me. If you obey the Bible you will see a miracle." She cried with tears in her eyes, "Dr. Bruno I only have until Saturday. Then they're going to take everything my family has built over the last 50 years." Suddenly, we began to pray and the wonderful presence of God invaded and infused the house and us too. That very night, Thursday, she came to the crusade. I preached a message that night against, alcohol, which I called; the sermon of the three kings: KING PHARAOH, KING SOLOMON AND KING JESUS

The message touched many people's hearts as I explained that the Lord Jesus Christ did not drink wine with alcohol. The wine he made in John 2 was real wine because it was fresh and brand new.

I looked in the Webster's dictionary and found that the word wine means fresh juice, glucose or wine without alcohol. I explained to the people that when the wine becomes fermented 3 days later through the process of fermentation in the air, it becomes alcohol. The Hebrew word alcohol means 'evil one'. So, in John 2 the real wine that Jesus made was fresh and brand new because the Lord cannot go contrary to His word. In many, many passages it indicates that wine is a mocker.

Proverbs 20:1
KJV
'Wine is a mocker; strong drink is raging: and whosoever is deceived thereby is not wise.'

I explained to the people that Jesus is God and He will not create anything outside of His scripture. The wine in John 2 was created by the power of the Holy Spirit when Jesus had gone to the wedding to make everything new. I explained to the people that alcohol was the number one killer because Taiwan has 12 tribes of mountain people with a population of almost 1 million and the majority of these men, in their religious doctrine, drink to a stupor, beat their wives and many times drive their scooters drunk and fall off the mountain to their deaths from being so intoxicated. People were touched in their hearts and a offering was taken. My lady friend Joyce came forth and whispered that she wanted to donate 50 thousand N.T, which is $1,500.00 in US money, to print books and to distribute them into the jail ministry.

The following day we received a phone call in the hotel room. When my wife picked the phone up, Joyce was on the phone and explained, "I only have two days left and then I will lose everything. My husband told me to give up on God and she also felt like she wanted to commit suicide." Immediately, I got on my knees and began to pray and make intercession to God for this lady. The following morning, while in the classroom with my students Joyce came in and after three hours of teaching, she approached me and said, "Dr. Bruno last night I vowed to the Lord to give you 50,000 N.T. I was going to pay my taxes with this money." She also said that she had two million dollars in jewelry and that she was going to sell them and keep her vow to God. I replied to her, you made a vow to the Lord; you should keep it and believe God that by tomorrow God will give you more than one hundredfold (100). She obeyed the command of my voice and God gave her; A MIRACLE.

READ ON AND YOU WILL SEE HOW YOU CAN GET A MIRACLE TOO!

She said, "Ok, Dr. Bruno, I believe you." As we all went for lunch, she drove to the bank and took out all the money she had, 50, 000N.T. She came back to the car and said, "Dr. Bruno this is God's money. I want to fulfill my vow." We were so surprised because we knew that God was looking down from heaven and that He desires OBEDIENCE from us. Immediately, I asked the Lord to release His angels to bring this lady her finances by tomorrow at 12:00 noon, in Jesus' name. As we continued our fellowship that afternoon, she mentioned to me that her factories had many idols from her husband's side, whose ancestor's worshipped idols for fifty years. We insisted that the idols be taken down so they would not stop the blessing and the money from coming.

She replied that they were not her idols. They belonged to her mother-in-law and her husband's brother prepared food for her mother-in-law to offer to the idols. I replied to her, "Take me there. I want to meet your family." She replied, "She's very sick and cannot walk right." I said, "Please take us there. Do not tell her I am a preacher but rather tell her I am a doctor." Within 30 minutes we reached the compound of factories. As we went inside the house to see her mother-in-law we were really, really praying. We were praying a storm. Once inside the house, I met mama, who was over 80 years old. After receiving us, she apologized saying, "Sorry, I cannot get up. I am a very sick woman." I said immediately, "God sent me here. The Lord Jesus Christ wants to heal you. Would you like that?" She replied, "Yes."

Immediately we took the oil and I opened up the Bible to James 5:13 and 14 which declares:

James 5:13-14
"Is anyone among you suffering? Let him pray. Is anyone cheerful? Let him sing Psalms. Is anyone among you sick? Let him call for the elders of the church, and let them pray over him, anointing him with oil in the name of the Lord."

While I was kneeling on the floor, anointing and praying for her, I declared that she could walk. I led her into the sinner's prayer and let her denounce all the idols and come to repentance. In a matter of seconds, the power of the Holy Spirit hit this lady like lightning and she began to walk, saying, thank you God. Her daughter came running inside the room and she kneeled down immediately because the power of God was so strong that people around me could hardly stand up. She said to me, "I want Jesus." We found out later that she was suffering from long – term depression and she would shut herself in the room for weeks at a time. She was a beautiful woman in her thirties, tall and beautiful. I anointed her with oil as well. I then advised them they should immediately be water baptized. I opened my 26 Translation Bible and she read to me from Mark 16:16:

Mark 16:16:
'He who believes and is baptized will be saved, but
he who does not believe will be condemned.'

In a matter of a few minutes we baptized both of them and the Lord Jesus baptized them with the Holy Spirit and power. We watched the glory of God transform these two souls. The sister – in – law, Joyce was doing the translation from Chinese to English. She was full of Joy, shouting to see the miracles that had taken place in her family after so many years of praying for them. While they were changing their clothes and drying their hair, I said to mama, "Now that you are a Christian." She responded, "Yes I am." I told her, "We need to take down the Idols." And she looked at me and said, "Is that in the bible?" I turned toExodus20:4- and she read it out loud three times:

Exodus20:4
'You shall not make for yourselves any carved image, or any
likeness of anything that is in heaven above, or that is in
the earth beneath, or that is in the water under the earth;'

Deuteronomy 7:25-26
"You shall burn the carved images of their gods with fire; you shall not covet the silver the silver or gold that is on them, nor take it for yourselves, lest you be snared by it; for it is an abomination to the Lord your God. Nor shall you bring an abomination into your house, lest you be doomed to destruction like it; but you shall utterly detest it and utterly abhor it for it is an Accursed thing.'

The look on her face was like an angel. She looked at me and said, "Burn them all!" It was about 4:30 pm. I would like to mention that in Taiwan it rains a lot. It was raining very heavy that afternoon. But in spite of the rain Joyce, my wife and I immediately went inside the very large factory and began to tear down the Idols. Within 3 hours, we tore down the Idols and carried them to the center of the compound. Even Joyce brought over a statue of Buddha that was 4 feet tall worth over $3,000.00 US Dollars. We lit them up and burned them. While the Idols were being burned, two of mama's sons and their wives came into the compound in their Mercedes. Upon seeing these strange Americans burning their mother's Idols, they questioned what was going on. But it was too late, mama was already water baptized and saved. The sons responded to us, "We want Jesus too." Hallelujah. We caught the whole nest in the net. That very night, during the healing crusade, Joyce shared the miracles that were taking place. The message God gave me that night was so divinely inspired. The message was out of Mark 5:22-23,36,41-42.

While I was walking up and down the platform I looked at the people's faces in the conference. There was an explosion of faith in the air. I looked at Joyce and decreed "Only believe that God will send the money tomorrow." She shouted publicly, "I believe, I believe." After the crusade was over we went home and the following day, at 12:00 noon on Saturday, we received a phone call from Joyce and she said, "A miracle! Somebody put five million N.T. in the bank." This equals $150,000 dollars in US money. This is big money. God gave Joyce one hundred-fold. We asked her, "How did this happen?" She said one of her clients ordered so much work in advance and paid in advance also.

No one had ever paid in advance before. She said, "Dr. Bruno you are my hero." I exclaimed this was the work of God and not the work of man. I told her that this was only the beginning of her and her family's honeymoon with the Holy Spirit of God. What can we learn from this? Here are ten points of illustration:

1. Obedience, honesty, integrity.
2. Get rid of all the idols in your life and in your home
3. Family repentance and salvation.
4. Giving and receiving.
5. God sending His angels.
6. Real miracle.
7. Faith in God.
8. L= love.
9. A= always.
10. W= wins.

Joyce has become a very good family friend of Everlasting Chip Ministry and we have experienced a wonderful warm love and friendship with her. We continue in the future to build a training school in Taiwan.

LESSON THIRTY

Bible Purpose Driven:
Daily Wisdom Key for Today:

CLEANING YOUR HOUSE & BRINGING IT TO GOD'S ORDER

Verse to Remember: Exodus 20:1-5
'And God spake all these words, saying, I am the Lord thy God, which have brought thee out of the land of Egypt, out of the house of bondage. Thou shalt have no other gods before me. Thou shalt not make unto thee any graven image, or any likeness of anything that is in heaven above, or that is in the earth beneath, or that is in the water under the earth: Thou shalt not bow down thyself to them, nor serve them: for I the Lord thy God am a jealous God, visiting the iniquity of the fathers upon the children unto the third and fourth generation of them that hate me;'

Question to Meditate On: I will consecrate myself and my household from any idol or anything that will take your place, in Jesus' name, amen and amen.

LESSON THIRTY-ONE

Genesis 1:11
'And God said, Let the earth bring forth grass, the herb yielding seed, and the fruit tree yielding fruit after his kind, whose seed is in itself, upon the earth: and it was so.'

GOD'S ETERNAL PROVISION & FINANCIAL PLAN FOR THE EARTH

We see that when the Lord replenished the earth, he put the seeds under the ground. He put the gold and all of the wealth. Everything is on the earth and is still in the earth and has not jumped out or fallen off the earth. It is available for those who are obedient and who are not rebels. The rebels are Satan's army. They steal, kill and destroy. The children of God are you and I and God has instituted the way to sow and reap and obtain what is on the earth

<u>Bible Financial Purpose Driven's</u> main purpose is to inspire the reader to apply God's principles in your own life and to acknowledge the love and the fear of God. The Hebrew word for 'fear' means to acknowledge and obey the principle of God. When we obey them, WE WILL WIN!

DEFINITION OF GOD'S FINANCIAL PLAN

Leviticus 27:30
KJV
"And all the tithes of the land...is the
Lord's: It is holy unto the Lord."

Numbers 18:21
KJV
"And behold I have given the children of Levi
all the tenth in Israel for an inheritance."

Numbers 18:24
KJV
"But the tithes of the children of Israel...I
have given to the Levites to inherit."

It is not necessary to state that the church has to have finances in order to carry on the great work of evangelizing the world. It is quite apparent that there has to be a financial plan. A study of God's Word reveals that the Lord has provided for this need by instituting a definite financial plan to finance His work upon the earth. God's plan is tithing. We shall study this plan by answering a number of questions.

What is a tithe?

A tithe is one-tenth of your increase (Num. 18:21). If a man's paycheck is $100, he should take out $10 (a tithe) for the Lord. Tithe is a seed for your next harvest. In 1990, I read an article in Charisma magazine that, unfortunately, 85% of Christians around the world do not tithe of their income. In doing so, they fall into a ditch and they become shipwrecked. Anyone who owns a business or has employees and does not pay his employees will fail.

Who should tithe?

Everyone should faithfully tithe, both Christians and non-Christians. No one is exempt. In the United States, we have well over 20 million Jewish people and the majority of them are not born-again Christians and yet they obey Malachi 3:10 and they tithe and give offerings to many, many foundations and they are the wealthiest and richest people in America and also around the world.

One of the problems of the body of Christ, in many, many denominations, is that they do not teach 4 spiritual laws of the bible which are found in the New Testament in Matthew, Mark, Luke, John and the epistles. There are many, many Pastors around the world who are holy and love God with all of their heart, mind and soul and yet are very, very poor. They have a broken down church, a broken down car, a broken down home and they live with a poverty-stricken mentality.

I remember in 2007, my staff and I received an invitation to go to Indonesia. On my arrival there, the Pastor and his staff picked us up from the airport and took us for dinner. He cried out to us over dinner and said that his church was very poor and that he had been trying to build a School of Biblical Theology for 20 years. He said to me, 'Dr. Bruno, we do not know you very well. Give us a message and if we like you and you do well, then we will open up the doors to you.' I just smiled and laughed and said, "Ok."

Later that evening, as 300 people began to worship, the power of God unfolded to the people. I began to pray for the sick and

I gave 4 points about Divine Healing. As I prayed for the sick, I took my oil and prayed for an 80-year-old man who looked like he was 100. He was crippled and banged up. He had suffered a stroke. I anointed him with oil and commanded the healing to come to his body and instantly he was totally healed and the church began to rejoice and celebrate this miracle. Some were weeping tears of joy and laughing and shouting to the Lord. I was overwhelmed with their excitement. For me it was normal.

When they gave a testimony, they said that he was stricken with a stroke for 20 years. Also, the Pastor said to me, 'We like you and we like your teaching, can you stay for 7 days and do teaching?" I responded, "Yes, I will." That afternoon he took me outside of the building, where there was a lot of jungle with many banana trees. He said to me very enthusiastically that this was his property and that he wanted to build the school here and he said, "I give the property to you to build the school." I said to him, "Pastor, how much many do you need to build this school?" He told me he needed $75,000.00 and that he had been waiting 25 years because his church was very poor and didn't have the money. I made a motion and said that the money to build was right here, as I reached in my back pocket to adjust my belt, he thought that I was reaching for the money to give to him. He asked me, "Where is the money?" I told him, "The money is right here in this building in your church." He looked at me attentively and I said, "Get everybody together and I will raise it for you." That night I gave a message about the laws of prosperity and sowing and reaping and within 3 hours people were inspired and moved by God and we raised up $90,000.00 The church and all the people celebrated for 7 days.

Today, as I write these lines to you, it has been 5 years and I recently returned from that village in Tangerang, Jakarta, Indonesia and now they have a bible school and training center and they reach the poor and Muslims with the gospel. Hallelujah.

Many of the congregation testified that they received 100-fold from the Lord. Our Ministry wishes to express thanks to Pastor Emus and his congregation for expanding our Ministry all over Indonesia and for the incredible contact with our current publisher in Indonesia who translated many of our books into Indonesian and we believe that the best is yet to come.

LESSON THIRTY-ONE

Bible Purpose Driven:
Daily Wisdom Key for Today:

GODS ETERNAL PROVISION & FINANCIAL PLAN FOR THE EARTH

Verse to Remember: Genesis 1:11
'And God said, Let the earth bring forth grass, the herb yielding seed, and the fruit tree yielding fruit after his kind, whose seed is in itself, upon the earth: and it was so.'

Question to Meditate On: I release my faith to GOD and take HIS righteousness in my life and walk through HIS righteousness so that HIS steps will be my steps. (meditate on the following scripture).

Psalms 85:13
'Righteousness shall go before him; and shall set us in the way of his steps.'

If you agree, shout HALLELUJAH 3 TIMES, In Jesus' name!

LESSON THIRTY-TWO

Nehemiah 10:35-37
KJV
'And to bring the first fruits of our ground, and the first fruits
of all fruit of all trees, year by year, unto the house of the
Lord: Also the firstborn of our sons, and of our cattle, as
it is written in the law, and the firstlings of our herds and
of our flocks, to bring to the house of our God, unto the
priests that minister in the house of our God: And that we
should bring the first fruits of our dough, and our offerings,
and the fruit of all manner of trees, of wine and of oil, unto
the priests, to the chambers of the house of our God; and
the tithes of our ground unto the Levites, that the same
Levites might have the tithes in all the cities of out tillage.'

TITHES AND FIRST FRUITS –
WHERE DO THEY GO?

You must choose to be honest with God and faithful with your
money and then you will begin to build a friendship with the
Lord. Be open to Him and be honest to Him in every situation.
God does not expect you to be perfect but he insists that you
be honest. In one incredible example of frank friendship God
honestly expressed His total disgust with Israel's disobedience.
He told Moses that He would keep His promise to give the
Israelites the promised land but He went one step further with
them in the desert. God was fed up and let Moses know exactly
how He felt. Moses, speaking as a friend of God responded
with equal candor. Moses said, "Look, you tell me to lead the

people but you do not let me know whom you are going to send with me.... if I am so special to you, let me in on your plans.... don't forget this is your people, your responsibility.... if your presence doesn't take the lead here call this trip off right now. How else will I know that you are with me and your people? Are you traveling with us or not?'. God said to Moses, 'Alright, just as you say; this also I will do for I know you well and you are special to me.'

YOUR BUSINESS IS GOD'S WORK

When you engage with God your true feeling it is good that you tell Him your comments and let Him know every situation and the circumstances of your work. The more you become God's partner and friend the more you will care about the things that God cares about. Please study the next set of principles on tithing which will instill in you an understanding of God's system of Kingdom finance. The more you read and re-read these points and apply the scripture and meditation for the lesson, the greater your Bible Purpose will be in the journey to obtain financial freedom that is only in Christ Jesus.

When should I tithe?

Upon the first day of the week (I Cor. 16:2).

Where shall I pay my tithes?

Into God's storehouse (Mal. 3:10). This is clearly your home church where you get your spiritual food. The Bible says, "Bring" not "Send" the tithes into the storehouse. The only time tithes should be sent is when one is sick and shut-in, away on vacation or visiting, then the tithes should be sent back to the home church (storehouse).

To whom does the tithe belong?

They belong to God (Lev. 27:30). They belong to the Levites (Num. 18:24). They are for the support of the ministry.

Should the ministry tithe?

Most certainly. They must practice tithing themselves before they can teach others to tithe. The Levites tithe to the descendants of Aaron. This teaches us that the ministry should tithe into their storehouse (their headquarters) to support the district and national work.

Was not tithing given under the law?

It belongs to the Abrahamic covenant and was instituted long before the law. Both Abraham and Jacob paid tithes (Gen. 14:20; Heb. 7:4; Gen. 28:22). The fact that Abraham tithed proved that it was the result of faith and not of law. What happens if I do not tithe? If one does not tithe he robs God (Mal. 2:8).

Should I pay my debts before I tithe?

Pay your debt to God first. The tithe is God's money. It is not permissible to use money that does not belong to you, whether it is to pay debts or not. Nine-tenths with God's blessings will go farther to meet your needs then ten-tenths with God's curse.

CAN I BEGIN TO TITHE NOW AND BE FORGIVEN OF MY PAST NON-TITHING?

The answer to that is YES! Simply cry out to the Lord and tell God that you are sorry for your ignorance and your foolishness and your pride and truly repent, bone deep, and re-dedicate yourself and everything that you have to the Lord. Acknowledge HIM, from this day forward, as your source and the only source and make God your partner. AMEN.

Proverbs 3:5
KJV
'Trust in the Lord with all thine heart; and lean not unto thine own understanding. In all thine ways acknowledge him, and he shall direct thy paths.'

When you do this, the Lord wipes away all of your sins and the rebellion of your past because you acted out of your ignorance. True repentance wipes out all of your past and the bibles declares that he does not remember your sins anymore.

Could I be too poor to tithe?

Absolutely not! You may be poor because you do not tithe. Poor people tithe more easily than rich people because they have less to be responsible for. While living in sin, most people no matter how poor spend far more than a tithe serving Satan. If we are poor, we have to trust God more; therefore, we should be more faithful.

Is my responsibility finished with tithing?

An offering is what you give above your tithe. We can rob God also by not giving offerings (Mal. 3:8). Stewardship requires that we handle all our finances wisely (I Cor. 4:2).

TITHING IS GOD'S FINANCIAL PLAN- IT WILL WORK ANY WHERE IN THE WORLD.

The church will be amply provided for if all would tithe. If all would tithe there would be no lack. There would be an abundance in your home, work, city, government and the nation.

Tithes and Offerings

God has, from the beginning, provided a means of financing his program through voluntary giving (offerings) and assessments called "Tithes." Contrary to the opinion of many, Tithes did not begin with the "Law", but was practiced by Abraham 430 years before the law (Gen. 14:18-20) and continued on through Jacob (Gen 28:20-22) and finally through Levi (law) and the Levitical Priesthood. God employs the principle of "Offerings" when instructing Moses on how to get the materials to build the tabernacle (Ex. 25:1-8) and later Solomon's Temple. The subject of "Tithes and Offerings" is widely practiced but often misunderstood as to its purpose and applications according to the scriptures. This lesson deals with the subject matter of Tithes and Offerings as two distinct sections. The first section will deal with "TITHES", covering the definition and purpose according to the scriptures. The second section will cover "OFFERINGS" and how they are used.

It is obvious that one cannot pay tithes or give offerings unless there is some manner of "Income" provided for the individual.

This income may be money or wages, interest or dividends from investments, Social Security and welfare checks, bonuses, produce from the fields (farming), livestock (cattle, sheep, etc.) or anything that represents an increase to the individual. In biblical times tithes consisted of things harvested, increases in the flocks and herds and money from the sale of their produce as well as wages. Today, tithes and offerings are almost always paid in the currency of the time and it is the exception to the rule to use commodities as the medium of exchange. As we begin, the first thing that must be established is, it is God who makes it possible for us to get wealth and is responsible for any increase one may enjoy. We see this illustrated beautifully in Deuteronomy 8:18:

Deuteronomy 8:18
KJV
'But though shalt remember the Lord thy God: for it is he that giveth thee power to get wealth, that he may establish his covenant which he sware unto thy fathers, as it is this day.'

All that we possess in reality belongs to God and He expects us to be faithful stewards over His things. Because of Him one has the strength, health and opportunity to get and hold a job. It is because of Him that the fields and trees provide a harvest and livestock reproduce to provide for our needs. In the final analysis, God owns everything and all we are able to enjoy is on "loan from Him" who provides for your daily needs.

Psalms 24:1
KJV
"The earth is the LORD's and the fullness thereof;
the world, and they that dwell therein"

Psalms 50:10-12
KJV
"For every beast of the forest is mine, and the cattle upon a thousand hills. I know all the fowls of the mountains: and the wild beasts of the field are mine. If I were hungry, I would not tell thee: for the world is mine, and the fulness thereof"

And finally,

I Timothy 6:17-19
KJV
"Charge them that are rich in this world, that they be not high minded, nor trust in uncertain riches, but in the living God, who giveth us richly all things to enjoy. That they do good, that they be rich in good works, ready to distribute, willing to communicate; Laying up in store for themselves a good foundation against the time to come, that they may lay hold on eternal life"

As these scriptures teach us, God is the owner, controller and generator of all that exists. These things are given to man for him to enjoy, but at the same time man has the obligation and responsibility to act as a good steward over God's abundant blessings. We are admonished not to put our trust in corruptible material things, for God can reclaim them as easy as He can provide them. He expects us to honor and give Him glory for the blessings we receive and one way to do this is to honor Him with our tithes and offerings!

LESSON THIRTY-TWO

Bible Purpose Driven:
Daily Wisdom Key for Today:

TITHES AND FIRST FRUITS - WHERE DO THEY GO?

Verse to Remember: Nehemiah 10:35-37
KJV

'And to bring the first fruits of our ground, and the first fruits of all fruit of all trees, year by year, unto the house of the Lord: Also the firstborn of our sons, and of our cattle, as it is written in the law, and the firstlings of our herds and of our flocks, to bring to the house of our God, unto the priests that minister in the house of our God: And that we should bring the first fruits of our dough, and our offerings, and the fruit of all manner of trees, of wine and of oil, unto the priests, to the chambers of the house of our God; and the tithes of our ground unto the Levites, that the same Levites might have the tithes in all the cities of our tillage.'

Question to Meditate On: My obedience in giving will draw me close to God and He will call me a friend.

LESSON THIRTY-THREE

Malachi 3:7-11
KJV
"Even from the days of your fathers ye are gone away from mine ordinances, and have not kept them. Return unto me, and I will return unto you, saith the Lord of hosts. But ye said, Wherein shall we return? Will a man rob God? Yet ye have robbed me. But ye say wherein have we robbed thee? In tithes and offerings. Ye are cursed with a cursed: for ye have robbed me, even this whole nation. Bring ye all the tithes into the storehouse, that there may be meat in mine house, and prove me now herewith, saith the Lord of hosts, if I will not open you the windows of heaven, and pour you out a blessing, that there shall not be room enough to receive it. And I will rebuke the devourer for your sakes, and he shall not destroy the fruits of your ground; neither shall your vine cast her fruit before the time in the field, saith the LORD of hosts"

TITHES – PART I

Perhaps the most familiar scripture on the subject of Tithes is Mal. 3:7-11. Unfortunately for some, this is the only scripture they know, but the purpose and procedure of dealing with tithes and offerings are unknown to them. First to be noticed is verse 7. God's indictment is "you have gone away from mine ordinances and not kept them. Will a man rob God? How? In tithes AND offerings." (Note the distinction between tithes AND offerings. The robbery involved both). They once did tithe, but now they have slacked off and are no longer fulfilling their obligation to God. He calls them "robbers." Does one dare rob God? What is the nature of this robbery? They did not pay their tenth or give offerings and as a result, the House of God went lacking and the priests were forced into the fields to work.

The results, "you are cursed with a curse (vs. 10), bring ALL the tithes into the STOREHOUSE (church) that there may be meat in my house – if you will, I will pour out a blessing more than you can contain." Paying tithes and giving offerings brings a blessing a blessing of the magnitude that there is not enough room to receive it, on the other hand, failing to pay tithes bring the individual a "curse," God's disfavor in all their activities.

Please note that Tithes are a DEBT one OWES to God. It is a fixed percentage of one's total increase. On the other hand, an Offering is the amount the individual chooses to give as a voluntary gift. One does not GIVE their tithes. Do you "give" the bank your mortgage loan payment or do you PAY your loan to the bank. This mortgage money does not belong to the individual borrower; it is a loan and a debt. The mortgagee is expected to return that money with interest by PAYING on their debt at an agreed upon date. SINCE TITHES ARE A DEBT, WE PAY TITHES, BUT WE GIVE OFFERINGS. When one fails to pay tithes, they are stealing from God. The nine tenths God allows us to keep coupled with his blessing is far better than keeping it all for yourself.

The eighth commandment reads, "Thou salt not steal." Since the tithe belongs to God, does not this commandment also apply to the things belonging to Him? Is robbing God any less a sin because it is God's stuff? NO! It is a dangerous thing to rob God. The first fruits belong to God and when we receive our increase, our obligation is to give God that which belongs to Him FIRST. First fruits is the gross amount of the paycheck, it is the first thing paid from the paycheck before the house note, car payment, grocery bill and credit card, etc. The IRS does not trust us to pay our taxes so they take their portion first to make sure they get it. Most never see the amount of deduction taken from their check. It is just a number. However, God is entitled to the first payment before anything else is paid and HE trusts the individual to pay on time.

Proverbs 3:9-10
KJV
"Honour the LORD with they substance, and with the first fruits of all thine increase: So, shall thy barns be filled with plenty, and thy presses shall burst out with new wine"

It Takes Faith to Give God The "Tenth" With A Willing Heart. It takes faith to give with a willing heart. This is the kind of faith that is pleasing to God and this is the only faith that will unlock the storehouse of heaven and which gives us a blessing that we cannot contain, WOW! Remember, God is the one who fights the battle for you, the battle belongs to the Lord. God set the principle of tithes in the garden when He reserved a portion for Himself and not for Adam or Eve; the tree of the "knowledge of good and evil." They were not to eat of this tree on penalty of death. It was reserved for God and God alone. As a result of partaking of this tree man received a death sentence and a curse was placed on the earth. Compare this principle with Mal. 3:9 where a curse is pronounced for robbing God of the tithes. The purpose of tithes was to insure "Meat in mine House" (Mal. 3:10). This is in reference to the Word & Truth dispensed by the ministry. This was God's financial way of compensating the Levitical Priests and the ministry of that day for their services for Him.

Matthew 24:45
KJV
"Who then is a faithful and wise servant, whom
his lord hath made ruler over his household,
to give them meat in due season?"

The reference here is of the responsibility of the ministry to feed the flock of God with the Word. While details of tithing are outlined in the Old Testament, not too much is stated in the New Testament. However, there are enough obvious references made in the New Testament to give authority for the ministry to collect the tithe from the children of God. Consider too, the Apostles, who were Jewish and well acquainted with the Old Testament system of tithing. They saw no problem in applying the same system in the church.

In Matthew 23 Jesus justified the paying of tithes. He accuses the Pharisees and hypocrites, who paid tithes of aromatic spices and herbs, of having left off the weightier matters of the law, judgment, mercy and faith. These (Tithing) they were to do and not leave the others undone. Note the following scriptures also:

Galatians 3:29
KJV
"If ye be Christ's, then ye are Abraham's seed...."

John 8:39
'If we are Abraham's children (seed) then we are to do the works of Abraham."

Please also read these scriptures which illustrate God's tithing system:

Genesis 14:18-20 - Abraham gave tithes of ALL to Melchizedek (God Himself).

Genesis 28:20-22 - Jacob made a vow which included giving a "tenth" unto God.

The definition of tithes is the "tenth" or one tenth of one's total increase. Increase is defined as "the gross amount that is added to one's possessions." This is not limited to just gross wages, but any other increase that is added to your total resources, taxable or not.

Leviticus 27:30-32
KJV
"And all the tithe of the land, whether of the seed of the land, or of the fruit of the tree, is the LORD's: it is holy unto the LORD. And if a man will at all redeem ought of his tithes, he shall add thereto the fifth part thereof. And concerning the tithe of the herd, or of the flock, even of whatsoever passeth under the rod, the tenth shall be holy unto the LORD"

Since the "tenth" belongs to God, He can dispose of it as He wishes. The "tenth" was given to the children of Levi for their service of the tabernacle. When one pays their tithes, the money is no longer theirs and they have no say so as to how it is to be used. It now belongs to God for His use and disbursement. God's system of tithing is equally applied to the rich and poor alike. It is equal sacrifice.

Numbers 18:20-21
"And the LORD spake unto Aaron, Thou shalt have no inheritance in their land, neither shalt thou have any part amongst them: I am thy part and thine inheritance among the children of Israel. And, behold I have given the children of Levi all the tenth in Israel for an inheritance, for their service which they service, even the services of the tabernacle of the congregation"

(Note: if something is mine, then I have the right to dispose of it as I see fit. Since the tenth or tithes belong to God, He has the right to dispose of it as He see fit. He in turn gives it to the ministry as their pay for service).

The "Law" Provided A "System" For Paying
Tithes and Not the Authority for Them

Both circumcision AND tithing came from Abraham. Please see the following scriptures:

John 7:22 – Moses provided circumcision

Romans 8:3-4 - The righteousness of the law is fulfilled in US, that is paying tithes.

Numbers 18 - The Levites were to TAKE tithes of the children of Israel. Note the following scripture and the tenses in the statement.

Hebrews 7:5-10
"And verily they that are of the sons of Levi, who receive the office of the priesthood, have a commandment to take tithes of the people according to the law, that is of their brethren, though they come out of the loins of Abraham: But he whose descent is not counted from them received tithes of Abraham, and blessed him that had the promises. And without all contradiction the less is blessed of the better. And here men that die receive tithes; but there he receiveth them, of whom it is witnessed that he liveth. And as I may so say Levi also, who receiveth tithes, payed tithes in Abraham. For he was yet in the loins of his father, when Melchisedec met him"

"And verily they that ARE (present tense) the "SONS OF LEVI" (the ministry Mal. 3:10) who RECEIVE (present tense) the office of the priesthood, HAVE (present tense) a COMMANDMENT TO TAKE TITHES of the people according to the law (system)." Note the use of the present tense in the above verse:

1. The ministry is now in the place of the Priesthood, who "are the sons of Levi."
2. The ministry is now instructed to "take tithes of the People."
3. Tithes are to be taken "according to the law" (System).
4. The ministry who takes tithes also PAYS tithes.

WHO ARE THE LEVITES, KINGS & PRIESTS TODAY?

The bibles declares in:

**Revelation 1:5-6
KJV
'and from Jesus Christ, the faithful witness, the firstborn from the dead, and the ruler over the kings of the earth. To Him who loved us and washed us from our sins in His own blood, and has made us kings and priests to His God and Father, to Him be glory and dominion forever and ever. Amen.'**

Every born-again believer who has been redeemed by the blood and the cross of Christ is a Levite, King and Priest unto the Lord today and qualifies to accept and receive gifts to and from one another. As we do it unto the Lord we are building His church and ALL THE BLESSINGS WILL COME DOWN!

LESSON THIRTY-THREE

Bible Purpose Driven:
Daily Wisdom Key for Today:

TITHES – PART I

Verse to Remember: Malachi 3:7-11
KJV
**"Even from the days of your fathers ye are gone away
from mine ordinances, and have not kept them. Return
unto me, and I will return unto you, saith the Lord of hosts.
But ye said, Wherein shall we return? Will a man rob
God? Yet ye have robbed me. But ye say wherein have we
robbed thee? In tithes and offerings. Ye are cursed with
a cursed: for ye have robbed me, even this whole nation.
Bring ye all the tithes into the storehouse, that there
may be meat in mine house, and prove me now herewith,
saith the Lord of hosts, if I will not open you the windows
of heaven, and pour you out a blessing, that there shall
not be room enough to receive it. And I will rebuke the
devourer for your sakes, and he shall not destroy the fruits
of your ground; neither shall your vine cast her fruit
before the time in the field, saith the LORD of hosts"**

Question to Meditate On: I am a Priest and a King and God wants me to prosper. I will do it <u>His way</u> and not my way.

If you are a female – I am a Priestess and a Princess and God wants me to prosper. I will do it <u>His way</u> and not my way and I will get the heavenly highway which is coming my way.

LESSON THIRTY-FOUR

Nehemiah 10:38
KJV
"And the priest the son of Aaron shall be with the Levites, when the Levites take tithes: and the Levites shall bring up the tithe of the tithes unto the house of our God, to the chambers, into the treasure house"

TITHES – PART II

Tithes are brought to the church and not sent to the foreign field, sent to support a TV broadcast, given to the poor or distributed as the individual chooses. The church is the "storehouse" or "treasure house" and it is the responsibility of the Pastor to disburse for the use of the ministry as he is directed of God.

We find in Numbers 18:26-31 that the Levites were to offer an "heave offering" consisting of a tenth part of the tithe. This tithe of the tithe was to be given to Aaron and included gifts they received. In verse 24 - the tithe of the people was given to the Levites as their inheritance. They were to tithe of this tithe, as it was their income, the equivalent to the people's increase. To deny or restrict the ministry of their income is wrong. Jealousy, envy, resentment are often the root causes behind such restrictions.

I Corinthians 9:13-14
KJV
"Do ye not know that they which minister about holy things live of the things of the temple? And they,

**which wait at the altar, are partakers with the altar?
Even so hath the Lord ordained that they which
preach the gospel should live of the gospel"**

If paying tithes and giving offerings was not required in the New Testament Church then where did the material substance (money) come from? What was there that provided a living for the preachers of the gospel if tithing was not practiced and a storehouse established to receive their contributions? The ministry is to live off of the things of the temple (church) and they that are ordained to preach the gospel should live of the gospel which indicates some form of systematized income. (The tithing system). Please also see Gal. 6:6 and Neh. 13:10-12.

These principles were in force BEFORE the law, DURING the law and AFTER the law. Under the law the use of tithes was for those who did the service (Levites and Priests) of the tabernacles/temple, however, the use of the tithe now is for the ministry of the church, that there may be "meat" in my house.

THE LAW OF TITHES

Consider the following scriptures on the "Law of Tithes" and open up your heart and let the Holy Spirit place this bone-deep inside of your heart and soul as you read these verses:

**Leviticus 27:30-32.
KJV
"And all the tithe of the land, whether of the seed of the land, or of the fruit of the tree, is the LORD's: it is holy unto the LORD. And if a man will at all redeem ought of his tithes, he shall add thereto the fifth part thereof. And concerning the tithe of the herd, or of the flock, even of whatsoever passeth under the rod, the tenth shall be holy unto the LORD."**

This passage states that <u>ALL</u> the tithes belong to the Lord. We pay our tithe to God, not the pastor. The pastor gets the use of it but it is God's payment for his service. The tithe is to be paid at the place God chooses (storehouse-church) and not where one may choose on their own.

Deuteronomy 12:5-8
KJV
"But unto the place which the LORD your God shall choose out of all your tribes to put his name there, even unto his habitation shall ye see, and thither thou shalt come: And thither ye shall bring your burnt offerings and your sacrifices, and your tithes, and heave offerings of your hand, and your vows, and your freewill offerings, and the firstlings of your herds and of your flocks: And there ye shall eat before the LORD your God, and ye shall rejoice in all that ye put your hand unto, ye and your households, wherein the LORD they God hath blessed thee. Ye shall not do after all the things that we do here this day, every man whatsoever is right in his own eyes"

Today, as stated previously, this place is the local church where the individual has placed their membership. Also see Deuteronomy 12:5-8, 10-14.

Numbers 18:21-31
KJV
"And, behold, I have given the children of Levi all the tenth in Israel for an inheritance, for their service which they serve, even the service of the tabernacle of the congregation. Neither must the children of Israel henceforth come nigh the tabernacle of the congregation, lest they bear sin, and die. But the Levites shall do the service of the tabernacle of the congregation, and they shall bear their iniquity: it shall be a state forever throughout your generations, that among the children of Israel they have no inheritance. But the tithes of the children of Israel, which

**they offer as a heave offering unto the LORD, I have given
to the Levites to inherit: therefore, I have said unto them,
Among the children of Israel they shall have no inheritance.**

And the LORD spoke unto Moses, saying, Thus speak unto the Levites, and say unto them, When ye take of the children of Israel the tithes which I have given you from them for your inheritance, then ye shall offer up a heave offering of it for the LORD, even a tenth part of the tithe. And this your heave offering shall be reckoned unto you, as though it were the corn of the threshing floor, and as the fullness of the winepress. Thus ye also shall offer a heave offering unto the LORD of all your tithes, which ye receive of the children of Israel; and ye shall give thereof the LORD's heave offering to Aaron the priest. Out of all your gifts ye shall offer every heave offering of the LORD, of all the best thereof, even the hallowed part thereof out of it. Therefore, thou shalt say unto them, when ye have heaved the best thereof from it, then it shall be counted unto the Levites as the increase of the threshing floor, and as the increase of the winepress. And ye shall eat it in every place, ye and your households: for it is your reward for your service in the tabernacle of the congregation.

In these verses God gives the "tenth" to the Levites (ministry) and gives instructions on how it is to be used and the freedom of its use. This is their paycheck for the service in the tabernacle. Also see Num. 18:26-31.

I Corinthians 9:8-11
KJV
"Say I these things as a man? Or saith not the law the same also? For it is written in the law of Moses, Thou shalt not muzzle the mouth of the ox that treadeth out the corn. Doth God take care of oxen? Or saith he it altogether for our sakes? For our sakes, no doubt, this is written: that he that ploweth should plow in hope;

and that he that thresheth in hope should be partaker
of hope. If we have sown unto you spiritual things, is
it a great thing if we shall reap your carnal things?"

If we sow spiritual things, it is then unreasonable to reap carnal things. We are not to muzzle the mouth of the ox that treadeth out the corn. The Pastor and the Ministry are not to be denied that which is their right to have. God will take good care of those who serve at His pleasure.

Remember this one thing, God is the Pastor's paymaster and He will not defraud anyone who has been commissioned by Him to do service for the people of God. Even if there is a shortage of tithes because the people fail to pay, God is still obligated to take care of His own "employees." There is however, one restriction. When God promises to take care of His servants, He does not intend for them to be extravagant or wasteful of the blessings that they receive. The Pastor must always remember that he is the steward of God's substance and is not to become greedy for filthy lucre or to strive to follow the trends and fashions of the world. That is the Bible Purpose that should drive the Ministry and those who do the work of the Lord.

Deuteronomy 14:22-23
KJV
"Thou shalt truly tithe all the increase of thy seed,
that the field bringeth forth year by year. And thou
shalt eat before the LORD thy God, in the place which
he shall choose to place his name there, the
tithe of thy corn, of thy wine, and of thine oil, and
the firstlings of thy herds and of thy flocks; that thou
mayest learn to fear the LORD thy God always"

To truly pay one's tithes is not to hold back but to consider all their increase, in whatever form, when paying tithes. (remember that tithes are paid on the gross earnings and any other form of increase). Finally, balance your budget. Here is a recommendation from the authors: Build yourself a desk and prayer room where you place all of your bills and all of your income and immediately separate the tithes and offerings which are the Lord's or you may be tempted to spend it all and burn the seed which is for your next harvest. Remember, do it by faith because your faith is obedience which will move the mountains of poverty away from you and your life.

LESSON THIRTY-FOUR

**Bible Purpose Driven
Daily Wisdom Key for Today:**

TITHES – PART II

**Verse to Remember: Nehemiah 10:38
KJV
"And the priest the son of Aaron shall be with the
Levites, when the Levites take tithes: and the Levites
shall bring up the tithe of the tithes unto the house of
our God, to the chambers, into the treasure house"**

Question to Meditate On: I will give more than 10 %to get the
OVERFLOW because that is the only way to go!

LESSON THIRTY-FIVE

Exodus 22:29-30
KJV
**"Thou shalt not delay to offer the first of thy ripe fruits,
and of thy liquors: the firstborn of thy sons shalt thou
give unto me. Likewise, shalt thou do with thine oxen,
and with thy sheep: seven days; it shall be with his
mother on the eighth day thou shalt give it me"**

'I WILL NOT FALL BEHIND'

One of the problems when paying tithes is when you put it off. God requires one to pay on time. To delay is to add a double burden the next time and often one becomes so far behind that they fail to pay at all. It is far better to pay one's tithes immediately as the income comes to them. There have been cases where one has fallen so far behind in paying their tithes and allowed the devil to discourage them into thinking there was no use to continue serving God. These kind of people then backslide from the church. Satan works on a guilty conscience and will use any and every ploy he can to recapture those who have once been delivered from his hand.

In Nehemiah 13: 5, 10-12 - The Levites had to return to the fields because the people failed to pay their tithes. This is the same as forcing the Pastor to return to his secular job in order to support his family because the church fails to tithe as they should. Many disgruntled church members have tried to use this tactic in an effort to force a Pastor to leave the church so they could get one to their own liking. If the Pastor is really God's person, he will stick it out and God will prove deliverance.

Please see some of the benefits, in scripture, regarding faithful tithing:

II Chronicles 31:4,10 -The Ministry is "encouraged" because the people paid their tithes.

Ezekiel 44:30 -By paying tithes, the ministry will "cause" a blessing to rest on your house.

Nehemiah 12:44 -When the Levites and Priests received their tithes, the people rejoiced for them.

I Thessalonians 5:12-13 -We are to "esteem" the ministry highly.

When the total tithe had been given, they were to testify to acknowledge that all had been paid. In other words, they had to give an account of the tithes paid. Today, this is done through our method of tithing envelopes. It is a necessity in today's time to keep accurate records of offerings. This is the basis for the administration to record and complete the books regarding the giving. It includes <u>ALL</u> gifts and donations recorded for tax purposes and also used to justify church income and expenditures in the event of potential government inspection of church finances. Please see Deuteronomy 26:12-14 for this teaching.

It is the responsibility of the Ministry to teach the people to tithe and if the Ministry fails, they will be asked to give an account for the lack of paying tithes. Please also see Nehemiah 10:32-39 and Numbers 18:26. The Ministry is also to pay tithes as do other people. Their tithe is given to the church treasury as part of their obligation for the "service of the sanctuary." As

Levi received tithes he also paid tithes in verse 32. The Levites were required to "charge themselves" to give a certain amount. This is the modern-day authority for pledging to help carry on the burden of the needs of the church.

Aaron was given the responsibility of managing the money that came to the temple by reason of the "anointing" that rested on him. Here again the managing of church finances is the responsibility of the Pastor by reason of the "anointing" invested in him or her. They may delegate the work to others, but it is their responsibility to oversee the affairs of the church.

Numbers 18:8
KJV
"And the LORD spake unto Aaron, Behold, I also have given thee the charge of mine heave offerings of all the hallowed things of the children of Israel; unto thee have I given them by reason of the anointing, and to the sons, by an ordinance forever

For those Pastors who have picked up this book in search of financial wisdom principles from the Lord, beware that you are not guilty of being greedy of "filthy lucre" and using all the tithes for yourself. They are for the MINISTRY, the assisting ministry in the local church and for the ministry in smaller churches where they are having a struggle. While it is true that smaller churches must use the majority of the tithe to support the Pastor, that Pastor must learn too, to live within his or her means and not try to compete with the larger churches with luxuries, big homes and "things" for the Ministry such as buildings, equipment, staff, supplies, etc., that are not yet within the 'immediate' budget to obtain.

We say 'immediate' because we want to remind you that, it is not because God does not want your Ministry to enjoy such benefits, but because the Lord has His timing and His will in how and when those things will manifest in your church. It could very well be that the Lord will raise up donors for those very necessities which you are praying and looking to purchase with the Church funds. In your haste, you could be guilty of cutting the church off from the very blessing that God is preparing to give the church <u>free of charge</u>! Remember that the tithe of the tithe belongs to the church treasury and God understands the needs of the Pastor, his family, the staff and the congregation, even better than YOU DO!

OFFERINGS & FREE WILL OFFERINGS - PART III

Over in Malachi 3:7-11 -In considering the subject of tithes and offerings we often make the mistake of emphasizing only the tithes portion and very rarely do we stress the OFFERINGS. The charge is: You have robbed me of tithes AND OFFERINGS. As shown in the previous section, tithes were used principally for the Priest and Levites which is the equivalent to today's ministry.

<u>Offerings are used to support the house of God, to supply the maintenance and other needs of the church building, utilities, service requirements, etc</u>. While we speak of free will offering as a general offering for the church, there may be a number of special offerings for specific needs as well as pledges designed to offset major costs of purchase and repair. Offerings are given according to the measure of God's blessing of an individual and are not a fixed percentage as the "one tenth" or tithe. In fact, offerings could well be MORE than tithes in some cases. In Numbers 18:8 God placed on Aaron the responsibility of overseeing the money by reason of the anointing resting on him as the High Priest. Now today - <u>the Pastor has that same anointing and responsibility.</u>

Individual persons, as a king or prophet of your household and your work, also have an anointing and responsibility. Your focus must be driven by the Holy Spirit and His leading. The church is an example to all of us of how to handle money. The bible declares that if anyone cannot manage his home how can they then manage the house of God? We are all accountable to be good stewards in every area of our life to be led and to be driven by God because we were all made by God and for God. Until you understand His purpose in life, life will never make sense and success starts with God's purpose.

The Pastor is held accountable by God, to use wisely, the revenue and assets of the church treasury and is not to be foolish or wasteful just because there is money to be used. God's house deserves the best but it requires one who is prudent and a skilled manager of those assets in his or her control. Because God has called and ordained the Pastor, He is holding that Pastor responsible for the entire business transactions of the church. The anointing rests upon the Pastor by virtue of their office and not because of who the person is. It is needful in most cases, to have a staff who can assist in church management, in order to relieve the Pastor for more spiritual duties but the responsibility still belongs to the Pastor.

Proverbs 3:9-10
KJV
"Honour the LORD with thy substance, and with the first fruits of all thine increase: So, shall thy barns be filled with plenty, and thy presses shall burst out with new wine"

These verses speak of three things: "Honor," "Substance" and "First fruits." To honor or give glory to God is to OBEY the commands He gives to us. In this verse, honoring God is through giving offerings and paying tithes. Substance is that part of our increase that remains after the tithes have been paid. It is from the substance that offerings of various descriptions are given. Substance belongs to the individual for their use as they see fit.

"First fruits" is the tithe. If one will be faithful in paying their tithes and generous in giving their offerings, God promised that they would be blessed in having the things that will make them "full and happy." Note also the instruction of:

Psalms 96:8
KJV
"Give unto the Lord the glory due unto his name:
bring an offering and come into his courts."

Moses was commissioned by God to build a "Sanctuary for Him." This required building materials of all kinds along with gold, silver, brass and also precious jewels and fine linen to fulfill the vision of God's sanctuary shown to Moses on the Mount. Moses never knew purpose until he found the purpose by the instructions of the Father. Before he could begin, Moses had to ask the people for offerings of all things required to build the Sanctuary as directed. This material came from Egypt and was carried by the people into the wilderness. Now God was to put all these things to use and commands Moses in Exodus –

Exodus 25:2-8
KJV
"Speak unto the children of Israel, that they bring me an offering: of every man that giveth it willingly with his heart ye shall take my offering. And this is the offering which ye shall take of them; gold, and silver, and brass, and blue, and purple, and scarlet, and fine linen, and goats' hair, and rams' skins dyed red, and badgers' skins and shittim wood, Oil for the light, spices for anointing oil, and for sweet incense, Onyx stones, and stones to be set in the ephod, and in the breastplate. And let them make me a sanctuary; that I may dwell among them"

How was Moses to acquire these things? <u>By asking the people to bring them with a willing heart.</u> This should be an answer to the critics who complain that "all the church does is ask for money," seeing that it was God who, in the beginning of constructing a structure for worship, asked for a freewill offering from the congregation. Later, Ezra was given a similar command when the temple was in the process of being rebuilt

Ezra 1:2-4
KJV
"Thus, saith Cyrus king of Persia, The LORD God of heaven hath given me all the kingdoms of the earth; and he hath charges me to build him an house at Jerusalem, which is in Judah. Who is there among you of all his people? His God be with him, and let him go up to Jerusalem, which is in Judah, and build the house of the LORD God of Israel, (he is the God) which is in Jerusalem. And whosoever remaineth in any place where he sojourneth, let the men of his place help him with silver, and with gold, and with goods, and with beasts, beside the freewill offfering for the house of God that is in Jerusalem"

We see that Ezra cried to the Lord in the sense that he was brokenhearted and he began to intercede for the children of Israel and the Lord inspired him and the king and his household and gave him all the supply that he need to build his purpose. Note the last part of verse 4. This offering was to be brought to Ezra BESIDES THE FREEWILL OFFERING FOR THE HOUSE OF GOD.

The offering that we give to the church is of an amount we choose to give, however, the special offering is given in ADDITION to our regular church offerings. One does not divide the original offering into little pieces, but it is kept whole and other offerings are the "little pieces." To pledge into the building fund, for example, is not at the expense of one's regular offering, but an amount in addition to their regular offering. The following verses are examples of the special offerings that were asked for:

Leviticus 23:37-38
KJV
"These are the feasts of the LORD, which ye shall proclaim to be holy convocations, to offer an offering made by fire unto the LORD, a burnt offering, and a meat offering, a sacrifice, and drink offerings, everything upon his day: Beside the sabbaths of the LORD, and beside your gifts and beside all your vows, and beside all your freewill offerings, which ye give unto the LORD"

Exodus 36:3
KJV
"And they received of Moses all the offering, which the children of Israel had brought for the work of the service of the sanctuary, to make it withal. And they brought yet unto him free offerings every morning"

"FREEWILL OFFERINGS" ARE THOSE REGULAR OFFERINGS FOR THE MAINTENANCE AND SUPPLY OF "GOD'S HOUSE."

Deuteronomy 16:10, 17
"And thou shalt keep the feast of weeks unto the LORD thy God with a tribute of a freewill offering of thine hand, which thou shalt give unto the LORD thy God, according as the LORD thy God hath blessed thee: Every man shall give as he is able, according to the blessing of the LORD thy God which he hath given thee"

II Corinthians 8:11-12
"Now therefore, perform the doing of it; that as there was a readiness to will, so there may be a performance also out of that which ye have. For if there be first a willing mind, it is accepted according to that a man hath, and not according to that he hath not"

Deuteronomy 23:21-23
"When thou shalt vow a vow unto the LORD thy God, thou shalt not slack to pay it: for the LORD, thy God will surely require it of thee; and it would be sin in thee. But if thou shalt forbear to vow, it shall be no sin in thee. That which is gone out of thy lips thou shalt keep and perform; even a freewill offering, according as thou hast vowed unto the LORD thy God, which thou hast promised with thy mouth"

The above scriptures are to be studied as they give the description of "freewill offerings" and the attitude by which they are to be given. In summary, they speak of giving as God has blessed; give according to one's ability; give with a willing mind; do not let emotions govern your giving, if you do not have it, do not promise it. Finally, if you make a promise to give a pledge, then pay what you have vowed.

II Kings 12:4-5
"And Jehoash said to the priests, All the money of the dedicated things that is brought into the house of the LORD, even the money of everyone that passeth the account, the money that every man is set at, and all the money that cometh into any man's heart to bring into the house of the LORD, Let the priests take it to them, every man of his acquaintance: and let them repair the breaches of the house, wheresoever any breach shall be found"

This verse deals with a repair problem and each one set for themselves a certain amount toward repairing the house of God. This is the same as making a pledge.

Nehemiah 10:32-33
"Also, we made ordinances for us, to charge ourselves yearly with the third part of a shekel for the service of the house of our God; For the shewbread, and for the continual meat offering, and for the continual burnt offering, of the sabbaths, of the new moons, for the set feasts, and for the holy things, and for the sin offerings to make an atonement for Israel, and for all the work of the house our God"

In addition to the previous verse, the Levites were to charge themselves or using the procedure of today, they were to "pledge" to give a certain amount of their "income" to provide for the necessary items used in the Temple of worship. For a Pastor to think that he or she is exempt from this kind of giving is a mistake as they are under the same obligation that the people must live by.

Exodus 30:16
KJV
"And thou shalt take the atonement money of the children of Israel, and shalt appoint it for the service of the tabernacle of the congregation; that it may be a memorial unto the children of Israel before the LORD, to make an atonement for your souls"

There are special offerings taken for specific purposes and they must be used for that purpose.

II Chronicles 24:4-6
KJV
"And it came to pass after this, that Joash was minded to repair the house of the LORD. And he gathered together the priests and the Levites, and said to them, go out unto the cities of Judah, and gather of all Israel money to repair the house of your God from year to year, and see that ye hasten the matter. Howbeit the Levites hastened it not. And the king called for Jehoiada the chief, and said unto him, Why has thou not required of the Levites to bring in out of Judah and out of Jerusalem the collection, according to the commandment of Moses the servant of the LORD, and of the congregation of Israel, for the tabernacle of witness?"

Those who are assigned a work or service in the House of God must give an account for the finances received to do the work. If they fail, they will be called into question and action will be taken against them. Dilatory attitudes should not be tolerated in the management of God's house (the church). When we give unto the Lord or make a vow to offer something to the church it should involve some sacrifice on our part. When David wanted to build an altar to offer sacrifices to God, he was offered the threshing floor of Araunah's as a gift, but David refused to accept it because "it did not cost him anything." –

II Samuel 24:24
KJV
"And the king said unto Araunah, Nay; but I will surely buy it of thee at a price: neither will I offer burnt offerings unto the LORD my God of that which doth cost me nothing. So, David bought the threshing floor and the oxen for fifty shekels of silver"

This should be a lesson for us in determining the generosity of our offerings to the church. There should be some "sacrifice" when one gives. It is not always how much (quantity) one gives, but the motive and attitude behind the giving. Jesus points out the widow woman who gave two mites, all that she had, which in God's sight was more than the abundance of the rich. As a rule, those with less often give more proportionally than those who have much to give.

Mark 12:41-44
KJV
"And Jesus sat over against the treasury, and beheld how the people cast money into the treasury: and many that were rich cast in much. And there came a certain poor widow, and she threw in two mites, which make a farthing. And he called unto him his disciples, and saith unto them, Verily I say unto you, that this poor widow hath cast more in, than all they which have cast into the treasury: For all they did cast in of their abundance; but she of her want did cast in all that she had, even all her living"

God loves a cheerful giver and is averse to the stingy one who is tight with their substance. If one does not sow many seeds, they will not reap a bountiful harvest. Little given, little received.

II Corinthians 9:6-8
KJV
"But this I say, He which soweth sparingly shall reap also sparingly; and he which soweth bountifully shall reap also bountifully. Every man according as he purposeth in his heart, so let him give; not grudgingly, or of necessity: for God loveth a cheerful giver. And God is able to make all grace abound toward you; that ye, always having all sufficiency in all things, may abound to every good work."

REMEMBER: THE OTHER OFFERINGS WE GIVEARE NOT TO BE GIVEN AT THE EXPENSEOF OUR REGULAR CHURCH OFFERING!

The following scriptures illustrate the blessings of liberality:

Proverbs 11:25
"The liberal soul shall be made fat: and he that watereth shall be watered also himself"

Luke 6:38
"Give, and it shall be given unto you; good measure, pressed down, and shaken together, and running over, shall men give into your bosom. For with the same measure that ye mete withal it shall be measured to your again"

Ecclesiastes 5:2
"Be not rash with thy mouth, and let not thine heart be hasty to utter any thing before God: for God is in heaven, and thou upon earth: therefore, let thy words be few"

This verse warns against being overtaken by emotions and promising more than one can deliver. When pledges are asked for, be generous but also be sensible. Pledge within your ability for God will hold everyone accountable for their failed promises. Paul knowing that there were some severe deficiencies in Jerusalem where the church was in dire need, organized an offering to be taken on a regular basis and set aside to be taken to the church at an appointed time. This illustrates the need for some sort of organized giving for the poor and other localities in need. During the time of national disaster, churches have collected monies to help alleviate the suffering of those who suffer in these disasters, be it flood, fire, or windstorm.

I Corinthians. 16:1
KJV
"Now concerning the collection for the saints, as I have given order to the churches of Galatia, even so do ye"

The Heave Offerings: (Gifts of God) Were those offerings which the children of Israel voluntarily gave or which were prescribed by the law. These offerings were separated from what was theirs and presented (given) to God, not as a sacrifice, but as an offering.

LESSON THIRTY-FIVE

**Bible Purpose Driven:
Daily Wisdom Key for Today:**

'I WILL NOT FALL BEHIND'

**Verse to Remember: Exodus 22:29-30
KJV
"Thou shalt not delay to offer the first of thy ripe fruits,
and of thy liquors: the firstborn of thy sons shalt thou
give unto me. Likewise, shalt thou do with thine oxen,
and with thy sheep: seven days; it shall be with his
mother on the eighth day thou shalt give it me"**

Question to Meditate On: All the Champions in the bible, from Adam and Eve to Apostle John, were inspired and God purpose driven to fulfill the destiny and journey and these are the historical men of faith. I want to be one too. WHAT ABOUT YOU? If you answered YES, shout HALLELUJAH 3 times and cry out to the Lord. He will fulfill HIS purpose in your life.

LESSON THIRTY-SIX

Psalms 112:1-3
KJV
'Praise the Lord! Blessed is the man who fears the Lord, who delights greatly in His commandments. His descendants will be mighty on the earth; The generation of the upright will be blessed. Wealth and riches will be in his house., And his righteousness endures forever.'

THE BENEFITS OF JUBILEE

Wealth and riches, wow, these are God's promises for all who obey His commands. Let's read more scripture:

Leviticus 25:10-22
KJV
'And you shall consecrate the fiftieth year, and proclaim liberty throughout all the land to all its inhabitants. It shall be a jubilee for you; and each of you shall return to his possession, and each of you shall return to his family. 11 That fiftieth year shall be a Jubilee to you; in it you shall neither sow nor reap what grows of its own accord, nor gather the grapes of your untended vine. 12 For it is the Jubilee; it shall be holy to you; you shall eat its produce from the field.13 In this Year of Jubilee, each of you shall return to his possession. And if you sell anything to your neighbor or buy from your neighbor's hand, you shall not oppress one another.15 According to the number of years after the Jubilee you shall buy from your neighbor, and according to the number of crops he shall sell to you. 16 According

BRUNO CAPORRIMO; DOMINIC CONTRERAS

to the multitude of years you shall increase its price, and according to the fewer number of years you shall diminish its price; for he sells to you according to the number of the years of the crops. 17 Therefore you shall not oppress one another, but you shall fear your God; for I am the Lord your God 18 So you shall observe my statutes keep my judgements, and perform them; and you will dwell in the land in safety. 19 Then the land will yield its fruit, and you will eat your fill and dwell in safety. 20 And if you say, "What shall we eat in the seventh year, since we shall not sow nor gather in our produce?" 21 Then I will command my blessing on you in the sixth year, and it will bring forth produce enough for three years. 22 And you shall sow in the eighth year, and eat old produce until the ninth year; until its produce comes in, you shall eat of the old harvest.'

Luke 4:18-21
KJV
"The Spirit of the LORD is upon me, because he has anointed me to preach the gospel to the poor; He has sent me to heal the broken hearted, to proclaim liberty to the captives and recovery of sight to the blind, to set at liberty those who are oppressed; 19 To proclaim the acceptable year of the LORD," 20 Then he closed the book, and gave it back to the attendant and sat down. And the eyes of all that were in the synagogue were fixed on Him. 21 And He began to say to them, "Today this Scripture is fulfilled in your hearing."

2 Corinthians 6:1-2
KJV
'We then, as workers together with Him also plead with you not to receive the grace of God in vain. 2 For he says: "In an acceptable time I have heard you, and in the day of salvation I have helped you." Behold, now is the accepted time; behold, now is the day of salvation.'

The Benefits of Jubilee

1. One hundred percent liberation from everything that has ever bound you.
2. Things previously owned will be restored.
3. All slavery is abolished.
4. There will be an increase of prosperity, including the transfer of wealth.
5. No more oppression or harassment (Acts 10:38)
6. Supernatural protection from harm.
7. Debt deliverance.

Three Things you must do to Prepare for Jubilee

1. You have to sow and be a sower.

Matthew 6:33
New Century Version (NCV)
³³ Seek first God's kingdom and what God wants.
Then all your other needs will be met as well

Mark 4:26-29
New Century Version (NCV)
Jesus Uses a Story About Seed
²⁶ Then Jesus said, "The kingdom of God is like someone who plants seed in the ground. ²⁷ Night and day, whether the person is asleep or awake, the seed still grows, but the person does not know how it grows. ²⁸ By itself the earth produces grain. First the plant grows, then the head, and then all the grain in the head. ²⁹ When the grain is ready, the farmer cuts it, because this is the harvest time."

Genesis 8:22
New Century Version (NCV)
22 "As long as the earth continues,
planting and harvest,
cold and hot,
summer and winter,
day and night
will not stop."

Amos 9:13
New Century Version (NCV)
13 The LORD says, "The time is coming when
there will be all kinds of food.
People will still be harvesting crops
when it's time to plow again.
People will still be taking the juice from grapes
when it's time to plant again.
Wine will drip from the mountains
and pour from the hills.

2. To benefit from Jubilee, you will have to increase your devotional and prayer time, day after day, until it becomes a living action in every area of your life.

Proverbs 13:22
New Century Version (NCV)
22 Good people leave their wealth to their grandchildren,
but a sinner's wealth is stored up for good people.

3. Increase your daily confession.

Acts 10:1-4
New Century Version (NCV)
Peter Teaches Cornelius
10 At Caesarea there was a man named Cornelius, an
officer in the Italian group of the Roman army. 2 Cornelius
was a religious man. He and all the other people who

lived in his house worshiped the true God. He gave much of his money to the poor and prayed to God often. ³ One afternoon about three o'clock, Cornelius clearly saw a vision. An angel of God came to him and said, "Cornelius!" ⁴ Cornelius stared at the angel. He became afraid and said, "What do you want, Lord?"

The angel said, "God has heard your prayers. He has seen that you give to the poor, and he remembers you.

Romans 13:11
New Century Version (NCV)
¹¹ Do this because we live in an important time. It is now time for you to wake up from your sleep, because our salvation is nearer now than when we first believed.

Luke 4:19
New Century Version (NCV)
¹⁹ and to announce the time when the Lord will show his kindness."

Romans 10:6-11
New Century Version (NCV)
⁶ But this is what the Scripture says about being made right through faith: "Don't say to yourself, 'Who will go up into heaven?'" (That means, "Who will go up to heaven and bring Christ down to earth?") ⁷ "And do not say, 'Who will go down into the world below?'" (That means, "Who will go down and bring Christ up from the dead?") ⁸ This is what the Scripture says: "The word is near you; it is in your mouth and in your heart."[a] That is the teaching of faith that we are telling. ⁹ If you declare with your mouth, "Jesus is Lord," and if you believe in your heart that God raised Jesus from the dead, you will be saved. ¹⁰ We believe with our hearts, and so we are made right with God. And we declare with our mouths that we believe, and so we are saved. ¹¹ As the Scripture says, "Anyone who trusts in him will never be disappointed."[b]

GOD'S WAY TO GET OUT OF DEBT

Luke 4:18-19
KJV
"The spirit of the LORD is upon me, because He has anointed Me to preach the gospel to the poor; He has sent Me to heal the brokenhearted, to proclaim liberty to the captives and recovery of sight to the blind, to set at liberty those who are oppressed; to proclaim the acceptable year of the LORD."

Confession of your faith - A new level to help the reader in expanding your faith by confession and prayer unto the Lord. This will help you to build character and faith. Repeat this prayer throughout the week as you meditate on this lesson:

TODAY I AM RELEASED AND DELIVERED FROM MY CAPTIVITY OF DEBT! IN JESUS NAME!

Now, keep in mind these principles:

1. Debt is a demonic spirit. Recognize that! Debt will not control my life any more.

2. Most of us have grown up in a cycle of debt that has been passed on from generation to generation.

Proverbs 22:6-7
KJV
'Train up a child in the way he should go, and when he is old he will not depart from it. The rich rules over the poor, and the borrower is servant to the lender.'

a. We should be training our children in the way of faith and knowing the principles of sowing and reaping.

3. There is an anointing to remove bondage and destroy the yoke of debt. The call of Abraham: blessed to be a blessing

4. Everything in the Kingdom of God operates by faith.

5. Being in debt is being in captivity.

Psalm 126:1-2
KJV
'When the LORD brought back the captivity of Zion,
we were like those who dream. Then our mouth was
filled with laughter, and our tongue with singing.'

If you follow the world's system, you will sow much and bring in little.

a. Don't abandon the will of God for your life, because you will also sink.
b. Then they said among the nations, "The LORD has done great streams in the South. Those who sow in tears shall reap in joy.'
c. We are sanctified by the Word; and we are cleansed by the Word.

6. The world has a way to get rid of debt.

Exodus 22:29-30
KJV
"Thou shalt not delay to offer the first of thy ripe fruits,
and of thy liquors: the firstborn of thy sons shalt thou
give unto me. Likewise, shalt thou do with thine oxen,
and with thy sheep: seven days; it shall be with his
mother on the eighth day thou shalt give it me"

a. You need another job.

7. If you follow the world's system, you will sow much and bring in little.

    a. Don't abandon the will of God for your life, because you will also abandon the power of God for your life!
    b. We need our mind and attitude set right to overcome the attacks on our mind.

John 17:14-16
Amplified Bible (AMP)
14 I have given *and* delivered to them Your word (message) and the world has hated them, because they are not of the world [do not belong to the world], just as I am not of the world.

15 I do not ask that You will take them out of the world, but that You will keep *and* protect them from the evil one.

16 They are not of the world (worldly, belonging to the world), [just] as I am not of the world.

    c. "World" - refers to a system of operation.

8. "Sanctify" - come out of; and come into.

    a. Separate yourself from the world; and come into God's way of doing things.
    b. Come out of sin; and come into the Word.
    c. Come out of the world's system of debt reduction; into God's way of supernatural debt cancellation.

PRINCIPLE: You will always get greater results from sowing something than from selling it.

9. If you do things the world's way, you will get the world's results. If you do things God's way you will get supernatural results.

    a. What have I been actively doing about my debt?

CONFESSION: I choose to do things the "Word way", not the world's way!

10. Kill the giant... and you will be free from all your debt!

1 Samuel 17:40
Amplified Bible (AMP)
40 Then he took his staff in his hand and chose five smooth stones out of the brook and put them in his shepherd's [lunch] bag [a whole kid's skin slung from his shoulder], in his pouch, and his sling was in his hand, and he drew near the Philistine.

1 Samuel 17:53
Amplified Bible (AMP)
53 The Israelites returned from their pursuit of the Philistines and plundered their tents.

FIVE HIGH POWERED TRUTHS CONCERNING DEBT CANCELLATION

1. Realize that God is a debt-canceling God.

2 Kings 6:5
Amplified Bible (AMP)
5 But as one was felling his beam, the ax head fell into the water; and he cried, Alas, my master, for it was borrowed!

a. God is no respecter of persons, He is a respecter of faith.
b. God wants me out of debt.

2. Two things that you must start doing:

a. Make a quality decision that you are going to do what it takes to get out debt. Decision is the open door into your reality. A quality decision always requires heaven's backup.
b. Start speaking your freedom. "Call those things that are not...." Deal with God on a daily basis to get daily results from a daily God. The same pressure debt is trying to put on you ...you need to put on debt. Set boundaries for yourself (have determination) e.g. Use your credit card like a check. Don't use it unless you have the money for it.

3. Create an open heaven by <u>tithing.</u> What do I do with unexpected income? Sow from it for the next harvest.

4. <u>Create an out-of-debt flow.</u>

Luke 6:31
(Amplified)
'And as you would like and desire that men
would do to you, do exactly so to them.'

IMPLEMENT THE PRINCIPLE OF SOWING AND REAPING.

When was the last time you forgave someone's debt? Wouldn't you like to have someone forgive you your debt?

Luke 6:38
(AMP)
'Give, and (gifts) will be given to you; good measure, pressed down, shaken together and running over, will they pour into (the pouch formed by) the bosom (of your robe and used as a bag). For with the measure you deal out (with the measure you use when you confer benefits on others), it will be measured back to you.'

Give! The only way to create an out-of-debt flow is by giving and sowing seed. Your job was not designed to meet your need. Your job was designed to give you seed. God meets your needs. Live by sowing and not by your job. Place heaven on notice of your intent to be debt-free.

II Kings 4:1-7
(KJV)
'A certain woman of the wives of the sons of the prophets cried out to Elisha, saying, „Your servant, my husband, is dead, and you know that your servant feared the LORD. And the creditor is coming to take my two sons to be his slaves." So, Elisha said to her, what shall I do for you? Tell me, what do you have in the house?" And she said, "Your maidservant has nothing in the house but a jar of oil." Then he said, 'Go borrow vessels from everywhere, from all your neighbors – empty vessels; do not gather just a few. And when you have come in, you shall shut the door behind you and your sons; then pour it into all those vessels, and set aside the full ones.' So, she went from him and shut the door behind her and her sons, who brought the vessels to her; and she poured it out. Now it came to pass, when the vessels were full, that she said to her son, "Bring me another vessel." And he said to her, "There is not another vessel." So, the oil ceased. Then she came and told the man of God. And he said, "Go, sell the oil and pay your debt; and you and your sons live on the rest."

Point of Contact:

1. Write on a clean piece of paper: DEBT FREE
2. Assemble all your bills in one place.
3. Put the paper on top of the bills and declare: "Debt cancellation has begun!"
4. Under Debt Free write:
   a. Favor
   b. Unexpected income
   c. Debt releasing anointing

Declaration:

In the name of Jesus, I declare right now that it is the will of the Father for me to be debt free. Therefore, I declare that my God is a debt-canceling God. He is no respecter of persons. He wants me out of debt. Therefore, in the Name of Jesus, I put heaven on notice, and I speak my freedom now from the spirit of debt. In the Name of Jesus, I receive the anointing for debt release. In the Name of Jesus, I receive the favor for debt release. In the Name of Jesus, I fully expect, unexpected income to come my way. In the Name of Jesus, this paper is my point of contact, and in Jesus' Name, when this paper hits my bills, I release my faith to receive favor, unexpected income, debt cancellation, and every anointing needed to remove the burden and destroy the yoke. Therefore, I declare before heaven and hell that this day, I proclaim and announce that I am free from debt. Free at last, free at last, free at last; thank God Almighty, from debt, I'm free at last. In Jesus' Name, it has begun!

LESSON THIRTY-SIX

Bible Purpose Driven:
Daily Wisdom Key for Today:

THE BENEFITS OF JUBILEE

Verse to Remember: Psalms 112:1-3
'Praise the Lord! Blessed is the man who fears the Lord, who delights greatly in His commandments. His descendants will be mighty on the earth; The generation of the upright will be blessed. Wealth and riches will be in his house., And his righteousness endures forever.'

Question to Meditate On: This is my time, this is my year for the financial wisdom anointing, that comes from above to bring financial freedom to me and my household.

LESSON THIRTY-SEVEN

Proverbs 16:3
Amplified Bible (AMP)
**³ Roll your works upon the Lord [commit and trust
them wholly to Him; He will cause your thoughts
to become agreeable to His will, and] so shall
your plans be established *and* succeed.**

GOD'S WAY TO GET OUT OF DEBT

<u>PRINCIPLE</u>: Debt removal requires focus. Violent Faith<u>:</u>

Examples of a point of contact – (Mark 5:21-43)

Jairus and the woman with the issue of blood.

    a. Violent faith targets the objective at hand – everyday.
    b. Violent faith is:
- consistent
- directed
- intense
- focused

    c. Intensity yields outstanding results.
    d. The enemy of 'violent faith' is complacency.

WHAT TO DO: Speak the Word.

Continually listen to faith-building cd's, songs and scriptures.
Apply these basic ideas, found in this lesson, as you speak out
the word of God with bible purpose and purposing yourself,

through and with the Lord, out of your financial stresses and strains.

1. Put continual pressure on getting out of debt.

Psalm 115:9-15
Amplified Bible (AMP)
⁹ O Israel, trust *and* take refuge in the Lord! [Lean on, rely on, and be confident in Him!] He is their Help and their Shield.

¹⁰ O house of Aaron [the priesthood], trust in *and* lean on the Lord! He is their Help and their Shield.

¹¹ You who [reverently] fear the Lord, trust in *and* lean on the Lord! He is their Help and their Shield.

¹² The Lord has been mindful of us, He will bless us: He will bless the house of Israel, He will bless the house of Aaron [the priesthood],

¹³ He will bless those who reverently *and* worshipfully fear the Lord, both small and great.

¹⁴ May the Lord give you increase more and more, you and your children.

¹⁵ May you be blessed of the Lord, who made heaven and earth!

2. God has made a covenant promise: I will bless you; I will increase you. In your debt release program, God is going to bring increase your way! You must believe that:

    a. Being blessed includes receiving increase.
    b. Expect and put faith pressure on receiving unexpected income.
    c. Praise is attached to receiving increase.

<u>Come on, say it</u>: LORD, I EXPECT UNEXPECTED INCOME!

Genesis 12:2-3
Amplified Bible (AMP)
² And I will make of you a great nation, and I will bless you [with abundant increase of favors] and make your name famous *and* distinguished, and you will be a blessing [dispensing good to others].

³ And I will bless those who bless you [who confer prosperity or happiness upon you] and [a]curse him who curses *or* uses insolent language toward you; in you will all the families *and* kindred of the earth be blessed [and by you they will bless themselves].

3. God has favors ready to give to those who will believe Him. Here are some points to help you catch this:

a. Envision walking in daily favors from God.
b. Receiving something that didn't require any effort or action from you.
c. Favors from God will help you get free from being locked down by contracts and debt.
d. Simplicity – focus in on the objective; become "violent" in your faith (speaking it, meditating on it, praying it, spending time on it).
e. Create an expectation flow for the Father to fill.

<u>PRINCIPLE</u>: Expectation that cannot be killed is expectation that cannot be denied.

f. Respond to and expect what you see in the Word. Example: building strong muscles (eating right; lifting weights).

4. "Press" into the things of God: Here are a few simple points that illustrate this powerful purpose:

    a. Press the root of "pressure"
    b. Apply pressure to your debt, through increase and promise.
    c. Great things come out of entering into the "press"

CONFESSION: I will press towards debt cancellation and I will add pressure on increase, unexpected income, prosperity, healing and debt cancellation, until I have reached the mark.

5. Great things don't happen by doing something <u>one</u> time.

    a. Stay focused; don't let it go until you achieve you goal.

6. Entering into covenant with God brings increase and expansion.

    Multiplication not addition.

    a. God's favor in your life opens doors no man can shut.

Philippians 3:12-16
Amplified Bible (AMP)
[12] Not that I have now attained [this ideal], or have already been made perfect, but I press on to lay hold of (grasp) *and* make my own, that for which Christ Jesus (the Messiah) has laid hold of me *and* made me His own.

[13] I do not consider, brethren, that I have captured *and* made it my own [yet]; but one thing I do [it is my one aspiration]: forgetting what lies behind and straining forward to what lies ahead,

**¹⁴ I press on toward the goal to win the
[supreme and heavenly] prize to which God
in Christ Jesus is calling us upward.**

**¹⁵ So let those [of us] who are spiritually mature *and*
full-grown have this mind *and* hold these convictions;
and if in any respect you have a different attitude
of mind, God will make that clear to you also.**

**¹⁶ Only let us hold true to what we have already
attained *and* walk *and* order our lives by that.**

7. You cannot reach to the things that are ahead if you haven't forgotten the things that are behind. Does that sound familiar to you? Everyone struggles with past defeats at some point in life.

   a. Don't let past debts and bad decisions keep you from pressing into increase and debt cancellation.
   b. If you don't cut off the past, it will press upon your future, and keep you from making progress.
   c. Debt turns people away from God.
   d. Don't miss the purpose for money: <u>money is no good without purpose.</u>
   e. Your attitude is <u>key</u> in getting out of debt.

QUESTION: What could I do if I were out of debt?

   f. When you are out of debt you will have freedom to obey God's voice without questions or worry.

8. So many of us have been in debt so long, that we have forgotten that the price of everything is negotiable. We must purpose to change our purpose in acquiring and spending. There must be a why to our what!

a. When you are debt-free you are servant to no one.
b. Debt is a spirit we need to be delivered from if we are to do what God wants us to accomplish in these last days.

CONFESSION: In the name of Jesus, I am out of debt. All of my needs are met. I have plenty more to put in store. I apply pressure to the Word of God on increase and debt-cancellation.

I have violent faith. I am intense with my debt release. In the name of Jesus, I am free from the spirit of debt, forever. I expect an increase of the favor of God. I press towards the mark of being debt free by forgetting the things that are behind and reaching to the things that are before.

I will obtain the prize of being free from the spirit of debt, that I may be a blessing until all the families of the earth are blessed. I thank you for it now Lord. As the redeemed of the Lord, I have what I say, in Jesus' name. AMEN.

GOD'S WAY TO GET OUT OF DEBT- SEVEN POWER-PRINCIPLES FOR DEBT CANCELLATION

Genesis 12:1-3
Amplified Bible (AMP)
12 Now [in Haran] the Lord said to Abram, go for yourself [for your own advantage] away from your country, from your relatives and your father's house, to the land that I will show you.

2 And I will make of you a great nation, and I will bless you [with abundant increase of favors] and make your name famous _and_ distinguished, and you will be a blessing [dispensing good to others].

3 And I will bless those who bless you [who confer prosperity or happiness upon you] and [a]curse him who curses *or* uses insolent language toward you; in you will all the families *and* kindred of the earth be blessed [and by you they will bless themselves].

PRINCIPLE #1: Decide to do it God's way.

1. God wants increase in your life for a purpose.

   a. We need a right motive and a right focus.

James 1:6-7
Amplified Bible (AMP)
6 Only it must be in faith that he asks with no wavering (no hesitating, no doubting). For the one who wavers (hesitates, doubts) is like the billowing surge out at sea that is blown hither *and* thither and tossed by the wind.

7 For truly, let not such a person imagine that he will receive anything [he asks for] from the Lord,

   b. The world's way versus God's way.
   c. Don't only start the process of debt cancellation, but stay with it until it is finished.

Hebrews 12:2
Amplified Bible (AMP)
2 Looking away [from all that will distract] to Jesus, who is the Leader *and* the Source of our faith [giving the first incentive for our belief] and is also its Finisher [bringing it to maturity and perfection]. He, for the joy [of obtaining the prize] that was set before Him, endured the cross, despising *and* ignoring the shame, and is now seated at the right hand of the throne of God.

d. There is something greater than God putting what you need into your hand, and that is being taught how to have the ability to get what you need.

e. God says to you: "I will empower you to get wealth."

CONFESSION: God is empowering me to prosper. Amen.

2. Our number one objective is to get out of debt so that we can be a blessing. You cannot be a blessing if your life is flooded with misfortune.

a. When we are in debt we are a slave to the lender.

b. The money God gave Israel was not used to take care of them. Money was not the source of their supply. God was the source.

c. The purpose of that money was to be used in the sanctuary of worship – to serve God.

CONFESSION: God is my source – not my paycheck – not my money.

d. Believe God to look after you – use your money to serve Him.

e. Over 95% of the Church today is in debt.

CONFESSION: I'm being delivered from average. I'm being promoted from mediocrity to magnificence.

f. envision what it will be like when you pay off your last debt!

Matthew 11:11-12
Amplified Bible (AMP)
10 Truly I tell you, among those born of women there has not risen anyone greater than John the Baptist; yet he who is least in the kingdom of heaven is greater than he.

12 And from the days of John the Baptist until the present time, the kingdom of heaven has endured violent assault, and violent men seize it by force [as a precious prize—a [a]share in the heavenly kingdom is sought with most ardent zeal and intense exertion].

PRINCIPLE # 2: You have to be violent and intense in your faith.

1. Intense exertion: investing everything; confession, praise, eye-gate, ear-gate 'prayer' reading time, listening time, fellowship time.

   Growth versus development (e.g. muscles) Growth happens naturally. Development requires pressure to produce Strength.

   a. Keep exerting pressure on your promise of debt cancellation!
   b. Violent = Enter into the press (root of pressure)

   - Peer pressure versus faith pressure
   - Forcibly get the manifestation of receiving your promise.
   - Temptation is pressure that is applied to your flesh.

Philippians 3:14
Amplified Bible (AMP)
14 I press on toward the goal to win the [supreme and heavenly] prize to which God in Christ Jesus is calling us upward.

CONFESSION: In Jesus' Name, I am intense and I will be out of debt!

PRINCIPLE # 3: Stay focused!

Proverbs 4:26-27
Amplified Bible (AMP)
[26] Consider well the path of your feet, and let all your ways be established *and* ordered aright.

[27] Turn not aside to the right hand or to the left; remove your foot from evil.

1. Remain on target

   a. Don't buy a new car just because you've paid off the old one.
   b. Don't put things on lay away.
   c. When you get extra money, don't take it easy and spend it.

CONFESSION: I am focused!

   d. It will take the anointing to get you out of debt. Your foot cannot be in evil at the same time you are looking for supernatural power for debt cancellation.
   e. Sin is a debt – but Jesus paid it!

PRINCIPLE # 4: Cast your debt upon the Lord

1. Read, believe and practice Peter 5:7

2. Casting all your care upon Him, for He cares for you. Our God is well and able.

   a. We are not designed to carry the stress of debt. Wisdom: Don't worry about the things you can do because you can do it. Don't worry about the things you cannot do because there isn't anything you can do about it. Worry is a sin. Roll the care of your debt on to God.

CONFESSION: In the Name of Jesus, I roll the care of every bill and every debt on to God right now. I cast my cares on to the Lord. I cast my debts on to the Lord because He cares for me and will deliver me.

PRINCIPLE # 5: Utilize the power of thanksgiving.

Psalm 50:14-15
Amplified Bible (AMP)
¹⁴ Offer to God the sacrifice of thanksgiving,
and pay your vows to the Most High,

¹⁵ And call on Me in the day of trouble; I will deliver
you, and you shall honor *and* glorify Me.

1. "Vow a vow"

   a. The vow becomes a voucher and is used to obtain provision from heaven. Then it is required from you to pay your promise. e.g. Hanna
   b. Get ready for heaven to accelerate the anointing when you are in "the day of trouble" (debt).

PRINCIPLE # 6: Stick with the Word on debt cancellation.

2 Timothy 3:16
Amplified Bible (AMP)
16 Every Scripture is God-breathed (given by His inspiration) and profitable for instruction, for reproof *and* conviction of sin, for correction of error *and* discipline in obedience, [and] for training in righteousness (in holy living, in conformity to God's will in thought, purpose, and action),

PRINCIPLE # 7: Don't be lazy.

1. Be faithful and you will inherit the promise.

    a. Power twins: Faith & Patience.
    b. The Word .and consistency.

2. Is there anything too hard for the Lord?

Genesis 18:14
Amplified Bible (AMP)
[14] Is anything too hard *or* too wonderful [a]for the Lord? At the appointed time, when the season [for her delivery] comes around, I will return to you and Sarah shall have borne a son.

    a. God can and will deliver us from every one of our debts.

LESSON THIRTY-SEVEN

Bible Purpose Driven:
Daily Wisdom Key for Today:

GOD'S WAY TO GET OUT OF DEBT

Verse to Remember: Proverbs 16:3
Amplified Bible (AMP)
[3] Roll your works upon the Lord [commit and trust them wholly to Him; He will cause your thoughts to become agreeable to His will, and] so shall your plans be established *and* succeed.

Question to Meditate On: My commitment is my integrity. The Lord will close all the doors of my past. I am looking to Him for the best.

LESSON THIRTY-EIGHT

Hebrews 6:12
: "That you do not become sluggish but imitate those who through faith and patience inherit the promises."

ALL SCRIPTURE IS <u>PROFITABLE</u> FOR GETTING YOU OUT OF DEBT

OUR TESTIMONY: Our pastor taught the Word, we received it, and God did it.

Declaration: In the Name of Jesus, I declare right now that I am out of debt. I call those things that be not as though they were. All of my needs are met. I have plenty more to put in store. I declare right now it is the will of the Father for me to be debt free. Therefore, I give thanksgiving. Thank You Lord that I am delivered from all of my debt and I make a vow before You now, in this day of debt, that You will deliver me from all of my debt. I vow to You now that when I am delivered from all of my debt that I will support the gospel in all the ways that I know of and in all the ways that You guide me into. I thank You in advance for deliverance and debt cancellation. I believe that I've received right now, complete freedom from captivity. Jesus has announced my release from captivity. Therefore, I agree with Him by declaring my freedom from debt.

GOD'S WAY TO GET OUT OF DEBT - THE KEY TO MIRACLE DEBT CANCELLATION

Luke 4:18-19
Amplified Bible (AMP)
[18] The Spirit of the Lord [is] upon Me, because He has anointed Me [the Anointed One, the Messiah] to preach the good news (the Gospel) to the poor; He has sent Me to announce release to the captives and recovery of sight to the blind, to send forth as delivered those who are oppressed [who are downtrodden, bruised, crushed, and broken down by calamity],

[19] To proclaim the accepted *and* acceptable year of the Lord [the day [a]when salvation and the free favors of God profusely abound].

1. Jesus was anointed.

    a. This anointing was first designated to the poor.
    b. Secondly, it was designated to the captive.
    c. It will take the anointing to bring debt-release.

Matthew 11:12
New King James Version (NKJV)
1 And from the days of John the Baptist until now the kingdom of heaven suffers violence, and the violent take it by force.

2. You have to apply "pressure" to your debt cancellation.

    a. It is not enough to merely talk about it.
    b. Unless you get violent about the promise you won't experience the promise.
    c. Follow up.

PRINCIPLE: Convenience will never move you into barrier-breaking harvest.

3. Recognize (judge yourself) the causes of your problem:

    a. Compulsive spending
    b. Habits and desires
    c. Lies and desires
    d. Credit (debt) cards
       • Though it has your name on it, it does not represent your money.
       • Treat your credit card like you would a check – don't use it unless you have the money to pay for it.

PRINCIPLE: We <u>pay</u> the world system to keep us enslaved.

    e. Don't cash your paycheck; deposit it in the bank.

4. Counterfeit miracle.

1 Corinthians 15:48
New King James Version (NKJV)
⁴⁸ As *was* the *man* of dust, so also *are* those who *are made* of dust; and as *is* the heavenly *Man*, so also *are* those *who are* heavenly.

    a. Satan can hold back the Gospel, if he can keep the Body of Christ in debt.
    b. We can only "do the minimum" while we are in debt.
    c. Am I earthly-minded or heavenly-minded?
    d. Bankruptcy is a counterfeit miracle, attempting to duplicate God's miracle of debt cancellation.
    e. Bankruptcy is immoral when it becomes an easy-fix for irresponsible, reckless spending.
    f. Bankruptcy is not a real way out.

5. You are caught in "The Debt Trap"

   a. When you pay more than 20% of your gross income on debt.
   b. When you can only afford to pay the monthly minimum on your credit cards.
   c. When you start using pre-approved credit cards because the other ones are all filled to the maximum.
   d. When you use one credit card (cash withdrawal) to pay the other.
   e. When you make alternating payments on your bills.

6. We need to change our way of doing things:

   a. I can do without it for now.
   b. Re-learn how to shop: for food, for gas, etc.

7. Debt brings problems

   a. Anxiety, divorce, divided families, broken friendships.
   b. Debt is a spirit – 90 % of our personal problems are connected to debt.

CONFESSION: Repeat this out loud three times: <u>God has a way out of the problem called debt.</u>

8. More than at any other time in history, we qualify for the miracle of debt cancellation.

   a. Supernatural intervention is available for us for debt cancellation.

Hebrews 11:40
King James Version (KJV)
**⁴⁰ God having provided some better thing for us,
that they without us should not be made perfect.**

b. God wants to provide something better for us than was provided for in the Old Covenant.

CONFESSION: God has something better for me. It is: *miracles, deliverance, prosperity, debt cancellation*.

Romans 3:4
New King James Version (NKJV)
⁴ Certainly not! Indeed, let God be true but
every man a liar. As it is written:
"That You may be justified in Your words,
And may overcome when You are judged."[a]

9. The Word says debt cancellation is <u>possible</u> for me. It is God's will for me to be out of debt.

a. Miracles are given by God, not men.

James 1:6
New King James Version (NKJV)
⁶ But let him ask in faith, with no doubting,
for he who doubts is like a wave of the
sea driven and tossed by the wind.

b. Patience: consistently constant in what you believe. You've got to be sure that God can do it.

10. Tradition (and the world system) will weaken your faith and keep you from getting out of debt.

Matthew 15:6
New King James Version (NKJV)
⁶ then he need not honor his father or mother.'[a]
Thus you have made the commandment[b]
of God of no effect by your tradition.

a. Tradition got you into debt!

b. Traditions of what you've "got to have"

c. Pressure to do certain things on Christmas, birthdays, etc.

11. Keys to the miracle of debt cancellation:

2 Kings 4:1-7
New King James Version (NKJV)
Elisha and the Widow's Oil
4 A certain woman of the wives of the sons of the prophets cried out to Elisha, saying, "Your servant my husband is dead, and you know that your servant feared the LORD. And the creditor is coming to take my two sons to be his slaves."

2 So Elisha said to her, "What shall I do for you? Tell me, what do you have in the house?" And she said, "Your maidservant has nothing in the house but a jar of oil."

3 Then he said, "Go, borrow vessels from everywhere, from all your neighbors—empty vessels; do not gather just a few. 4 And when you have come in, you shall shut the door behind you and your sons; then pour it into all those vessels, and set aside the full ones."

5 So she went from him and shut the door behind her and her sons, who brought *the vessels* to her; and she poured *it* out. 6 Now it came to pass, when the vessels were full, that she said to her son, "Bring me another vessel."

And he said to her, "*There is* not another vessel." So, the oil ceased. 7 Then she came and told the man of God. And he said, "Go, sell the oil and pay your debt; and you *and* your sons live on the rest."

Never lose reverence for the prophet and for the anointing upon what he says.

    a. The woman did exactly what she was told to do.

    b. What are you going to do with the first thing God told you to do?

    c. The key to this miracle: The woman <u>trusted</u> the man of God with the last thing of value she had.

1 Kings 17:9-16
New King James Version (NKJV)

9 "Arise, go to Zarephath, which *belongs* to Sidon, and dwell there. See, I have commanded a widow there to provide for you." 10 So he arose and went to Zarephath. And when he came to the gate of the city, indeed a widow *was* there gathering sticks. And he called to her and said, "Please bring me a little water in a cup, that I may drink." 11 And as she was going to get *it,* he called to her and said, "Please bring me a morsel of bread in your hand."

12 So she said, "As the Lord your God lives, I do not have bread, only a handful of flour in a bin, and a little oil in a jar; and see, I *am* gathering a couple of sticks that I may go in and prepare it for myself and my son, that we may eat it, and die."

13 And Elijah said to her, "Do not fear; go *and* do as you have said, but make me a small cake from it first, and bring *it* to me; and afterward make *some* for yourself and your son. 14 For thus says the Lord God of Israel: 'The bin of flour shall not be used up, nor shall the jar of oil run dry, until the day the Lord sends rain on the earth.'"

¹⁵ So she went away and did according to the word of Elijah; and she and he and her household ate for *many* days. ¹⁶ The bin of flour was not used up, nor did the jar of oil run dry, according to the word of the Lord which He spoke by Elijah.

d. First, God told the woman that Elijah was coming, and that she should take care of him.

2 Chronicles 20:20
New King James Version (NKJV)
²⁰ So they rose early in the morning and went out into the Wilderness of Tekoa; and as they went out, Jehoshaphat stood and said, "Hear me, O Judah and you inhabitants of Jerusalem: Believe in the Lord your God, and you shall be established; believe His prophets, and you shall prosper."

e. The key to this miracle: she trusted the man of God with the last thing of value she had.
f. The master key to your debt cancellation is to trust what God has said, enough to do it.
g. According to 2. Chron. 20:20, when you believe that God's Word is coming through the man of God, it guarantees that what comes out of his spirit is going to be directed from God, because you have applied faith pressure to the scripture.
h. Do exactly what the man of God tells you to do (by the Word), then you will be blessed.
i. If you want to be blessed, you are under obligation God to do what you were told to do in faithfulness.

Hebrews 13:12
New King James Version (NKJV)
¹² Therefore Jesus also, that He might sanctify the people with His own blood, suffered outside the gate.

12. If God did it once, he'll do it again.

   a. No more . . . "I'm coming out of debt", now it is: "I am out of debt."
   b. We call those things that be not as though they are.

NOTES for Lesson 38: Please read and re-read these scriptures as you complete this lesson.

Strategies for Debt Release – Strategy #1

Romans 9:28
New King James Version (NKJV)
28 For He will finish the work and cut *it* short in righteousness, Because the Lord will make a short work upon the earth."[a]

Ephesians 5:27
New King James Version (NKJV)
27 that He might present her to Himself a glorious church, not having spot or wrinkle or any such thing, but that she should be holy and without blemish.

Isaiah 10:27
New King James Version (NKJV)
27 It shall come to pass in that day
***That* his burden will be taken away from your shoulder,**
And his yoke from your neck,
And the yoke will be destroyed because of the anointing oil.

Romans 13:8
New King James Version (NKJV)
Love Your Neighbor
8 Owe no one anything except to love one another, for he who loves another has fulfilled the law.

Romans 13:11
New King James Version (NKJV)
Put on Christ
[11] **And *do* this, knowing the time, that now *it is* high
time to awake out of sleep; for now, our salvation
is nearer than when we *first* believed.**

Make a DECISION to be debt free.

LESSON THIRTY-EIGHT

Bible Purpose Driven:
Daily Wisdom Key for Today:

ALL SCRIPTURE IS <u>PROFITABLE</u> FOR GETTING YOU OUT OF DEBT

Verse to Remember: Hebrews 6:12
: "That you do not become sluggish but imitate those
who through faith and patience inherit the promises."

Question to Meditate On: I will meditate day and night, through faith and into faith, and God will make a champion out of me. Say HALLELUJAH 3 times if you agree!

LESSON THIRTY-NINE

Joel 3:14
New King James Version (NKJV)
¹⁴ Multitudes, multitudes in the valley of decision!
For the day of the Lᴏʀᴅ *is* near in the valley of decision.

WHEN I AM IN THE VALLEY I WILL CLIMB THE MOUNTAIN

<u>PRINCIPLE</u>: Every time you make a decision in line with the Word of God, things begin to happen. Because the bible <u>IS </u>the ultimate purpose. Study the following points:

a. The Power of Decision: Heaven and earth are making a record of your decisions.

Deuteronomy 30:19-20
KJV
I call heaven and earth as witnesses today against you, that I have set before you life and death, blessing and cursing; therefore, choose life, that both you and your descendants may live; that you may love the Lord your God, that you may obey His voice, and that you may dwell in the land which the Lord swore to your fathers, to Abraham, Isaac, and Jacob to give them.

b. Faith never goes past the question mark. Remember the words Jesus spoke to the leper in Mathew 8:2-3: "Lord, if you are willing . . . Jesus said, I am willing."

c. Salvation –Includes deliverance, victory, health prosperity, help, material and temporal deliverance, restoration and pardon.

Hebrews 1:13
New King James Version (NKJV)
But to which of the angels has He ever said: "Sit at My right hand, till I make Your enemies Your footstool?" Are they not all ministering spirits sent forth to minister for those who will inherit salvation?

Hebrews 2:3
New King James Version (NKJV)
How shall we escape, if we neglect so great a salvation, which at the first began to be spoken by the Lord, and was confirmed to us by those who heard Him.

Psalm 103:20
New King James Version (NKJV)
Bless the lord, you His angels, who excel in strength, who do His word, heeding the voice of His word.

d. Decision is the point of action.
e. Christianity is a series of decisions.
    • Being saved
    • Water baptism
    • Decision opens the door into reality.
f. It doesn't only take a decision – but a decision of quality. We see this in James 1:7-8: For let not that man suppose that he will receive anything from the Lord; he is a double-minded man, unstable in all his ways.
g. Your decision summons the anointing to get the job done.

h. Decision is illustrated in scripture:

Mark 5:1-43
New King James Version (NKJV)

'Then they came to the other side of the sea, to the country of the Gadarenes. And when He had come out of the boat, immediately there met Him out of the tombs a man with an unclean spirit, who had his dwelling among the tombs; and no one could bind him, not even with chains because he had often been bound with shackles and chains. And the chains have been pulled apart by him, and the shackles broken in pieces; neither could anyone tame him. And always, night and day, he was in the mountains and in the tombs, crying out and cutting himself with stones. When he saw Jesus from afar, he ran and worshipped Him. And he cried out with a loud voice and said, "What have I to do with You, Jesus, son of the Most High God? I implore You by God that You do not torment me." For He said to him, "Come out of the man, unclean spirit!" Then He asked him, "What is your name?" And he answered, saying, "My name is Legion; for we are many." Also, he begged Him earnestly that He would not send them out of the country. Now a large herd of swine was feeding there near the mountains. So, all the demons begged Him, saying, "Send us to the swine, that we may enter them." And at once Jesus gave them permission. Then the unclean spirits went out and entered the swine (there were about two thousand); and the herd ran violently down the steep place into the sea, and drowned in the sea. So those who fed the swine fled, and they told it in the city and in the country. And they went out to see what it was that had happened. Then they came to Jesus, and saw the one who had been demon-possessed and had the legion, sitting and clothed and in his right mind. And they were afraid. And those who saw it told them how it happened to him who had been demon-possessed, and about the swine. Then they began to plead with Him to depart from their region. And when He got into the boat, he who had been demon-possessed begged Him that he might be with Him. However, Jesus did not permit him, but said to him, "Go home to your friends, and tell them what great things the Lord has done for you, and how He has had compassion on you." And he departed and began to proclaim in Decapolis all that Jesus had done for him, and all marveled. Now when Jesus had crossed over again by boat to the other side, a great multitude gathered to Him; and He was by the sea. And behold, one of the rulers of the synagogue came, Jairus by name. And when he saw Him, he fell at His feet and begged Him earnestly, saying, "My little daughter lies at the point of death. Come and lay Your hands on her, that she may be healed, and she will live." So, Jesus went with him, and a great multitude followed Him and thronged Him. Now a certain woman had a flow of blood for twelve Years, and had suffered many things from many physicians. She had spent all that she had and was no better, but rather grew worse. When she heard about Jesus, she came behind Him in the crowd and touched His garment. For she said, "If only I may touch His clothes, I shall be made well." Immediately the fountain of her blood was dried up, and she felt in her body that she was healed of the affliction. And Jesus, immediately knowing in Himself that power had gone out of Him, turned around in the crowd and said, "Who touched My clothes?" But His disciples said to Him, "You see the multitude thronging You, and You say, Who touched Me?'" And He looked around to see her who had done this thing. But the woman, fearing and trembling, knowing what had happened to her, came and fell down before Him and told Him the whole truth. And He said to her, "Daughter, your faith has made you well. Go in peace, and be healed of your affliction." While He was still speaking, some came from the ruler of the synagogue, "Do not be afraid; only believe." And He permitted no one to follow Him except Peter, James and John the brother of James. Then He came to the house of the ruler of the synagogue, and saw a tumult and those who wept and wailed loudly. When He came in, He said to them, "Why make this commotion and weep? The child is not dead, but sleeping." And they ridiculed Him. But when He had put them all outside, He took the father and the mother of the child, and those who were with Him, and entered where the child was lying. Then He took the child by the hand, and said to her, "Talitha, cumi," which is translated, "Little girl, I say to you, arise." Immediately the girl arose and walked, for she was twelve years of age. And they were overcome with great amazement. But He commanded them strictly that no one should know it, and said that something should be given her to eat.'

TAKING INVENTORY

1. Know the Word: It is the only source for standing firmly and standing in faith concerning any life-issue.

   Balance the Word: However Biblical their source, lopsided ideas produce lopsided living. Only the Word brings real life.

   Apply the Word: We need to act on what we find. God's promises are not merely for repeating or reviewing, but for revealing a course of action.

2. Debt is a demonic spirit. God is a debt- canceling God.

3. Two things you must do:

   a. Make a quality decision that you are going to do what it will take to get out of debt. Decision is the open door into your reality.
   b. Start <u>speaking</u> your freedom.
      • Call those things that be not. Say: "I will never be broke another day in my life!"

4. The same pressure debt is trying to put on you, you need to put on debt.

5. Create an open heaven by tithing. This is your covenant connector.

6. Seven principles:

   a. Decide to do it God's way.
   b. You have to become violent in your faith:
      • intense, consistent, directed.
   c. Stay focused.
   d. Cast your debt upon the Lord (1. Peter 5:7)
   e. Utilize the power of thanksgiving.
   f. Stick with the Word on debt cancellation.
   g. Don't be lazy and be faithful with money and He will trust you with true riches (the anointing).

7. Sacrifice: an act or offering to God; a precious gift to God; surrendering that which means something to you.

   a. Every time a sacrifice was offered – God showed up.

8. The anointing will support money with a mission but it will not support greed or selfishness.

9. Strategies for Debt Release –

a. Strategy #1: Make a DECISION to be debt-free.
b. Strategy #2: Become debt-free through the Kingdom of God's system, instead of the world's system. The world's way of doing things always has a dead end.

6 POINTS TO FOCUS ON FOR YOUR DIVINE PROVISION

1. People in the world's system have more confidence and act smarter than people in God's Kingdom.

Luke 16:1-8
New King James Version (NKJV)
'He also said to His disciples: "There was a certain rich man who had a steward, and an accusation was brought to him that this man wasting his goods. So, he called him and said to him, "What is this I hear about you? Give an account of your stewardship, for you can no longer be steward." Then the steward said within himself, "What shall I do? For my master is taking the stewardship away from me. I cannot dig; I am ashamed to beg. I have resolved what to do, that when I am put out of the stewardship, they may receive me into their houses." So, he called every one of his master's debtors to him, and said to the first, "How much do you owe my master?" And he said, "A hundred measures of oil." So, he said to him, "Take your bill and sit down quickly and write fifty." Then he said to another, "And how much do you owe?" So, he said "A hundred measures of wheat." And he said to him, "Take your bill, and write eighty." So, the master commended the unjust steward because he had dealt shrewdly. For the sons of this world are more shrewd in their generation than the sons of light.'

2. We have been born again out of the world's system into God's system of operation.

John 18:36
New King James Version (NKJV)
'Jesus answered, "My kingdom is not of this world.
If My kingdom were of this, My servants would
fight, so that I should not be delivered to the
Jews; but now My kingdom is not from here.'

Colossians 1:13
New King James Version (NKJV)
He has delivered us from the power of darkness and
conveyed us into the kingdom of the Son of His love.

Samuel 22:28-32
New International Version (NIV)
You will save those in trouble, but you bring down the
haughty; for you watch their every move. O Lord, you
are my light! You make my darkness bright. By your
power I can crush an army; By your strength I leap
over a wall. As for God, his way is perfect; the Word of
the Lord is true. He shields all who hide behind him.
Our Lord alone is God. We have no other Savior.

3. Seek first the Kingdom of God.

Mathew 6:33-34
Amplified Bible (AMP)
But seek (aim at and strive after) first of all His Kingdom
and His righteousness (His way of doing and being
right), and then all these things taken together will be
given you besides. So, do not worry or be anxious about
tomorrow, for tomorrow will have worries and anxieties
of its own. Sufficient for each day is its own trouble.

If you do it God's way, all these things will be added. When will it be added? When you do it God's way.

4. Promotion Money Added Favor - The Grandfather Parable of all Parables

Mark 4:11-19
New International Version (NIV)
And He said to them, "To you it has been given to know the mystery of God; but to those who are outside, all things come in parables, so that Seeing they may see and not perceive, and hearing they may hear and not understand; lest they should turn, and their sins be forgiven them." And He said to them, "Do you not understand this parable? How then will you understand all the parables? The sower sows the word. And these are the ones by the wayside where the word is sown. When they hear, Satan comes immediately and takes away the word that was sown in their hearts. These likewise are the ones sown on stony ground who, when they hear the word, immediately receive it with gladness; and they have no root in themselves, and so endure only for a time. Afterward, when tribulation or persecution arises for the word's sake, immediately they stumble. Now these are the ones sown among thorns; they are the ones who hear the word and the cares of this world, the deceitfulness of riches, and the desires for other things entering in choke the word and it becomes unfruitful."

Mark 4:21-29
Amplified Bible (AMP)
21 And He said to them, Is the lamp brought in to be put under a [a]peck measure or under a bed, and not [to be put] on the lampstand?

22 [b]Things are hidden temporarily only as a means to revelation.] For there is nothing hidden except to

be revealed, nor is anything [temporarily] kept secret
except in order that it may be made known.

²³ If any man has ears to hear, let him be listening
and let him perceive *and* comprehend.

²⁴ And He said to them, be careful what you are
hearing. The measure ⁽ᶜ⁾[of thought and study] you
give [to ⁽ᵈ⁾the truth you hear] will be the measure ⁽ᵉ⁾
[of virtue and knowledge] that comes back to you—
and more [besides] will be given to you *who hear*.

²⁵ For to him who has will more be given; and from him who
has nothing, even what he has will be taken away [⁽ᶠ⁾by force],

²⁶ And He said, The kingdom of God is like a
man who scatters seed upon the ground,

²⁷ And then continues sleeping and rising night
and day while the seed sprouts and grows
and⁽ᵍ⁾increases—he knows not how.

²⁸ The earth produces [acting] by itself—first the
blade, then the ear, then the full grain in the ear.

²⁹ But when the grain is ripe *and* permits, immediately
he ⁽ʰ⁾sends forth [the reapers] *and* puts in the
sickle, because the harvest stands ready.

Galatians 6:2
Amplified Bible (AMP)
² Bear (endure, carry) one another's burdens *and*⁽ᵃ⁾
troublesome moral faults, and in this way fulfill *and*
observe perfectly the law of Christ (the Messiah) *and*
complete ⁽ᵇ⁾what is lacking [in your obedience to it].

5. You have to have seed before you can have debt-cancellation.

Luke 6:31-38
Amplified Bible (AMP)
[31] And as you would like *and* desire that men would do to you, do exactly so to them.

[32] If you [merely] love those who love you, what [a]quality of credit *and* thanks is that to you? For even [b]the [very] sinners love their lovers (those who love them).

[33] And if you are kind *and* good *and* do favors to *and* benefit those who are kind *and* good *and* do favors to *and* benefit you, what [c]quality of credit *and* thanks, is that to you? For even [d]the preeminently sinful do the same.

[34] And if you lend money [e]at interest to those from whom you hope to receive, what [f]quality of credit *and* thanks is that to you? Even notorious sinners lend money [g] at interest to sinners, so as to recover as much again.

[35] But love your enemies and be kind *and* do good [doing favors [h]so that someone derives benefit from them] and lend, expecting *and* hoping for nothing in return but[i] considering nothing as lost *and* despairing of no one; and then your recompense (your reward) will be great (rich, strong, intense, and abundant), and you will be sons of the Most High, for He is kind *and* charitable *and* good to the ungrateful *and* the selfish and wicked.

[36] So be merciful (sympathetic, tender, responsive, and compassionate) even as your Father is [all these].

[37] Judge not [neither pronouncing judgment nor subjecting to censure], and you will not be judged; do not condemn *and* pronounce guilty, and you will not be condemned *and* pronounced guilty; acquit *and*

forgive *and*[i]release (give up resentment, let it drop), and you will be acquitted *and* forgiven *and*[k]released.

[38] Give, and [gifts] will be given to you; good measure, pressed down, shaken together, and running over, will they pour [l]into [the pouch formed by] the bosom [of your robe and used as a bag]. For with the measure you deal out [with the measure you use when you confer benefits on others], it will be measured back to you.

6. Seed time and harvest time is a Life Principle. The Great Escape – Debt Free Forever

Genesis 8:22
Amplified Bible (AMP)
[22] While the earth remains, seedtime and harvest, cold and heat, summer and winter, and day and night shall not cease.

I. Debt free forever!
   a. Debt removing anointing
   b. Supernatural favor
   c. Unexpected income

II. The Lord will help me get out of debt.

Isaiah 50:7
Amplified Bible (AMP)
[7] For the Lord God helps Me; therefore, have I not been ashamed *or* confounded. Therefore, have I set My face like a flint, and I know that I shall not be put to shame.

Romans 13:8
Amplified Bible (AMP)
[8] Keep out of debt *and* owe no man anything, except to love one another; for he who loves his neighbor [who

practices loving others] has fulfilled the Law [relating to one's fellowmen, meeting all its requirements].

Deuteronomy 28:12
Amplified Bible (AMP)
¹² The Lord shall open to you His good treasury, the heavens, to give the rain of your land in its season and to bless all the work of your hands; and you shall lend to many nations, but you shall not borrow.

a. God wants us in a position where we are able to step into what He is getting ready to do in these last days. (Wealth is never transferred in good times).

b. What one does for the sake of tomorrow is an investment. What one does to enjoy today, at the expense of tomorrow, is called debt.

c. The moment you make the quality decision to live debt-free, God sees you debt-free.

d. What you need to do, is to walk this out by faith believe in God's Word, and be obedient to whatever He tells you to do.

CONFESSION: I decide now to live debt-free!

e. Now you must become a 'barefooted priest' – one who is sensitive to where he goes and what he does.

f. You don't need many ways to get out of debt. <u>You only need one!</u>

III. Our thinking has to change.

1 Samuel 17:25
Amplified Bible (AMP)
²⁵ And the Israelites said, have you seen this man who has come out? Surely, he has come out to defy Israel; and the man who kills him

the king will enrich with great riches, and will give him his daughter and make his father's house free [from taxes and service] in Israel.

1 Samuel 17:40
Amplified Bible (AMP)
⁴⁰ Then he took his staff in his hand and chose five smooth stones out of the brook and put them in his shepherd's [lunch] bag [a whole kid's skin slung from his shoulder], in his pouch, and his sling was in his hand, and he drew near the Philistine.

Proverbs 22:6-7
Amplified Bible (AMP)
⁶ Train up a child in the way he should go [and in keeping with his individual gift or bent], and when he is old he will not depart from it.

⁷ The rich rule over the poor, and the borrower is servant to the lender.

3 John 1:2
Amplified Bible (AMP)
² Beloved, I pray that you may prosper in every way and [that your body] may keep well, even as [I know] your soul keeps well *and* prospers.

a. We are changed by the renewing of our mind. Our thinking has to change.

Romans 12:2
Amplified Bible (AMP)
² Do not be conformed to this world (this age), [fashioned after and adapted to its external, superficial customs], but be transformed (changed) by the [entire] renewal of your mind [by its new

ideals and its new attitude], so that you may prove [for yourselves] what is the good and acceptable and perfect will of God, *even* the thing which is good and acceptable and perfect [in His sight for you]

b. The Word is able to save your mind (soul).

James 1:21
Amplified Bible (AMP)
[21] So get rid of all uncleanness and the rampant outgrowth of wickedness, and in a humble (gentle, modest) spirit receive *and* welcome the Word which implanted *and* rooted [in your hearts] contains the power to save your souls.

Proverbs 23:7
Amplified Bible (AMP)
[7] For as he thinks in his heart, so is he. As one who reckons, he says to you, eat and drink, yet his heart is not with you [but is grudging the cost].

LESSON THIRTY-NINE

Bible Purpose Driven:
Daily Wisdom Key for Today:

WHEN I AM IN THE VALLEY I WILL CLIMB THE MOUNTAIN

Verse to Remember: Joel 3:14
'Multitudes, multitudes in the valley of decision! For the day of the Lord is near in the valley of decision.'

Question to Meditate On: My waiting and meditation in the Valley is waiting on the Lord. In my waiting HE will anoint me to go through every situation that comes my way. Now read this scripture and ingest its purpose and truth! Amen.

Mark 11:23-24
Amplified Bible (AMP)
23 Truly I tell you, whoever says to this mountain, be lifted up and thrown into the sea! and does not doubt at all in his heart but believes that what he says will take place, it will be done for him.

24 For this reason I am telling you, whatever you ask for in prayer, believe (trust and be confident) that it is granted to you, and you will [get it].

LESSON FORTY

Proverbs 8:18-21
'Riches and honor are with me, Enduring riches and righteousness. My fruit is better than gold, yes, than fine gold, And my revenue than choice silver. I traverse the way of righteousness, in the midst of the paths of justice, That I may cause those who love me to inherit wealth, That I may fill their treasuries.'

IT'S ALL IN A STATE OF MIND

We've got to think differently

- If you think you're beaten, then you are.
- If you think you dare not, then you won't.
- If you like to win but don't think you can, then you won't.
- If you think you'll lose, you've already lost.
- Success begins with a man's will.
- If you think you're outclassed, then you are.
- You've got to think high to rise.
- You've got to be sure of yourself to win a prize.
- Think big and your deeds will grow.
- Think small and you'll fall behind.
- Think that you can and you will.
- Life's battles don't always go to the stronger, faster man.
- The man who wins is the man who thinks he can.
    . . . for as he thinks in his heart, so is he!

1. 6 stones to kill the Giant of Debt.

Hebrews 13:8
Amplified Bible (AMP)
[8] Jesus Christ (the Messiah) is [always] the same,
yesterday, today, [yes] and forever (to the ages)

a. Stone #1 - God is a debt-canceling God.

If God cancelled debt for anyone, anywhere, anytime ever he has to do it for me today!

- God is no respecter of persons.
- What he does for one, He has to do for me.

Acts 10:34
Amplified Bible (AMP)
[34] And Peter opened his mouth and said: Most certainly *and* thoroughly I now perceive *and* understand that God shows no partiality *and* is no respecter of persons,

2 Kings 4:1-7
Amplified Bible (AMP)
4 Now the wife of a son of the prophets cried to Elisha, your servant my husband is dead, and you know that your servant feared the Lord. But the creditor has come to take my two sons to be his slaves.

[2] Elisha said to her, What shall I do for you? Tell me, what have you [of sale value] in the house? She said, Your handmaid has nothing in the house except a jar of oil.

[3] Then he said, Go around and borrow vessels from all your neighbors, empty vessels—and not a few.

⁴ And when you come in, shut the door upon you and your sons. Then pour out [the oil you have] into all those vessels, setting aside each one when it is full.

⁵ So she went from him and shut the door upon herself and her sons, who brought to her the vessels as she poured the oil.

⁶ When the vessels were all full, she said to her son, Bring me another vessel. And he said to her, There is not a one left. Then the oil stopped multiplying.

⁷ Then she came and told the man of God. He said, Go, sell the oil and pay your debt, and you and your sons live on the rest.

- Common denominator: There was an anointed man of God.
- God knows how to inspire people to buy what you've got
- What have you got in your house. Giftings? Talent? Ability?
- The Key to Debt Deliverance: Whatever He asks you to do, do it.
- Your connection with the man of God and the House of God matters.

2 Kings 6:1-7
Amplified Bible (AMP)

6 The sons of the prophets said to Elisha, Look now, the place where we live before you is too small for us.

² Let us go to the Jordan, and each man get there a [house] beam; and let us make us a place there where we may dwell. And he answered, Go.

³ One said, Be pleased to go with your servants. He answered, I will go.

**⁴ So he went with them. And when they came
to the Jordan, they cut down trees.**

**⁵ But as one was felling his beam, the ax
head fell into the water; and he cried, Alas,
my master, for it was borrowed!**

**⁶ The man of God said, Where did it fall? When
shown the place, Elisha cut off a stick and
threw it in there, and the iron floated.**

**⁷ He said, Pick it up. And he put
out his hand and took it.**

This story illustrates God's attitude to His children
when they are in debt.

- The anointing causes something supernatural to happen
  (it goes against the natural law).

CONFESSION: I am out of debt. Debt-free forever!

God wants you out of debt.

  b. Stone #2

  (1) Do what will get you out of debt.

    - Stop doing the old things like: impulsive buying,
      credit cards, etc.
    - Close any open charge accounts.
    - No more lay away plans.

  (2) Start speaking your freedom.

    - There is a debt-free language.

- Proverbs 18:21. Remember that death and life are in the power of the tongue, and those who love it will eat its fruit.
- Even God called the things 'that be not as though they were.' If you're not saying anything, you're not creating anything. You need to create with your speech, your debt freedom. Call the thing that be not. Call in what is not there. 'I am healed. I am debt-free.'

1 Corinthians 1:28
Amplified Bible (AMP)
28 And God also selected (deliberately chose) what in the world is lowborn *and* insignificant and branded *and* treated with contempt, even the things that are nothing, that He might depose *and* bring to nothing the things that are,

c. Stone#3 - Create an open heaven.

Malachi 3:10
Amplified Bible (AMP)
10 Bring all the tithes (the whole tenth of your income) into the storehouse, that there may be food in My house, and prove Me now by it, says the Lord of hosts, if I will not open the windows of heaven for you and pour you out a blessing, that there shall not be room enough to receive it.

BLESSINGS WITHOUT LIMIT

- Make sure the heavens are not closed over your life.
- How much of God's money is hidden?

- How can God help you get out of debt if you are stealing from Him?
- Covenant connection; connection with the anointing.

d. Stone#4 - Create an out-of-debt flow.

Luke 6:31
Amplified Bible (AMP)
31 And as you would like *and* desire that men would do to you, do exactly so to them.

When was the last time you helped someone else get out of debt?

- The quickest way to get your prayers answered is to pray for someone else and help them to get out of debt.

Galatians 6:7
Amplified Bible (AMP)
7 Do not be deceived *and* deluded *and* misled; God will not allow Himself to be sneered at (scorned, disdained, or mocked [a]by mere pretensions or professions, or by His precepts being set aside.) [He inevitably deludes himself who attempts to delude God.] For whatever a man sows, that *and*[b]that only is what he will reap.

Ephesians 6:8
Amplified Bible (AMP)
8 Knowing that for whatever good anyone does, he will receive his reward from the Lord, whether he is slave or free.

Matthew 6:12
Amplified Bible (AMP)
[12] **And forgive us our debts, as we also have forgiven**
([a]left, remitted, and let go of the debts, and have
[b]given up resentment against) our debtors.

The limited force you exert in helping someone else out of debt will release God's unlimited force to get you out of debt!

- The law of the Anointing: Bear one another burdens, and so fulfill the law of Christ. (Galatians 6:2) Sow and believe for the flow to be created by following the leading of the Lord.

e. Stone #5 - Place heaven on notice of your serious intent to be debt-free. Make a memorial. Give a memorial offering that says, 'I'm serious about this.'

f. Stone #6 - Violent Faith:

Matthew 11:12
Amplified (AMP)
And from the days of John the Baptist until the
present time, the kingdom of heaven has endured
violent assault, and violent men seize it by force (as
a precious prize) - a share in the heavenly kingdom is
sought with most ardent zeal and intense exertion).

- Apply intensity to debt-release. Seize it by force.
- Make your decision to be debt-free.
- Find scriptures regarding debt-freedom and constantly read them, pray them, speak them, praise, sing them, praying in the Holy Spirit and speaking aloud.

- Take the Word of God (shield of faith); stand in the righteousness of God; say "I am the righteousness of God. I have a right to be debt-free"
- Seize your debt freedom – healing, deliverance and what you are believing God for.
- Don't let go of it.

THE WISE AND FAITHFUL SERVANT - STEWARDSHIP AND THE COMING OF THE LORD

Matthew 24:44-51
King James Version (KJV)
"Therefore, you also be ready, for the Son of Man is coming at an hour when you do not expect Him. Who then is a faithful and wise servant, whom his master made ruler over his household, to give them food in due season? Blessed is that servant whom his master, when he comes, will find doing. Assuredly, I say to you that he will make him ruler over all his goods. But and if that evil servant shall say in his heart, My lord delayeth his coming; And shall begin to smite his fellow servants, and to eat and drink with the drunken; the lord of that servant shall come in a day when he looketh not for him, an in a hour that he is not aware of, and shall cut him asunder, and appoint him his portion with the hypocrites: there shall be weeping and gnashing of teeth."

Mattthew 26:1
Amplified bible (AMP)
"Who then is the faithful, thoughtful, and wise servant, whom his master has put in charge of his household to give to others the food and supplies at the proper time? Blessed (happy, fortunate, and to be envied) is that servant whom, when his master comes, he will find so doing."

1. Stewardship -The manager of the household, church, business, etc. and its affairs (free man or slave); Has a leadership role by which God has entrusted with the management of his affairs including: the care of receipts and expenditures and the duty of dealing out the proper portion to every soul.

   a. Traditional interpretation of the Word of God: one thing that is more powerful than the Devil.
   b. Can God depend on you to give the supplies in the proper time?
   c. Altar: the place of the greatest deliverances.
   d. "Blessed" – empowered to succeed and prosper; empowered to do what he could not do.

2. Illustration of The Wise Servant –

Matthew 25:1-4
King James Version (KJV)
"Then the kingdom of heaven shall be likened to ten virgins who took their lamps and went out to meet the bridegroom. Now five of them were wise, and five were foolish. Those who were foolish took their lamps and took no oil with them, but the wise took oil in their vessels with their lamps."

The Faithful Servant -

Matthew 25:14-30
"For the kingdom of heaven is like a man traveling to a far country, who called his own servants and delivered his goods to them. And to one he gave five talents, to another two, and to another one, to each according to his own ability; and immediately he went on a journey.

"Then he who had receive the five talents went and traded with them, and made another five talents. And likewise he who had received two gained two more also. "But he

who had received one went and dug in the ground, and hid his lord's money. "After a long time the lord of those servants came and settled accounts with them. "So, he who had received five talents came and brought five other talents, saying, "Lord, you delivered to me five talents, look, I have gained five more talents besides them. His lord said to him, "Well done, good and faithful servant; you were faithful over a few things, I will make you ruler over many things. Enter into the joy of your lord." "He also who had received two talents came and said, "Lord, you delivered to me two talents; look, I have gained two more talents besides them.' "His lord said to him, "Well done, good and faithful servant; you have been faithful over a few things, I will make you ruler over many things. Enter into the joy of your lord." "Then he who had received the one talent came and said, "Lord, I knew you to be a hard man, reaping where you have not sown, and gathering where you have not scattered seed. "And I was afraid, and went and hid your talent in the ground. Look, there you have what is yours." "But his lord answered and said unto him, "You wicked and lazy servant, you knew that I reap where I have not sown, and gather where I have not scattered seed. "Therefore, you ought to have deposited my money with the bankers, and at my coming I would have received back my own with interest. 'Therefore, take the talent from him, and give it to him who has ten talents. "For to everyone who has, more will be given, and he will have abundance; but from him who does not have, even what he has will be taken away. 'And cast the unprofitable servant into the outer darkness, 'There will be weeping and gnashing of teeth."

How He will Judge –

Matthew 25:31-46
"When the Son of Man comes in His glory, and all the holy angels with, then He will sit on the throne of His glory. "All the nations will be gathered before Him, and He will separate them one from another, as a shepherd divides his sheep

from the goats. "And He will set the sheep on His right hand, but the goats on the left. "Then the King will say to those on His right hand, 'Come you blessed of My Father, inherit the kingdom prepared for you from the foundation of the world: for I was hungry and you gave me food; I was thirsty and you gave Me drink; I was a stranger and you took Me in; I was naked and you clothed Me; I was sick and you visited Me; I was in prison and you came to Me,' "Then the righteous will answer Him, saying, 'Lord, when did we see You hungry and feed You, or thirsty and give You drink? 'When did we see You a stranger and take You in, or naked and clothe You?' "And the King will answer and say to them, 'Assuredly, I say to you, in as much as you did it to one of the least of these My brethren, you did it to Me.' "Then He will also say to those on the left hand, "Depart from Me, you cursed, into the everlasting fire prepared for the devil and his angels: 'for I was hungry and you gave Me no food; I was thirsty and you gave Me no drink; 'I was a stranger and you did not take Me in, naked and you did not clothe Me, sick and in prison and you did not visit Me.' "Then they also will answer Him, saying; 'Lord, when did we see You hungry or thirsty or a stranger or naked or sick or in prison, and did not minister to You?' "Then He will answer them, saying, 'Assuredly, I say to you, in as much as you did not do it to one of the least of these, you did not do it to Me.' "And these will go away into everlasting punishment, but the righteous into eternal life."

The Judgment –

Matthew 25:1-13
Then the kingdom of heaven shall be likened to ten virgins who took their lamps and went out to meet the bridegroom. 'Now five of them were wise, and five were foolish. "Those who were foolish took their lamps and took no oil with them, "but the wise took oil in their vessels with their lamps. "But while the bridegroom was delayed they all slumbered and slept. "And at midnight a cry was heard 'Behold, the bridegroom is coming; go out to meet him!' "Then all those

virgins arose and trimmed their lamps. "And the foolish said to the wise, 'Give us some of your oil, for our lamps are going out.' "But the wise answered, saying, 'No, lest there should not be enough for us and you; but go rather to those who sell, and buy for yourselves.' "And while they went to buy, the bridegroom came, and those who were ready went in with him to the wedding; and the door was shut. "Afterward the other virgins came also, saying 'Lord, Lord, open to us!' "But he answered and said, 'Assuredly, I say to you, I do not know you.' "Watch therefore, for you know neither the day nor the hour in which the Son of Man is coming.

a. Oil: a type of the anointing. How did they relate to the anointing?
b. Wise: already had made an investment in oil, "Go and use your money to get your oil."
c. When Jesus comes, how will He find you investing your funds?

The Good and Faithful Servant –

Matthew 25:14-30
King James Version (KJV)
[14] For the kingdom of heaven is as a man travelling into a far country, who called his own servants, and delivered unto them his goods.

[15] And unto one he gave five talents, to another two, and to another one; to every man according to his several abilities; and straightway took his journey.

[16] Then he that had received the five talents went and traded with the same, and made them other five talents.

[17] And likewise he that had received two, he also gained other two.

¹⁸ But he that had received one went and digged
in the earth, and hid his lord's money.

¹⁹ After a long time the lord of those servants
cometh, and reckoneth with them.

²⁰ And so he that had received five talents came and brought
other five talents, saying, Lord, thou deliveredst unto me five
talents: behold, I have gained beside them five talents more.

²¹ His lord said unto him, Well done, thou good
and faithful servant: thou hast been faithful over
a few things, I will make thee ruler over many
things: enter thou into the joy of thy lord.

²² He also that had received two talents came and said,
Lord, thou deliveredst unto me two talents: behold,
I have gained two other talents beside them.

²³ His lord said unto him, Well done, good and faithful servant;
thou hast been faithful over a few things, I will make thee
ruler over many things: enter thou into the joy of thy lord.

²⁴ Then he which had received the one talent
came and said, Lord, I knew thee that thou art
a hard man, reaping where thou hast not sown,
and gathering where thou hast not strawed:

²⁵ And I was afraid, and went and hid thy talent in
the earth: lo, there thou hast that is thine.

²⁶ His lord answered and said unto him, thou wicked
and slothful servant, thou knewest that I reap where
I sowed not, and gather where I have not strawed:

²⁷ Thou oughtest therefore to have put my money
to the exchangers, and then at my coming I
should have received mine own with usury.

**²⁸ Take therefore the talent from him, and give
it unto him which hath ten talents.**

**²⁹ For unto everyone that hath shall be given, and he
shall have abundance: but from him that hath not
shall be taken away even that which he hath.**

**³⁰ And cast ye the unprofitable servant into outer darkness:
there shall be weeping and gnashing of teeth.**

    d. Prophesy: You are not ready for investment until you
have decided to establish God as your source. You must
first learn how to harvest from God before you learn
how to harvest from the world. If you learn how to
harvest from God first, then if the investment doesn't
go right you won't be the one climbing on a building and
jumping off, because you know how to sow a seed and
get a harvest. Harvest from God first – then investment
second.

    e. Real Bible worship includes what you do with your
money.

3. Money with a mission.

Luke 12:13-21
**Then one from the crowd said to Him "Teacher, tell my
brother to divide the inheritance with me." But He said to him,
"Man, who made Me a judge or an arbitrator over you?" And
He said to them, "Take heed and beware of covetousness,
for one's life does not consist in the abundance of things
he possesses." Then He spoke a parable to them, saying**

**"The ground of a certain rich man yielded plentifully. "And
thought within himself, saying, 'What shall I do, since I have
no room to store my crops?' "So, he said, 'I will do this: I will
pull down my barns and build greater, and there I will store
all my crops and my goods. 'And I will say to my soul, "Soul,**

you have many goods laid up for many years; take your ease; eat, drink, and be merry.'" "But God said to him, 'You fool! This night your soul will be required of you; then whose will those things be which you have provided? "So is he who lays up treasure for himself, and is not rich toward God."

a. We are to be distribution centers.
b. We are to begin to distribute when He gives the orders!
c. When the owner shows up to tell you to give something, He knows what you are going to need in your future.
d. Whenever you look in your hand and it is not enough, it is not your harvest – it is your seed.

4. Watching Servants

Luke 12:35-42
Amplified bible (AMP)
And the Lord said, "Who then is that faithful steward, the wise man whom his master set over those in his household service to supply them their allowance of food at the appointed time?"

Luke 19:1-11
New King James Version (NKJV)
Then Jesus entered and passed through Jericho. Now behold, there was a man named Zacchaeus who was a chief tax collector, and he was rich. And he sought to see who Jesus was, but could not because of the crowd, for he was of short stature. So, he ran ahead and climbed up into a sycamore tree to see Him, for He was going to pass that way. And when Jesus came to the place, He looked up and saw him, said to him, "Zacchaeus, make haste and come down, for today I must stay at your house." So, he made haste and came down, and received Him joyfully. But when they saw it, they all murmured, saying, "He has gone to be a guest with a man who is a sinner." Then Zacchaeus stood and said to the Lord, "Look, Lord, I give

**half my goods to the poor; and if I have taken anything
from anyone by false accusation, I restore fourfold." And
Jesus said to him, "Today salvation has come to this
house, because he also is a son of Abraham; "for the
Son of Man has come to seek and to save that which was
lost." Now as they heard these things, He spoke another
parable, because He was near Jerusalem and because they
thought the kingdom of God would appear immediately.**

    a. They thought the end was coming because wealth was being transferred – a sign of the times.

**Luke 19:12-13
He said therefore, A certain nobleman went
into a far country to receive for himself a
kingdom, and to return. And he called his ten
servants, and delivered them ten pounds,
and said unto them, Occupy till I come.**

    b. Go, sell and trade. Busy yourself. What is your gift? You have to step out in order to step up!

      • Anointing, healing, deliverance, finances

**Romans 8:32
Amplified bible (AMP)
He who did not withhold or spare (even His own Son)
but gave Him up for us all, will He not also with Him
freely and graciously give us all (other) things?**

    c. What is there that He won't give us, when He already given us His own Son?

The Money & Anointing Connection

1. Money is tied to the issues of life.

Isaiah 10:27
King James Version (KJV)
It shall come to pass in that day that his burden will be taken away from your shoulder, and his yoke from your neck, and the yoke will be destroyed because of the anointing oil.

2. Destroyed – no more usefulness.

    a. Anointing – God's ability added to your ability to give you the ability to do what you didn't have the ability to do before!
        -   Burden removing,
        -   Yoke destroying power.
    b. Sweatless victories: the anointing added to your work.
    c. Whatever the burden is, there is an anointing available to remove it.

John 14:12
King James Version (KJV)
Verily, verily, I say unto you, He that believeth on me, the works that I do shall he do also; and greater works than these shall he do; because I go unto My Father.

Luke 16:1-10
And He said to His disciples: "There was a certain rich man who had a steward, and an accusation was brought to him that this man was wasting his goods. "So, he called him and said to him, "What is this I hear about you? Give an account of your stewardship, for you can no longer be steward.' "Then the steward said within himself, 'What shall I do? For my master is taking the stewardship

away from me. I cannot dig; I am ashamed to beg. I have resolved what to do, that when I am put out of the stewardship, they may receive me into their houses.' "So, he called every one of his master's debtors to him, and said to the first, "How much do you owe my master? "And he said a hundred measures of oil.' So, he said to him, 'Take your bill, and sit down quickly and write fifty.' "Then he said to another, 'And how much do you owe?' So, he said, 'A hundred measures of wheat.' And he said to him,

'Take your bill, and write eighty.' "So, the master commended the unjust steward because he had dealt shrewdly. For the sons of this world are more shrewd in their generation than the sons of light.

3. Good stewardship over goods.

    a. Make good use of worldly riches. What are you doing with the worldly wealth God has put into your hands?
    b. Use your money to get people into this covenant.
    c. Friend – a covenant term.
    d. "Least" and "Much" rather than quantities, refer to categories or <u>distinctions</u>: Least, Much, Unrighteous mammon, True riches
    e. Your faithfulness with money will determine whether you enter into the greater. e.g. Tithing.
    f. Wrong relationship with material wealth (love of money) is the root of every evil and wicked thing the Devil does.

Colossians 1:27
To them God willed to make known what are the riches of the glory of this mystery among the Gentiles: which is Christ in you, the hope of glory.

4. Riches of His glory

   a. "The riches" – Christ in you.
   b. Christ – The anointed One <u>and</u> His anointing.
   c. "True riches" = the anointing.

Ephesians 3:8
'To me, whom am less than the least of all the saints,
this grace was given, that I should preach among
the Gentiles the unsearchable riches of Christ'

5. Christ's riches.

   a. Unsearchable riches = the anointing
   b. Riches of wisdom . . . riches of knowledge... (burden removing, yoke destroying anointing).

Luke 16:11
'Therefore, if you have not been faithful
in the unrighteous mammon, who will
commit to your trust the true riches?'

6. Faithfulness is required.

   a. "True riches" = anointing
   b. If you have not been faithful (dependable and trustworthy) with money, who will commit to your trust the anointing?
   c. Do the "life test": Are burdens being removed? Are yokes being destroyed?

7. Every time somebody needed God to show up and show out they gave a sacrificial gift.

II Chronicles 20:20
New King James Version (NKJV)
Believe in the LORD your God, and you shall be established; believe His prophets, and you shall prosper.

   a. Ignorance breeds mistrust.
   b. Your prosperity is in the hands of God.

LESSON FORTY

Bible Purpose Driven:
Daily Wisdom Key for Today:

IT'S ALL IN A STATE OF MIND:

Verse to Remember: Proverbs 8:18-21
**'Riches and honor are with me, Enduring riches
and righteousness. My fruit is better than gold, yes,
than fine gold, And my revenue than choice silver. I
traverse the way of righteousness, in the midst of the
paths of justice, That I may cause those who love me
to inherit wealth, That I may fill their treasuries.'**

Question to Meditate On: I will be a giver and not a taker because God is a giving GOD. Like Father, like Son because we are in HIS purpose. It is what drives me to be a mouthpiece for HIM. Hallelujah, Hallelujah, Hallelujah.

LESSON FORTY-ONE

Matthew 6:19-20
New King James Version (NKJV)
**'Do not lay up for yourselves treasures on earth,
where moth and rust destroys and where thieves
break in and steal; but lay up for yourselves treasures
in heaven, where neither moth nor rust destroys
and where thieves do not break in and steal.'**

THE KINGDOM LAW OF RICHES

There is a peace that comes to us when we know we are doing ok financially. Likewise, there is an anxiety that plagues our lives when we are not quite sure how ends are going to be met. When we have money, we feel in control. But Jesus tells us to store up treasures for ourselves in heaven. Where moth and rust do not destroy, and where thieves do not break in. And Peter tells us that as a part of our adoption as God's children, we have a heavenly inheritance that is incorruptible, untouchable. The inheritance and God's provision for us, in general, is completely reliable and brings a greater sense of assurance and peace than any amount of money.

Hebrews 7:25
New King James Version (NKJV)
**'Therefore, He is also able to save to the uttermost
those who come to God through Him, since He
always lives to make intercession for them.'**

From the above scripture is crystal clear that when you and I do alms and tithes and sow seed to others, the Lord takes them through intercession, to the Father and the Father sends His angel and His anointing to bring you and I the harvest. Hallelujah. We must be doers and press in. Don't give up, continue to sow your seed. Just like a farmer who farms the land, place your seed in a good ground, be patient and confess and believe that your harvest is on its way.

JESUS PROMISED US AN INHERITANCE THAT WILL NEVER SPOIL OR FADE

Ephesians 5:2
Amplified Bible (AMP)
2 And walk in love, [esteeming and delighting in one another] as Christ loved us and gave Himself up for us, a [a]slain offering and sacrifice to God [for you, so that it became] a sweet fragrance.

Hebrews 13:15
Amplified Bible (AMP)
15 Through Him, therefore, let us constantly *and* at all times offer up to God a sacrifice of praise, which is the fruit of lips that thankfully acknowledge *and* confess *and* glorify His name.

Philippians 4:18
Amplified Bible (AMP)
18 But I have [your full payment] and more; I have everything I need *and* am amply supplied, now that I have received from Epaphroditus the gifts you sent me. [They are the] fragrant odor of an offering *and* sacrifice which God welcomes *and* in which He delights.

1. Sacrifice: an act or offering to God, a precious gift to God, surrendering that which means something to you.

   a. Who is the master of your life?

Luke 16:11-14
Amplified Bible (AMP)

11 Therefore if you have not been faithful in the [case of] unrighteous mammon ([a]deceitful riches, money, possessions), who will entrust to you the true riches?

12 And if you have not proved faithful in that which belongs to another [whether God or man], who will give you that which is your own [that is, [b]the true riches]?

13 No servant is able to serve two masters; for either he will hate the one and love the other, or he will stand by *and* be devoted to the one and despise the other. You cannot serve God and mammon (riches, or [c]anything in which you trust and on which you rely).

14 Now the Pharisees, who were covetous *and* lovers of money, heard all these things [taken together], and they began to sneer at *and* ridicule *and* scoff at Him.

   b. Elijah/Elisha: see eye to eye, then you will receive my anointing.
   c. How do I know if I am serving two masters?

CONFESSION: God is my source!

Malachi 3:3-5:
Amplified Bible (AMP)

3 He will sit as a refiner and purifier of silver, and He will purify the priests, the sons of Levi, and refine them like gold and silver, that they may offer to the Lord offerings in righteousness.

⁴ Then will the offering of Judah and Jerusalem be pleasing to the Lord as in the days of old and as in ancient years.

⁵ Then I will draw near to you for judgment; I will be a swift witness against the sorcerers, against the adulterers, against the false swearers, and against those who oppress the hireling in his wages, the widow and the fatherless, and who turn aside the temporary resident from his right and fear not Me, says the Lord of hosts.

    d. Monies given out of the comfort zone, and in obedience to God, set yourself up for God to come near and are a <u>connection.</u>

2. Cornelius gave and prayed and God showed up.

Acts 10:1-4
Amplified Bible (AMP)
10 Now [living] at Caesarea there was a man whose name was Cornelius, a centurion (captain) of what was known as the Italian Regiment,

² A devout man who venerated God *and* treated Him with reverential obedience, as did all his household; and he gave much alms to the people and prayed continually to God.

³ About the ninth hour (about 3:00 p.m.) of the day he saw clearly in a vision an angel of God entering and saying to him, Cornelius!

⁴ And he, gazing intently at him, became frightened and said, What is it, Lord? And the angel said to him, Your prayers and your [generous] gifts to the poor have come up [as a sacrifice] to God *and* have been remembered by Him.

3. Sacrifice offered, God showed up.

Genesis 46:1-4
Amplified Bible (AMP)
**46 So Israel made his journey with all that he had and
came to Beersheba [a place hallowed by sacred memories]
and offered sacrifices to the God of his father Isaac.**

**² And God spoke to Israel in visions of the night,
and said, Jacob! Jacob! And he said, Here am I.**

**³ And He said, I am God, the God of your father;
do not be afraid to go down to Egypt, for I
will there make of you a great nation.**

**⁴ I will go down with you to Egypt, and I will also surely bring
you [your people Israel] up again; and Joseph will put his
hand upon your eyes [when they are about to close in death].**

4. Solomon tapped into the power God at Gibeon.

II Chronicles 1:3
King James Version (KJV)
**'Then Solomon, and all the congregation with him,
went to the high place that was at Gibeon; for the
tabernacle of meeting with God was there, which Moses
the servant of the Lord had made in the wilderness'**

II Chronicles 1:6-7
King James Version (KJV)
**'And Solomon went up there to the bronze altar before the
Lord, which was at the tabernacle of meeting, and offered a
thousand burnt offerings on it. - On that night God appeared
to Solomon and said to him, "Ask! What shall I give you?"**

5. Every time Solomon gave a sacrificial offering God showed up.

I Kings 8:63
King James Version (KJV)
And Solomon offered a sacrifice of peace offerings, which he offered to the Lord, twenty-two thousand bulls and one hundred and twenty thousand sheep. So, the king and all the children of Israel dedicated the house of the Lord.

I Kings 9:12
King James Version (KJV)
Then Hiram went from Tyre to see the cities which Solomon had given him, but they did not please him.

I Kings 9:1-2
King James Version (KJV)
And it came to pass, when Solomon had finished building the house of the Lord and the king's house, and all Solomon's desire which he wanted to do, that the Lord appeared to Solomon the second time, as He appeared to him at Gibeon.

6. The power of a sacrificial offering.

I Kings 17:8-10
King James Version (KJV)
Then the word of the Lord came to him, saying "Arise, go to Zarephath, which belongs to Sidon, and dwell there. See, I have commanded a widow there to provide for you." So he arose and went to Zarephath. And when he came to the gate of the city, indeed a woman was there gathering sticks. And he called to her and said, "Please bring me a little water in a cup, that I may drink."

a. The Lord had already told the widow to look after the prophet's needs.

b. The prophet challenged the two areas that were of greatest need: water and food.

c. The number one enemy of giving something out of your comfort zone is 'fear'. How am I going to make it if I give this?

d. Put your 'not enough' into anointed hands and it will become the 'more than enough' and 'over and above'.

e. Your future provision is based upon your present-day obedience.

f. Nothing 'just happens'. A man's heart is based solely on the seeds he sows.

g. The widow obeyed and gave . . . and God showed up with oil, a meal and her son!

7. I Kings 18:21-24; 26-27; 31-46 -

1 Kings 18:21-24
Amplified Bible (AMP)
21 Elijah came near to all the people and said, how long will you halt *and* limp between two opinions? If the Lord is God, follow Him! But if Baal, then follow him. And the people did not answer him a word.

22 Then Elijah said to the people, I, I only, remain a prophet of the Lord, but Baal's prophets are 450 men.

23 Let two bulls be given us; let them choose one bull for themselves and cut it in pieces and lay it on the wood but put no fire to it. I will dress the other bull, lay it on the wood, and put no fire to it.

24 Then you call on the name of your god, and I will call on the name of the Lord; and the One Who answers by fire, let Him be God. And all the people answered, It is well spoken.

1 Kings 18:26-27
Amplified Bible (AMP)

26 So they took the bull given them, dressed it, and called on the name of Baal from morning until noon, saying, O Baal, hear *and* answer us! But there was no voice; no one answered. And they leaped upon *or* limped about the altar they had made.

27 At noon Elijah mocked them, saying, Cry aloud, for he is a god; either he is musing, or he has gone aside, or he is on a journey, or perhaps he is asleep and must be awakened.

1 Kings 18:31-46
Amplified Bible (AMP)

31 Then Elijah took twelve stones, according to the number of the tribes of the sons of Jacob, to whom the word of the Lord came, saying, Israel shall be your name.

32 And with the stones Elijah built an altar in the name [and self-revelation] of the Lord. He made a trench about the altar as great as would contain two measures of seed.

33 He put the wood in order and cut the bull in pieces and laid it on the wood and said, fill four jars with water and pour it on the burnt offering and the wood.

34 And he said, Do it the second time. And they did it the second time. And he said, Do it the third time. And they did it the third time.

35 The water ran round about the altar, and he filled the trench also with water.

36 At the time of the offering of the evening sacrifice, Elijah the prophet came near and said, O Lord, the God of Abraham, Isaac, and Israel, let it be known this day

that You are God in Israel and that I am Your servant
and that I have done all these things at Your word.

³⁷ Hear me, O Lord, hear me, that this people
may know that You, the Lord, are God, and
have turned their hearts back [to You].

³⁸ Then the fire of the Lord fell and consumed the burnt
sacrifice and the wood and the stones and the dust,
and also licked up the water that was in the trench.

³⁹ When all the people saw it, they fell on their faces and
they said, The Lord, He is God! The Lord, He is God!

⁴⁰ And Elijah said, Seize the prophets of Baal; let
not one escape. They seized them, and Elijah
brought them down to the brook Kishon, and
[as God's law required] slew them there.

⁴¹ And Elijah said to Ahab, Go up, eat and drink,
for there is the sound of abundance of rain.

⁴² So Ahab went up to eat and to drink. And Elijah went
up to the top of Carmel; and he bowed himself down
upon the earth and put his face between his knees

⁴³ And said to his servant, Go up now, look toward
the sea. And he went up and looked and said, there
is nothing. Elijah said, Go again seven times.

⁴⁴ And at the seventh time the servant said, A cloud
as small as a man's hand is arising out of the sea.
And Elijah said, Go up, say to Ahab, Hitch your
chariot and go down, lest the rain stop you.

⁴⁵ In a little while, the heavens were black with wind-swept
clouds, and there was a great rain. And Ahab went to Jezreel.

**⁴⁶ The hand of the Lord was on Elijah. He
girded up his loins and ran before Ahab to the
entrance of Jezreel [nearly twenty miles].**

a. They were in a drought situation.
b. You will never give something sacrificially, and not see that same thing come back to you in a flood!
c. You don't give away in God's Kingdom –you <u>sow</u> into a gain, not a loss. When you sow, expect it to come back greater than when it left.
d. vs. 38 – 'The fire of God fell' ... God showed up and He accepted the sacrifice.
e. Offering – to make an offer.
f. If you don't see anything the first time you look then keep going back until you see something! Because surely the sound of Abundance will show up in your life because you obeyed God.
g. When you <u>sow</u>, you <u>know</u> that there will be a harvest.
h. When you give as God has instructed you to give, there will be an anointing upon your life and the hand of God will be upon your life.
i. Must be able to distinguish from average results vs. hearing the sound of abundance.
j. We serve God <u>with</u> money - not – We serve God <u>and</u> money.
k. Just enough is not enough.

8. II Chronicles 5:6, 13,14

a. Why did the glory of the Lord fill the temple?
b. Sacrifice was made . . . and God showed up.
c. There is something greater than money – the anointing (burdens removed, yokes destroyed). I declare it now!

1. Restoration – whatever is lost will be restored.
2. Supernatural Progress – 'speed it up!'
3. Supernatural Favor – divinely arranged.
4. A change of status – changed into another man.

Congratulations, you finished another lesson and by now are beginning to incorporate these teachings into your financial life. You almost done with this book and will soon be ready to pass it on to a friend and get them out of debt and into God's promises! Now re-read these points this week in this lesson and then repeat this bible purpose driven prayer to the Lord:

I BELIEVE I'VE RECEIVED THIS DAY, RESTORATION, SUPERNATURAL PROGRESS, SUPERNATURAL FAVOR AND A CHANGE OF STATUS UPON ME NOW, IN JESUS' NAME, AMEN.

LESSON FORTY-ONE

Bible Purpose Driven:
Daily Wisdom Key for Today:

THE KINGDOM LAW OF RICHES

Verse to Remember: Matthew 6:19-20
King James Version (KJV)
'Do not lay up for yourselves treasures on earth,
where moth and rust destroys and where thieves
break in and steal; but lay up for yourselves treasures
in heaven, where neither moth nor rust destroys
and where thieves do not break in and steal.'

Question to Meditate On: Open your front door and say this out loud:

'SICKNESS, POVERTY AND DISEASE, YOU
ARE NOT WELCOMED IN MY HOUSE ANY
MORE. THERE'S THE DOOR, GO!' THEN LIFT
UP YOUR FINGER IN THE AIR AND MAKE
A CIRCLE MOTION AND CONFESS THIS,
"HEALTH, WEALTH AND PROSPERITY

WONDER NO MORE, YOU ARE WELCOMED IN MY
HOUSE FOREVER MORE, IN JESUS' NAME, AMEN.

LESSON FORTY-TWO

Numbers 25:12
King James Version (KJV)
Therefore say, "Behold, I give to him My covenant of peace."

THE PEACE & PROSPERITY CONNECTION

1. Covenant of Peace.

Ezekiel 34:25
King James Version (KJV)
"I will make a covenant of peace with them, and cause wild beasts to cease from the land; and they will dwell safely in the wilderness and sleep in the woods."

Malachi 2:5
King James Version (KJV)
"My covenant was with him, one of life and peace, and I gave them to him that he might fear Me; so he feared Me; and was reverent before My name."

Isaiah 54:10
King James Version (KJV)
"For the mountains shall depart and the hills removed, but My kindness shall not depart from you, nor shall My covenant of peace be removed", says the LORD, who has mercy on you.

    a. Covenant: pledge, vow promise between two or more parties to carry out terms agreed upon; only broken by death.

    b. Peace: calmness of mind, serenity.

2. The anointing will support money with a mission – but not greed or selfishness.

Colossians 1:27
Amplified Bible (AMP)
'To them God will make known what are the riches of the glory of this mystery among the Gentiles: which is Christ (the Anointed One, and His anointing) in you, the hope of glory.'

    a. The riches = the anointing.

    b. This anointing will be so heavy on our lives that sinners will take notice. Your presence among Gentiles (sinners) will demand an explanation.

    c. We are pregnant with the power of God. Bone-deep anointing.

    d. The anointing is in you for a purpose. The anointing brings results.

    e. Hope: earnest expectation; looking and expecting to receive something.

    f. The anointing gives us the right to expect glory and we're going to do this amongst sinners!

    g. Glory: weight; the manifested Word; the manifested presence of God in our lives!

    h. God wants the sinners to see the glory that you expected.

3. Genesis 30:43–31:1

King James Version (KJV)
Thus the man became exceedingly prosperous, and had large flocks, female and male servants, and camels and donkeys. – Now Jacob heard the words of Laban's sons,

saying, "Jacob has taken away all that was our father's, and from what was our father's he has acquired all this wealth."

a. First time the word 'glory' is used in scripture.

Psalm 49:16-17
King James Version (KJV)
Do not be afraid when one becomes rich,
when the glory of his house is increased; for
when he dies he shall carry nothing away;
his glory shall not descend after him.

b. Glory – refers to material wealth that comes from God's blessing

c. Glory - chabod (kah-vohd): Weightiness; that which is substantial or heavy; glory, honor, splendor, power wealth, authority, magnificence, fame, dignity, riches and excellency. The root of chabod is chabad, 'to be heavy, glorious, notable,' or 'to be renowned' In the OT, 'heaviness' represented honor and substance, while 'lightness' was equated with vanity, instability, temporariness and emptiness.

4. Isaiah 60:1-3

Arise, shine; for your light has come! And the glory of
the Lord is risen upon you. For behold, the darkness
shall cover the earth, and deep darkness the people;
But the Lord will arise over you, and His glory will
be seen upon you. The Gentiles shall come to your
light, and kings to the brightness of your rising.

a. Those without Christ will see His glory upon you, and be drawn to you.

b. Problem: If this glory has to be spiritually discerned, then sinners won't be able to recognize it and come to it.

I Corinthians 2:14
But the natural man does not receive the things of the Spirit of God, for they are foolishness to him; nor can he know them, because they are spiritually discerned.

5. Isaiah 60:4-5

Amplified Bible (AMP)
[4] **Lift up your eyes round about you and see! They all gather themselves together, they come to you. Your sons shall come from afar, and your daughters shall be carried and nursed in the arms.**

[5] **Then you shall see and be radiant, and your heart shall thrill and tremble with joy [at the glorious deliverance] and be enlarged; because the abundant wealth of the [Dead] [a]Sea shall be turned to you, unto you shall the nations come with their treasures.**

a. The glory that shall be seen by the Gentiles is the wealth that will come unto you!
b. Abundance: the noise of the great mass of people coming to see the glory on our lives.
c. Fight the spirit of shame.

6. Haggai 2:6-9

Amplified Bible (AMP)
[6] **For thus says the Lord of hosts: Yet once more, in a little while, I will shake and make tremble the [starry] heavens, the earth, the sea, and the dry land;**

[7] **And I will shake all nations and the [a]desire and the precious things of all nations shall come in, and I will fill this house with splendor, says the Lord of hosts.**

[8] **The silver is Mine and the gold is Mine, says the Lord of hosts.**

⁹ The latter glory of this house [with its successor, to which Jesus came] shall be greater than the former, says the Lord of hosts; and in this place will I give peace *and* prosperity, says the Lord of hosts.

a. Latter house: me/us
    Former house: Solomon, Job, Abraham, Elijah, Jesus . . .
b. My peace is directly connected to my prosperity.

Lamentations 3:17
Amplified Bible (AMP)
¹⁷ And You have bereaved my soul *and* cast it off far from peace; I have forgotten what good *and* happiness *are*.

7. Definitions:

a. Peace (shalom): similar to (Greek) soteria – salvation; completeness; prosperity; for a man to have his peace there can be nothing missing (nothing missing, nothing broken). E.g. ox for an ox; eye for an eye.
b. Prosperity: having a good trip; bringing your monies together; prospering in every area of your life.

1 Thessalonians 5:23
Amplified Bible (AMP)
²³ And may the God of peace Himself sanctify you through and through [separate you from profane things, make you pure and wholly consecrated to God]; and may your spirit and soul and body be preserved sound *and* complete [and found] blameless at the coming of our Lord Jesus Christ (the Messiah).

8. I Samuel 10:1-6

Then Samuel took a flask of oil and poured it on his head, and kissed him and said: "Is it not because the Lord has

anointed you commander over His inheritance? "When you have departed from me today, you will find two men by Rachel's tomb in the territory of Benjamin at Zelzah; and they will say to you, "The donkeys which you went to look for have been found. And now your father has ceased caring about the donkeys and is worrying about you saying, "What shall I do about my son?" "Then you shall go on from there and come to the Terebinth tree of Tabor. There three men going up to God at Bethel will meet you, one carrying three young goats, another carrying three loaves of bread, and another carrying a skin of wine. "And they will greet you and give you two loaves of bread, which you shall receive from their hands. "After that you shall come to the hill of God where the Philistine garrison is. And it will happen, when you have come there to the city, that you will meet a group of prophets coming down from the high place with a stringed instrument, a tambourine, a flute, and a harp before them; and they will be prophesying. Then the Spirit of the Lord will come upon you, and you will prophesy with them and be turned into another man. "And let it be, when these signs come to you, that you do as the occasion demands, for God is with you. "You shall go down before me to Gilgal; and surely I will come down to you to offer burnt offerings and make sacrifices of peace offerings. Seven days you shall wait, till I come to you and show you what you should do." And so, it was, when he had turned his back to go from Samuel that God gave him another heart; and all those signs came to pass that day. When they came to the hill, there was a group of prophets to meet him; and the Spirit of God came upon him, and he prophesied among them.

The anointing will bring:

- Restoration – that which was lost will be found.
- Progress – to move forward.
- Favor – you didn't even ask for it.
- Change of status – changed into another man.

Genesis 15:13-15
Amplified Bible (AMP)
¹³ And [God] said to Abram, know positively that your descendants will be strangers dwelling as temporary residents in a land that is not theirs [Egypt], and they will be slaves there and will be afflicted *and* oppressed for 400 years. [Fulfilled in Exod. 12:40.]

¹⁴ But I will bring judgment on that nation whom they will serve, and afterward they will come out with great possessions.

¹⁵ And you shall go to your fathers in peace; you shall be buried at a good old (hoary) age.

a. What the Church is about to go through, has already been foreshadowed in the Old Testament.
b. Go to your fathers in peace: nothing missing or broken.

Ephesians 5:27
Amplified Bible (AMP)
²⁷ That He might present the church to Himself in glorious splendor, without spot or wrinkle or any such things [that she might be holy and faultless].

Psalm 105:37
Amplified Bible (AMP)
³⁷ He brought [Israel] forth also with silver and gold, and there was not one feeble person among their tribes.

LESSON FORTY-TWO

Bible Purpose Driven:
Daily Wisdom Key for Today:

The Peace and Prosperity Connection

Verse to Remember: Numbers 25:12
Therefore say, "Behold, I give to him My covenant of peace."

Question to Meditate On: Financial support - I DECLARE:

I AM OUT OF DEBT AND ALL MY NEEDS ARE MET;
THERE IS MUCH MORE IN THE STOREHOUSE,
MY FATHER'S HOUSE, WHERE IT CAME FROM.
THEREFORE, IN JESUS' NAME I COMMAND
THE ANGELS OF THE LORD TO GO FORTH
AND CAST OUT AND CAST DOWN ALL THE
STRONGHOLDS OF THE SPIRIT OF POVERTY.
AND I COMMAND MINISTERING ANGELS TO
GO FORWARD TO BRING FINANCIAL BLESSINGS
TO ME TO INHERIT MY PROVISION NOW.

Hebrews 1:13,14
But to which of the angels has He ever said: "sit at My
right hand, till I make Your enemies Your footstool"?
Are they not all ministering spirits sent forth to
minister for those who will inherit salvation?

LESSON FORTY-THREE

Zechariah 14:13-14
It shall come to pass in that day that a great panic from the Lord will be among them. Everyone will seize the hand of his neighbor, And raise his hand against his neighbor's hand; Judah also will fight at Jerusalem. And the wealth of all the surrounding nations shall be gathered together: Gold, silver, and apparel in great abundance.

MONEY IS LOOKING FOR ME

1.   There is a soon-coming wealth transfer!

Isaiah 60:5-
Then you shall see and become radiant, and your heart shall swell with joy; because the abundance of the sea shall be turn to you, the wealth of the Gentiles shall come to you.

   a.   Money is moving! Money is crying:

James 5:1-8
Come now, you rich, weep and howl for your miseries that are coming upon you! your riches are corrupted, and your garments are moth-eaten. Your gold and silver are corroded, and their corrosion will be a witness against you and will eat your flesh like fire. You have heaped up treasure in the last days. Indeed the wages of the laborers who mowed your fields, which you kept back by fraud, cry out; and the cries of the reapers have reached the ears of the Lord of Sabbath. You have lived on the earth in pleasure

and luxury; you have fattened your hearts as in a day of slaughter. You have condemned, you have murdered the just; he does not resist you. Therefore, be patient, brethren, until the coming of the Lord. See how the farmer waits for the precious fruit of the earth, waiting patiently for it until it receives the early and latter rain. You also be patient. Establish your hearts, for the coming of the Lord is at hand.

b. vs. 4: The money is crying; and the laborers are crying.
c. Money cometh is the battle cry of the Body of Christ in these last days. We've got to release the battle cry! Wealth and riches shall be in my house! "Psalm 112:3
d. We've been aggressive about our giving but we need to be aggressive about our harvest.

CONFESSION: I'm a money magnet! Money, thou art loosed! Money cometh to me now! I harvest money because I sow money.

e. The money is crying. and the laborers are crying into the ears of the Lord of Sabbath (Lord of the Heavenly Host).
f. See yourself harvesting. Get your expectations up.
g. Get out of Lodebar tonight (II Sam. 9:3-13) Then the king said, "Is there not still someone of the house of Saul, to whom I may show kindness of God?" And Ziba said to the king,

CONFESSION: I'll never be broke another day in my life!

2. Initiate a change of status. Reach out beyond everything that says, "You're not" and "You won't be"

a. All this is going to happen before the coming of the Lord. Wait patiently for the seed to manifest.
b. Establish the time zone.

Hebrews 11:1
Now faith **is the substance of things hope**
for, the evidence of things not seen.

Romans 3:23-25
for all have sinned and fall short of the glory of
God, being justified freely by His grace through the
redemption that is in Christ Jesus, whom God set
forth to be a propitiation by His blood, through faith,
to demonstrate His righteousness, because in
His forbearance God had passed over the
sins that were previously committed,

Genesis 21:1-2
And the Lord visited Sarah as He had said, and the
Lord did for Sarah as He had spoken. For Sarah
conceived and bore Abraham a son in his old age,
at the set time of which God had spoken to him.

c.   Laughter is a symptom of victory being at hand.

Galatians 4:4
But when the fullness of the time had come, God sent
forth His Son, born of a woman, born under the law.

Matthew 3:1-2
In those days John, the Baptist came preaching
in the wilderness of Judea, and saying, "Repent,
for the kingdom of heaven is at hand!"

Psalm 102:13
You will arise and have mercy on Zion; for the
time to favor her, yes, the set time, has come.

d.   The set time to favor Zion has come!

e. If you are going to get your harvest, you need to get in the 'Now Zone'

Psalm 118:23-25
This was the Lord's doing; It is marvelous in our eyes. This is the day which the Lord has made; we will rejoice and be glad in it. Save now, I pray, O Lord; O Lord, I pray, send now prosperity.

f. Rejoice now! Praise Him now! I receive now Prosperity!

3. What do I do between 'now by faith' and the manifestation?

a. Rejoice: brighten up; leap, spin around.

Rejoice always (I Thess. 5:16).

Isaiah 40:28-31
King James Version (KJV)
Have you not known? Have you not heard? The everlasting God, the Lord, the Creator of the ends of the earth, neither faints nor is weary. There is no searching of His understanding. He gives power to the weak, and to those who have no might He increases strength. Even the youths shall faint and be weary, and young men shall utterly fall, but those who wait on the Lord shall renew their strength.

Job 27:8-17
For what is the hope the hypocrite, though he may gain much, if God takes away his life? Will God hear his cry when trouble comes upon him? Will he delight himself in the Almighty? Will he always call on God? I will teach you about the hand of God; What is with the Almighty I will not conceal. Surely all of you have seen it; why then do you behave with complete nonsense? "This

is the portion of a wicked man with God, And the heritage of oppressors, received from the Almighty: If his children are multiplied, it is for the sword; and his offspring shall not be satisfied with bread. Those who survive him shall be buried in death,

And their widows shall not weep, though he heaps up silver like dust and piles up clothing like clay- He may pile it up, but the just will wear it, And the innocent will divide the silver.

Proverbs 13:22
A good man leaves an inheritance to his children's children, But the wealth of the sinner is stored up for the righteous.

b. Money is looking for you right now!

Proverbs 28:8
One who increases his possessions by usury and extortion Gathers it for him who will pity the poor.

Ecclesiastes 2:26
For God gives wisdom and knowledge and joy to a man who is good in His sight; but to the sinner He gives the work of gathering and collecting, that he may give to him who is good before God. This also is vanity and grasping for the wind.

Isaiah 45:2-3
I will go before you and make the crooked places straight; I will break in pieces the gates of bronze and cut the bars of iron. I will give you the treasures of darkness and hidden riches of secret places, that you may know that I, the Lord, who call you by your name, Am the God of Israel.

Psalm 73:3
For I was envious of the boastful, when
I saw the prosperity of the wicked.

Isaiah 51:3
For the Lord will comfort Zion, He will comfort
all her waste places; He will make her wilderness
like Eden, and her desert like the garden of
the Lord; joy and gladness will be found in it,
Thanksgiving and the voice of melody.

4. Wait upon the Lord: minister to the Lord, like a waiter serving in a restaurant.

   a. Worship Him, praise Him, minister to Him and glorify His Name.
   b. Between the 'now of faith' and the manifestation, your job is to 'wait' on the Lord.
   c. As the righteousness of God put on your eagle wings and fly high above the turbulence (debt, poverty, trouble). Rather than being part of the turbulence you'll be part of the victory!

LESSON FORTY-THREE

Bible Purpose Driven:
Daily Wisdom Key for Today:

MONEY IS LOOKING FOR ME

Verse to Remember: Zechariah 14:13-14
It shall come to pass in that day that That a great panic
from the Lord will be among them. Everyone will seize
the hand of his neighbor, and raise his hand against his
neighbor's hand; Judah also will fight at Jerusalem. And
the wealth of all the surrounding nations shall be gathered
together: Gold, silver, and apparel in great abundance.

Question to Meditate On: I am in the 'now-zone'.

"I CALL THOSE THINGS THAT ARE NOT AS THOUGH THEY ARE, MONEY BE LOOSED TO ME AND COME TO ME _NOW_, IN JESUS' NAME."

Hebrews 11:1
<u>Now faith</u> is the substance of things hope
for, the evidence of things not seen.

LESSON FORTY-FOUR

Mark 4:23-24
"If anyone has ears to hear, let him hear." Then
He said to them, "Take heed what you hear. With
the same measure you use, it will be measured to
you; and to you who hear, more will be given.

THE BLESSINGS OF THE LORD

1. Faith comes by hearing.

   a. hear = understand(ing)
   b. Satan cannot take from you what you understand; he can take away from you what you don't understand.
   c. We need to be careful in our getting of understanding.

   Proverbs 4:7
   Wisdom is the principle thing; therefore, get wisdom.
   And in all your getting, get understanding.

2. The power of tradition.

   Mark 7:13
   Making the word of God of no effect through your tradition
   which you have handed down. And many such things you do.

   a. There is something as destructive as the Devil – traditional interpretation of the scripture.
   b. e.g. Christ is not Jesus' last name. Definition: The Anointed One and His anointing.

    c. Peace – not just serenity of mind and calmness. Definition: wholeness, prosperity and completeness
    d. Revelation will take you to another level of existence. Traditional interpretation will hinder what God wants to do in your life.

3. What is The Blessing

Prov. 10:22
The blessing of the LORD makes rich,
and He adds no sorrow with it.

    a. 'Blessing' is one of the most used words in the Christian world;
    b. mistakenly used to describe the <u>results or effects</u> of the blessing.
    c. Blessing: an empowerment of God to have success and prosper In every area of life.
    d. The blessing is responsible for the <u>results</u> in your life (promotion, wisdom, finances, success in business, favor).
    e. 'Makes one rich' – it will propel you to another level of life existence.
    f. Adds no sorrow with it ": there is no substitute for it.
    g. Curse: means being empowered to fail and without bible purpose by missing the mark of what the word says about blessing.

Ephesians 1:3
Blessed be the God and Father of our Lord Jesus
Christ, who has blessed us with every spiritual
blessing in the heavenly places in Christ.

    a. The blessing is already on the inside of me!

CONFESSION: The deposit has been made

b. You need more information than just the knowledge that blessing has been given to you, to be able to make a withdrawal.

4. The pattern of blessing - God's blessing upon Abraham, Isaac, Jacob, Joseph, Jesus and you!

Genesis 12:1-3
Now the Lord had said to Abram: "Get out of your country, from your kindred and from your father's house, to a land that I will show you. I will make you a great nation; I will bless you and make your name great; and you shall be a blessing. I will bless those who bless you, and I will curse him who curses you; and in you all the families of the earth shall be blessed."

Genesis 12:16
He treated Abram well for her sake. He had sheep, oxen, male donkeys, male and female servants, female donkeys, and camels.

Genesis 13:1-2, 5
Then Abram went up from Egypt, he and his wife and all that he had, and Lot with him, to the south. Abram was very rich in livestock, in silver, and in gold. Lot also, who went with Abram, had flocks and herds and tents.

a. God had a covenant with Abraham.
b. Lot prospered in a similar way because of his connection with Abraham.

5. How do I qualify for the blessing?

Genesis 14:18-20
Then Melchizedek king of Salem brought out bread and wine; he was the priest of God Most High. And he blessed him and said: "Blessed be Abram of God Most High,

**possessor of heaven and earth; and blessed be God Most
High, who has delivered your enemies into your hand."**

    a. How do I set myself up to receive the blessing?

**Prov. 28:20
A faithful man shall abound with blessing.**

    b. The medium of exchange in the Kingdom of God is
<u>obedience.</u>

    c. When you are obedient to God in the financial realm,
you set yourself up to receive an exchange.

    d. There was <u>an exchange</u> between Melchizedek and
Abraham. Abraham brought the tithe . . . Melchizedek
blessed Abraham.

6. Malachi 3:10

**"Bring all the tithes into the storehouse, that there
may be food in My house and try Me now in this",
says the LORD of hosts, "If I will not open for you the
windows of heaven and pour out for you such blessing
that there will not be room enough to receive it."**

    a. Exchange the tithe and God will pour out the
empowerment for you to have success. A blessing
without limits.

7. Genesis 25:5-6

**And Abraham gave all that he had to Isaac. But Abraham
gave gifts to the sons of the concubines which Abraham
had; and while he was still living he sent them eastward,
away from Isaac his son, to the country of the east. And
it came to pass, after the death of Abraham, that God
blessed his son Isaac. And Isaac dwelt at Beer LahaiRoi.**

a. Abraham gave all that he had: Abraham gave Isaac the ability that enabled him to prosper.
b. If you have the blessing, you have the root to get everything you need. When Isaac empowered Jacob, Esau knew that Jacob now had the birthright and the blessing. (The root to get fruit).
c. The blessing comes with the exchange of obedience in the financial realm.
d. If you are obedient, you will not have a wrong relationship with money.

I Timothy 6:10
For the love of money is a root of all kinds of evil.

When you obey God in the financial realm, you are Declaring, "Jesus is LORD over my life (not money or material things)."

LESSON FORTY-FOUR

Bible Purpose Driven:
Daily Wisdom Key for Today:

THE BLESSINGS OF THE LORD

Verse to Remember: Mark 4:23-24
"If anyone has ears to hear, let him hear," And He
said to them, "Take heed what you hear. With the
same measure you use, it will be measured to you;
and to you who hear, more will be given."

Question to Meditate On: My Faith is getting stronger and stronger and God is positioning me in a NEW LEVEL of abundance. Confess out-loud 3 times: HALLELUJAH, HALLELUJAH, HALLELUJAH!

LESSON FORTY-FIVE

Genesis 15:1; 5-11
After these things, the word of the Lord came to Abram in a vision, saying, "Do not be afraid, Abram. I am your shield, your exceedingly great reward."- Then He brought him outside and said, "Look now toward heaven, and count the stars if you are able to number them." And He said to him, "So shall your descendants be."- And he believed in the Lord, and He accounted it to him for righteousness. Then He said to him, "I am the Lord, who brought you out of Ur of Chaldees, to give you this land to inherit it." And he said, "Lord God, how shall I know that I will inherit it?" So, He said to him, "Bring Me a three-year-old heifer, a three-year-old female goat, a three –year-old ram, a turtledove, and a young pigeon." Then he brought all these to Him and cut them in two, down the middle, and placed each piece opposite the other; but he did not cut the birds in two. And when the vultures came down on the carcasses, Abram drove them away.

I AM WALKING WITH THE BLESSING & WILL OCCUPY

1. Beware of the Seed Eater

   a. Abram prepares to enter into covenant with God.
      - Fowls: birds of prey (AMP)
      - Swoop: snatch or seize suddenly.
   b. Covenant cannot come into effect without the shedding of blood.

c. Abram follows God's instructions with his sacrifice and offering.
d. While Abram prepared his offering, the birds attempted to consume it before he could offer it to God.
e. If he hadn't driven them away, Abram could not have completed his covenant with God (his supernatural link to God).
f. Our offerings are not just a religious obligation. They are our link to the supernatural. Our covenant of increase is in force now!

2. Satan is the seed eater.

Mark 4:1-4
'And again, He began to teach by the sea. And a great multitude was gathered to Him, so that He got into a boat and sat in it on the sea; and the whole multitude was on the land facing the sea. Then He taught them many things by parables, and said to them in His teaching: "Listen! Behold, a sower went out to sow. And it happened, as he sowed, that some seed fell by the wayside; and the birds of the air came out and devoured it."

Mark 4:10-11
'But when He was alone, those around Him with the twelve asked Him about the parable. And He said to them, "To you it has been given to know the mystery of the kingdom of God; but to those who are outside, all things come in parables."

Mark 4:14- 15
"The sower sows the word. And these are the ones by the wayside where the word is sown. When they hear, Satan comes immediately and takes away the word that was sown in their hearts."

a. Seed is designed to reproduce and grow.
b. Fowl of the air: Satan is just like a bird of prey. He is after your seed (offering).
c. You must know that Satan is determined to steal your seed. You've got to be alert, wise and firm.
d. As soon as you get your paycheck, the birds of prey begin to swoop down (they talk).
e. Devourer = seed eater. Satan is the seed eater. If he can steal your seed, he can rob you of: potential increase and financial well-being, joy, happiness, relationships, business, job and Mission work.
f. Your seed makes you a threat to Satan.

3. Satan looks for opportunities to devour.

I Peter 5:8
Be sober, be vigilant; because your adversary the devil walks about like a roaring lion, seeking whom he _may_ devour.

a. Satan is seeking someone whom he _may_ devour.
b. Make a <u>firm commitment</u> to tithe, or the birds of prey will swoop down and successfully consume your seed.
c. If you don't tithe, you're on your own. You cannot expect the help of God in your finances because you haven't done anything that enforces your covenant.
d. If you do not tithe, you will eventually reach the point in your life and finances where you are not smart enough,
e. you will not have expertise or talent, to fix the financial problems or meet the need.
f. You can go further on 90% of your income, then you can on 100% because you are linked to the supernatural through your tithes.

g. When you tithe, God will personally rebuke the seed eater for your sake even making him repay seven times what was stolen.

h. Genesis 15 comes before Genesis 17 (when El Shaddai shows up).

4. The Word promises that a sower will <u>never</u> be without seed.

a. Ask in faith for seed to sow.

b. Any time a Christian gets money the seed eater will try to show up and swoop down.

c. Once the birds know you can be devoured, they will come back. It gets easier every time, until after a while, you won't even resist anymore.

5. Smite Your Debt

a. We have obtained an inheritance (Ephesians 1:3-11)

b. I am redeemed, I am forgiven, and I have already obtained an inheritance.

c. This has already happened – past tense.

d. When are God's people going to walk in the fullness of their inheritance?
  - Joint heir = heir
  - inheriting = taking possession

e. The heirs are not taking possession of everything that rightfully belongs to them.

f. vs. 11: have obtained This inheritance. It belongs to us right now, in this present time.

6. Lord, show me what I'm missing and I will correct it now.

Hosea 4:6
My people are destroyed for lack of knowledge.

a. destroyed = ruined or devoured.
b. Satan is a devourer.

I Peter 5:8
Be sober, be vigilant because your adversary
the devil walks about like a roaring lion,
seeking whom he may devour.

c. A lack of knowledge will cause us, or the things that belong to us, to be devoured.
d. The knowledge of God and wisdom of God will cause us to inherit substance.

Proverbs 8:21
That I (wisdom) may cause those who
love me (wisdom) to inherit wealth
that I may fill their treasuries.

e. How much longer are you going to be slack about possessing your inheritance.

Joshua 18:2-3
Amplified Bible (AMP)
² And there remained among the Israelites seven
tribes who had not yet divided their inheritance.

³ Joshua asked the Israelites, how long will you
be slack to go in and possess the land which the
Lord, the God of your fathers, has given you?

f. Has given to you: past tense. The land already belonged to them. It was not God or Joshua who was keeping them from receiving it.
g. Slack: slow to move; idle; inactive; sluggish, slothful, easily influenced and easily changed.
h. If we are not enjoying something that God says is ours, it is not God's fault. It is our fault.

Luke 24:25
Then He said to them, "O foolish ones, and slow of heart to believe in all that the prophets have spoken."

i. Jesus called them 'fools' because they couldn't believe what God had said in His Word. If we can't believe what God has said in His Word, we are fools; slow of heart to believe and dull of perception.

j. If you can't perceive it in your heart, you will never have it in your hand.

    - How long will you be slack?
    - The Church has largely been a 'sleeping giant; since
    - Jesus left the earth.

Proverbs 19:15
Laziness (slothfulness) casts one
into a deep sleep, and
and idle person will suffer hunger.

LESSON FORTY-FIVE

Bible Purpose Driven:
Daily Wisdom Key for Today:

I AM WALKING WITH THE BLESSING & WILL OCCUPY

Verse to Remember: Genesis 15:1; 5-11
After these things, the word of the Lord came to Abram
in a vision, saying, "Do not be afraid, Abram. I am your
shield, your exceedingly great reward."- Then He brought
him outside and said, "Look now toward heaven, and count
the stars if you are able to number them." And He said to
him, "So shall your descendants be."- And he believed in
the Lord, and He accounted it to him for righteousness.
Then He said to him, "I am the Lord, who brought you out
of Ur of Chaldees, to give you this land to inherit it." And
he said, "Lord God, how shall I know that I will inherit
it?" So, He said to him, "Bring Me a three-year-old heifer,
a three-year-old female goat, a three –year-old ram, a
turtledove, and a young pigeon." Then he brought all these
to Him and cut them in two, down the middle, and placed
each piece opposite the other; but he did not cut the
birds in two. And when the vultures came down
on the carcasses, Abram drove them away.

Question to Meditate On: No more slow to believe for me! No more dull of perception for me! Abraham was a doer and so will I be. If the Bible says it, that settles it, and I believe it! If God says it's mine then it's mine now!

LESSON FORTY-SIX

Galatians3:29
And if you are Christ's, then you are Abraham's
seed, and heirs according to the promise.

THE BLESSINGS OF ABRAHAM ARE OUR FULL INHERITANCE

1. Develop a consciousness and your faith regarding each of the blessings of God.

   a. The Lord has promised to smite the enemies that come against us.

   b. What are the greatest enemies of the Church and God's people?
      - Debt
      - Lack

   c. "Why don't you ask Me to smite them?" is what God says.

   d. You have to decide — Wouldn't you rather go from miracle to miracle and live in divine prosperity?

   e. Smite: quick, sudden decisive blow, with the intent to destroy.

   f. Hate lack! Hate debt!

2. Lacking Nothing! -

Luke 22:35
And He said to them, "When I sent you without
a money bag, knapsack and sandals, did you
lack anything?" So, they said, "Nothing."

a. When Jesus sent the disciples out to minister, they lacked nothing.
b. We lack because we have been too slack in possessing our inheritance.
c. God will smite the enemy before your face. He will give us evidence that it has been done. and He will do it in the now!
d. The only thing that has kept God from doing it, is that we have been slack in receiving it.

3. Making a memorial.

Exodus 12:13-14
'Now the blood shall be a sign for you on the houses where
you are. And when I see the blood, I will pass over you; and
the plague shall not be on you to destroy you when I strike
the land of Egypt. So, this shall be to you a memorial; and
you shall keep it as a feast by an everlasting ordinance.'

a. Memorial: that which preserves a memory of something special.
b. After a great victory in battle, the people of God often gave the place a special name or they would leave a pile of stones to mark the spot, so that when they or their descendants came again, it would remind them of the special event that took place there.
c. Where miracles are recorded in the Bible, they are usually preceded by a "point of contact".
   • The woman who determined to touch Jesus' clothes.

- Jesus made a mixture of spit and clay and put it on the blind man's eyes.
- At the man's request, Jesus spoke the Word only, and his servant was healed.

d. A 'point of contact' is a reference point, where you release your faith. It also creates a memorial – it preserves a memory of something special.

e. Memorial: a written representation of facts accompanied with a petition (a formal, written request).

f. It is written!

g. God wants to bring you out and into.

Psalm 105:37
He also brought them out with silver and gold,
and there was none feeble among His tribes.

h. God's will is to bring us into a wealthy place.

4. A Wealthy Place -

Psalm 66:11-12
Thou brought us into the net; thou laid affliction
upon our loins. Thou hast caused men to ride over
our heads; we went through fire and through water:
but thou brought us out into a <u>wealthy place</u>.

a. Land of Not Enough – Egypt

b. Land of Just Enough – Wilderness (Where men were satisfied.)

c. Land of More Than Enough – Promised Land - (Where God is glorified)

d. Money has to have a mission (purpose).

Deut. 8:18
And you shall remember the LORD your God,
for it is He who gives you power to get wealth,

**that He may establish His covenant which He
swore to your fathers, as it is this day.**

 e. God puts wealth into our hands to <u>serve Him</u>.
- You can have a wrong relationship with material wealth (root of all evil).
- Wealth cannot have first place in your life over God; self has got to die.
- Fight the Poverty Spirit that keeps you from entering into the wealthy place. Just enough is not enough.

5. God is restoring <u>all</u> of His gifts to the Church in these last days.

 a. Deliverance, Healing, Gifts of the Spirit and the gift of Prosperity.

 b. God will fulfill His promise of wholeness to the Church.

**Lamentations 3:17
You have moved my soul far from peace;
I have forgotten prosperity.**

 c. We can enter the Promised Land!

6. Traits of a Poverty Spirit: You justify and make excuses for where you are (false humility).

 a. You are critical of those who preach or teach prosperity (supported by jealousy).

 b. You don't think a man of God should live in abundance.

 c. You question, "Does it take all of that?" or "That man is only after your money (tithing, special offerings, etc.)."

 d. You are afraid to give under the direction of the Holy Spirit or the written Word of God.

e. You govern your finances with a lack of trust regarding God as your source (living dependent upon your paycheck).

f. You are suspicious and insecure of those around you, fearful that they are taking your money (suspicious).

LESSON FORTY-SIX

Bible Purpose Driven:
Daily Wisdom Key for Today:

THE BLESSINGS OF ABRAHAM
ARE OUR FULL INHERITANCE

Verse to Remember: Galatians3:29
And if you are Christ's, then you are Abraham's
seed, and heirs according to the promise.

Question to Meditate On: CONFESSION -

I DECLARE ACCORDING TO THE WORD OF GOD: I declare now in the Name of Jesus and by the power of the anointing of the Father Almighty, of Abraham, Isaac and Jacob, that every man, woman, boy, girl or child right now, who are reading this chapter, in Jesus' Name – I take authority by the Word of God and the Name of Jesus, and come into an agreement with them, that the spirit of poverty and lack be cast out of your people right now. In the Name of Jesus I adjure you right now – you must go and not come back.

And we decree God's purpose and that all of the blessings of Abraham, Isaac and Jacob be upon me and my household, in Jesus' name. Whom the son sets free is free indeed! AMEN Now Shout HALLELUJAH 3 times.

LESSON FORTY-SEVEN

Proverbs 3:9
Honor the LORD with your possessions, and
with the first fruits of all your increase.

MEDITATE ON THESE PRINCIPLES; TITHES, FIRST FRUITS & OFFERINGS

1. There is a distinction between first fruit offerings and the tithe. Many assume that first fruit offerings are the same as the tithe.

    a. God often works in threes: Father, Son, Holy Spirit and First fruit, tithe and offerings.
    b. Tithe = 10 % of your income.
    c. First Fruit = the very first of the produce that comes from the land. e.g. The first paycheck, first profit of a business, time, etc.
    d. Tithes and first fruit offerings are two different things.

II Chronicles 31:5
As soon as the commandment was circulated,
the children of Israel brought in abundance
the first fruits of grain and wine, oil and honey,
and of all the produce of the field; <u>and</u> they
brought in abundantly the tithe of everything.

Nehemiah 12:44
**And at the same time some were appointed over
the rooms of the storehouse for the <u>offerings,</u> the
<u>first fruits,</u> and the <u>tithes,</u> to gather into them from
the fields of the cities the portions specified by the
Law for the priests and Levites; for Judah rejoiced
over the priests and Levites who ministered.**

e. The <u>tithe</u> is holy to the Lord.

Leviticus 27:30
**And all the tithe of the Land, whether of the
seed of the land or of the fruit of the tree,
is the LORD'S. It is holy to the LORD.**

f. Holy to the Lord = it belongs to Him. e.g. Achan keeping
what was God's.

2. First fruit offerings are holy to the Lord.

Ezekiel 48:14
**'And they shall not sell or exchange any of it; they may not
alienate this best part of the land, for it is holy to the Lord.'**

a. God is serious about what belongs to Him.

Jeremiah 2:3
**Israel was holiness to the LORD, the first fruits
of His increase. "All that devour him will offend;
disaster will come upon them", says the LORD.**

3. How is abundance released in our lives?

Proverbs 3:9-10
**Honor the LORD with your possessions and with the
first fruits of all your increase; so, your barns will be
filled with, and your vats will overflow with new wine.**

a. This is an abundance of wealth so great that it is being forced out of the cracks.

Isaiah 1:19
'If you are willing and obedient, you
shall eat the good of the land.'

b. Honor the Lord with your possessions: you give Him authority to speak in your life with regards to giving and the use of your money; and you obey Him.
c. <u>And</u> the first fruits of all your increase: something you get for the first time. God is trying to take care of us now and in the future.
d. Result: barns (more than one) filled with plenty.

4. The bridge between God and our money.

Ezekiel 44:28-30
"It shall be, in regard to their inheritance, that I am
their inheritance. You shall give them (the priests) no
possession in Israel, for I am their possession. They
shall eat the grain offering, the sin offering and trespass
offering; every dedicated thing in Israel shall be theirs.
The best of all first fruits of any kind, and every sacrifice
of any kind from all your sacrifices, shall be the priest's;
also you shall give to the priest the first of your ground
meal, to cause a blessing to rest on your house."

a. The first of all the first fruits of any kind: shall be the priest's.
b. God has put a bridge between man and heaven – the five-fold ministry gifts.
c. To give God offerings, it must go through His ministry representatives on the earth.
d. Attacks to discredit ministries have been against the God-connection for our giving – to cut us off from the

Source of our supply. Insufficiency can be met through that bridge. Wealth can be met through that bridge.

5. The widow gave a first fruit offering to the man of God. Elijah was fed at Zarephath

I Kings 17:8-16
'Then the word of the Lord came to him, saying "Arise, go to Zarephath, which belongs to Sidon, and dwell there. See, I have commanded a widow there to provide for you." So he arose and went to Zarephath. And when he came to the gate of the city, indeed a widow was there gathering sticks. And he called to her and said, "Please bring me a little water in a cup, that I may drink." And as she was going to get it, he called to her and said, "Please bring me a morsel of bread in your hand." So, she said, "As the Lord your God lives, I do not have bread, only a handful of flour in a bin, and a little oil in a jar; and see I am gathering a couple of sticks that I may go in and prepare it for myself and my son, that we may eat it, and die." And Elijah said to her, "Do not fear; go and do as you have said, but make me a small cake from it first, and bring it to me; and afterward make some for yourself and your son. For thus says the Lord God of Israel: The bin of flour shall not be used up, nor shall the jar of oil run dry, until the day the Lord sends rain on the earth." So, she went away and did according to the word of Elijah; and she and he and her household ate for many days. The bin of flour was not used up, nor did the jar of oil run dry, according to the word of the Lord which He spoke by Elijah.'

    a. The widow had an opportunity to Honor God (doing what he said). Give a first fruit offering (the first cake).
    b. What would happen to her barns?
    c. The man of God confronted the Spirit of Fear (the giant in our land today): 'Fear not!'

d. Make me the <u>first one;</u> after that make one for you and your son.

e. He did according to the word of Elijah: her barns were running over!

6. The first fruit will cause the anointing to prosper in your house.

Ezekiel 44:28-30
The best of all first fruits of any kind, and every sacrifice of any kind from all your sacrifices shall be the priest's; also, you shall give to the priest the first of your ground meal to cause a blessing to rest on your house.

a. The priest can cause the blessing to <u>stay</u> in your house.

b. Blessing: anointing to prosper.

7. First fruit offerings will handle future dilemmas.

1 Kings 17:17, 20-22
'Now it happened after these things that the son of the woman who owned the house became sick. And his sickness was so serious that there was no breath left in him.'
'Then he cried out to the Lord and said, "O Lord my God, have you also brought tragedy on the widow with whom I lodge, by killing her son? And he stretched himself out on the child three times, and cried out to the Lord and said, "O Lord my God, I pray, let this child's soul come back to him. Then the Lord heard the voice of Elijah; and the soul of the child came back to him, and he revived.'

a. The widow's first fruit offering not only took care of her present situation but it also took care of her future dilemma.

b. The same man of God who received the first fruit offering was responsible for raising her son from the dead.

c. Jesus could do no miracles among the people who knew Him as He grew up because of familiarity.
d. The degree that is received of the anointing upon the life of a man or woman of God, is the same degree to which the Anointing will be released from his life to them.

LESSON FORTY-SEVEN

Bible Purpose Driven:
Daily Wisdom Key for Today:

MEDITATE ON THESE PRINCIPLES: TITHES, FIRST FRUITS & OFFERINGS

Verse to Remember: Proverbs 3:9
Honor the LORD with your possessions, and
with the first fruits of all your increase.

Question to Meditate On: I will ponder on this principle and remember now that Jesus, our Mediator and Prophet and GOD, is OUR FIRST FRUIT who was raised from the dead and we, through HIM, have a direct line to God. My giving will unleash the anointing and the blessing for God's purpose in MY LIFE!

LESSON FORTY-EIGHT

Romans 11:16
For if the first fruit is holy, the lump is also holy;
and if the root is holy, so are the branches.

I AM FIRST FRUIT MINDED
BECAUSE GOD IS MY SOURCE

1. The first fruit offering becomes the <u>root</u> to your fruits.

    a. The first fruit becomes the foundation of your future.
    b. If you want your lump to turn out right, it is <u>dependent</u> upon your first fruit.

2. God is trying to set us up so that our barns will flow over.

    Numbers 15:20-21
    'You shall offer up a cake of the first of your ground
    meal as a heave offering; as a heave offering of the
    threshing floor, so shall you offer it up. Of the first
    of your ground meal you shall give to the Lord a
    heave offering throughout your generations.'

    a. Why did God respect Abel's offering but reject Cain's?

    Genesis 4:1-8
    Amplified Bible (AMP)
    4 And Adam knew Eve as his wife, and she became
    pregnant and bore Cain; and she said, I have gotten
    ***and* gained a man with the help of the Lord.**

**² And [next] she gave birth to his brother
Abel. Now Abel was a keeper of sheep,
but Cain was a tiller of the ground.**

**³ And in the course of time Cain brought to the
Lord an offering of the fruit of the ground. ⁴ And
Abel brought of the firstborn of his flock and
of the fat portions. And the Lord had respect
and regard for Abel and for his offering,**

**⁵ But for [a]Cain and his offering He had no respect
or regard. So, Cain was exceedingly angry *and*
indignant, and he looked sad *and* depressed.**

**⁶ And the Lord said to Cain, why are you angry? And
why do you look sad *and* depressed *and* dejected?**

**⁷ If you do well, will you not be accepted? And if
you do not do well, sin crouches at your door;
its desire is for you, but you must master it.**

**⁸ And Cain said to his brother, [b]Let us go out to
the field. And when they were in the field, Cain
rose up against Abel his brother and killed him.**

b. Abel brought a first fruit offering; Cain did not.
c. We have to become first fruit minded.
d. Who is God in your life – really? When you get
something, how do you react?

3. Jesus was a first fruit offering.

Deuteronomy 18:1-5
**The priests, the Levites – all the tribe of Levi – shall have no
part nor inheritance with Israel; they shall eat the offerings of
the Lord made by fire, and His portion. Therefore, they shall**

have no inheritance among their brethren; the Lord is their inheritance, as He said to them. "And this shall be the priest's due from the people, from those who offer a sacrifice, whether it is bull or sheep: they shall give to the priest the shoulder, the cheeks, and the stomach. The first fruits of your grain and your new wine and your oil, and the first of the fleece of your sheep, you shall give him. For the Lord, your God has chosen him out of all your tribes to stand to minister in the name of the Lord, him and his sons forever."

    a. God sowed His Son in order to secure a future harvest.
    b. Christ the first fruits, afterward those who are Christ's at His coming.

4. What to do when everything seems to be shut up.

I Samuel 1:5, 11, 19-20

"But to Hannah he would give a double portion, for he loved Hannah, although the Lord had closed her womb.' 'Then she made a vow and said, "O Lord of hosts, if you will indeed look on the affliction of your maidservant and remember me, and not forget Your maidservant, but will give Your maidservant a male child, then I will give him to the Lord all the days of his life, and no razor shall come upon his head." 'They they arose early in the morning and worshipped before the Lord, and returned and came to their house at Ramah. And Elkanah knew Hannah his wife, and the Lord remembered her. So it came to pass in the process of time that Hannah conceived and bore a son, and called his name Samuel, saying, "Because I have asked for him from the Lord.'"

    a. Hannah vowed a vow.
    b. After Samuel, Hannah bore seven more children.

1 Samuel 2:5.
'.... Even the barren has borne seven....'

  c. Hannah came into completion number (7) because of
    her first fruit offering.

5. What do we do now? "Lord, I repent."

Matthew 3:8
Therefore, bear fruits worthy of repentance.

In the Old Testament, it was possible to recompense year by
year <u>or</u> you can begin afresh today!

6. The First Fruit Offering - How to be Led by the Spirit

  a. The Old Testament not only contains the Law but also
    God's covenant with us.

Romans 15:4
For whatever things were written before were
written for our learning that we through the patience
and comfort of the Scriptures might have hope.

  b. Covenant was established in the Old Testament. It is
    called the "Everlasting Covenant"
  c. Old Testament concepts lay the foundation for New
    Testament teaching.

    • 'But' = Zero.
    • Dove vs. sparrow: the dove comes back.
    • Woman with the issue of blood.
    • Israel was the first fruit to come out of Egypt and to
     enter their Promised Land
    • 'First fruit' always indicates that you are coming out
     of . . . and into Canaan land.

7. The distinction between first fruits and the tithe.

Proverbs 3:9-10
Honor the LORD with your possessions and with the first
fruits of all your increase; so, your barns will be filled
with plenty and your vats will overflow with new wine.

    a. 'Honor the Lord with your capital'- to do what God says concerning your money.

    b. Tithe: the tenth part.

    c. First fruit: the first of your increase; the first one produced.

    d. The promise: If you honor the Lord concerning your money and with the first fruit offerings, your barns will be filled with plenty and your presses will overflow with new wine.

LESSON FORTY-EIGHT

Bible Purpose Driven:
Daily Wisdom Key for Today:

I AM FIRST FRUIT MINDED
BECAUSE GOD IS MY SOURCE

Verse to Remember: Romans 11:16
For if the first fruit is holy, the lump is also holy;
and if the root is holy, so are the branches.

Question to Meditate On: God is my source and all of the blessings have been deposited into me. HE will see me through my destiny and purpose for my life.

SAY IT AGAIN & AGAIN & AGAIN:
GOD IS MY SOURCE!

LESSON FORTY-NINE

Ezekiel 44:30
The best of all first fruits of any kind and every sacrifice of any kind from all your sacrifices shall be the priest's; also you shall give to the priest the first of your ground meal, to cause a blessing to rest on your house.

THE PRINCIPLE OF FIRST FRUITS – CONSISTENT IN THE OLD AND NEW TESTAMENTS

1. What happens with the first one, determines what happens to the lump. Our money must have a mission.

   a. Our mission: blessed – so we can BE a blessing.
   b. Prosper: excel up.
   c. Philippian church ministered to Paul.

Philippians 4:15-16, 19
'Now you Philippians know also that in the beginning of the gospel when I departed from Macedonia, no church shared with me concerning giving and receiving but you only. For even in Thessalonica you sent aid once and again for my necessities.'
'And my God shall supply all your need according to His riches in glory by Christ Jesus.'

2. Paul pronounced a blessing over the church (vs. 19).

    a. Paul had financial resources
    b. Peace: nothing missing; nothing broken.
    c. The last thing God did for Israel before they exited Egypt, was to put great substance into their hands.

Acts 24:24-27
Amplified Bible (AMP)

24 Some days later Felix came with his wife Drusilla, who was a Jewess; and he sent for Paul and listened to him [talk] about faith in Christ Jesus.

25 But as he continued to argue about uprightness, purity of life (the control of the passions), and the judgment to come, Felix became alarmed *and* terrified and said, Go away for the present; when I have a convenient opportunity, I will send for you.

26 At the same time he hoped to get money from Paul, for which reason he continued to send for him and was in his company *and* conversed with him often.

27 But when two years had gone by, Felix was succeeded in office by Porcius Festus; and wishing to gain favor with the Jews, Felix left Paul still a prisoner in chains.

    d. Felix was actually trying to get money from Paul.
    e. People in the New Testament Church were cautioned against getting into the ministry for the finances that were connected with it.
    f. Knowledge on a matter is not enough. You must be led by the Spirit of the God.
    g. Your giving must be done in faith. Your faith comes by hearing the Word on that matter.
    h. You must rely upon the leading of the Spirit of God.

3.   Your success is dependent upon your relationship with the Holy Spirit.

II Corinthians 3:3,6
'Clearly you are an epistle of Christ, ministered by us, written with ink but by the Spirit of the Living God, not on tablets of stone but on tablets of flesh, that is, of the heart.........'
'Who also made us sufficient as ministers of the new covenant, not of the letter but of the Spirit; for the letter kills but the Spirit gives life.'

   a.   When you get a first fruit, find out what God wants you to do with it.
   b.   Follow Mary's advice "Whatever He says to do, do it."
   c.   Do not cut out the abundance of your harvest by not allowing the Holy Spirit to give you guidance and council. E.g. regulations regarding marriage and divorce, etc.

4.   The first step to being led by God is to be conscious that God lives in you.

   a.   How would you act if Jesus were to come to your house today?
   b.   You have to be so conscious of what you are doing because God is there in you.

5.   How God leads us.

Proverbs 20:27
The Spirit of a man is the lamp of the LORD, searching all the inner depths of his heart.

   a.   We need to keep from living a driven life. Don't work harder; work smarter.
   b.   God uses our born-again spirit–man as a candle.

c. He enlightens that candle with knowledge and information to provide guidance for our life.
d. The Spirit is the inner Guide for your life.
e. Don't receive guidance through your intellect or flesh.
f. The intellect – is not enlightened.
g. The flesh – is moved by feelings.

Psalm 18:28
For you will light my lamp; the LORD my God will enlighten my darkness.

h. The Holy Spirit will "light" your Spirit-man.

Romans 8:16
The Spirit Himself bears witness with our spirit that we are children of God.

i. 'Bears witness': gives an 'amen.'

6. Having confidence in coming to God

Romans 9:1
I tell you the truth in Christ, I am not lying, my conscience also bearing me witness in the Holy Spirit.

a. Not lying: agreeing with what the Word says about it.
b. Good conscience: approves.
c. Guilty conscience: reproves; brings correction.

Acts 23:1
Then Paul, looking earnestly at the council, said, "Men and brethren, I have lived in all good conscience before God until this day."

I John 3:20, 21
For if our heart condemns us, God is greater than our heart, and knows all things. Beloved, if our heart does not condemn us, we have confidence toward God.

d. e.g., Some people have no confidence in prayer because of guilt or condemnation.
e. Confidence comes through our understanding of our position in God.
f. Become tender-hearted so God can lead you.

I Timothy 4:2
Speaking lies in hypocrisy, having their own conscience seared with a hot iron.

g. Scorched, hardened – by not agreeing with what the Word says.
h. Do not seek guidance from outside voices – live by the Word.

John 16:13
However, when He, the Spirit of truth, has come, He will guide into all truth; for He will not speak on His own authority, but whatever He hears He will speak; and He will tell you things to come.

I Corinthians 14:10
'There are, it may be, so many kinds of languages in the world, and none of them is without significance.

i. Satan will take advantage of your seeking to hear from God.
j. Examine what you hear in light of what God's Word says.

7. Rules to Develop Your Human Spirit to be led by God.

Joshua 1:8
This Book of the Law shall not depart from your mouth, but you shall meditate in it day and night, that you may observe to do all that is written in it. For then you will make your way prosperous, and then you will have good success.

    a. Despite what is freely given in the Kingdom of God – some things will cost you. Are you willing to make the investment to hear from and be led by God as Joshua did?

    b. Train your spirit to hear from God by meditating in the Word of God.
- Time in the Word tunes your spirit to hear from the Spirit of God.
- Fill your mind with the Word until it fills your spirit.

    c. Train your spirit to hear from God by practicing the Word.
- If you will consistently do what is in the written Word, then you will obey when you hear from God.

James 1:22
But be doers of the Word, and not hearers only, deceiving yourselves.

- Do what you know to do from the Word.

    d. Give the Word first place in your life.
- Go to the Word first before you try everything else.
- Try prayer with bible purpose!
- Honor God and He will honor you.

    e. Train your spirit by instantly obeying the voice of the Spirit.
- 'Hunches' – learn to act on them.
- Use the Word as a safeguard to measure what you hear.
- Many times, the things you are told by the Spirit will contradict your intellect.

LESSON FORTY-NINE

Bible Purpose Driven:
Daily Wisdom Key for Today:

THE PRINCIPLE OF FIRST FRUITS IS CONSISTENT IN THE OLD AND NEW TESTAMENTS

Verse to Remember: Ezekiel 44:30
The best of all first fruits of any kind and every sacrifice of any kind from all your sacrifices shall be the priest's; also, you shall give to the priest the first of your ground meal, to cause a blessing to rest on your house.

Question to Meditate On: Service is the pathway to real significance. What is holding me back from accepting God's call to serve Him? To fulfill my purpose in my life.

LESSON FIFTY

Romans 5:1
Therefore, having been justified by faith, we have peace with God through our Lord Jesus Christ.

MY FAITH IS THE MASTER KEY

Romans 10:6-10
Amplified Bible (AMP)
⁶ But the righteousness based on faith [imputed by God and bringing right relationship with Him] says, do not say in your heart, who will ascend into Heaven? that is, to bring Christ down;

⁷ Or who will descend into the abyss? that is, to bring Christ up from the dead [as if we could be saved by our own efforts].

⁸ But what does it say? The Word (God's message in Christ) is near you, on your lips and in your heart; that is, the Word (the message, the basis and object) of faith which we preach,

⁹ Because if you acknowledge *and* confess with your lips that Jesus is Lord and in your heart, believe (adhere to, trust in, and rely on the truth) that God raised Him from the dead, you will be saved.

¹⁰ For with the heart a person believes (adheres to, trusts in, and relies on Christ) and so is justified (declared righteous, acceptable to God), and with the mouth he confesses (declares openly and speaks out freely his faith) *and* confirms [his] salvation.

2 Corinthians 5:17-21
Amplified Bible (AMP)

[17] Therefore if any person is [engrafted] in Christ (the Messiah) he is a new creation (a new creature altogether); the old [previous moral and spiritual condition] has passed away. Behold, the fresh *and* new has come!

[18] But all things are from God, who through *Jesus* Christ reconciled us to Himself [received us into favor, brought us into harmony with Himself] and gave to us the ministry of reconciliation [that by word and deed we might aim to bring others into harmony with Him].

[19] It was God [personally present] in Christ, reconciling *and* restoring the world to favor with Himself, not counting up *and* holding against [men] their trespasses [but cancelling them], and committing to us the message of reconciliation (of the restoration to favor).

[20] So we are Christ's ambassadors, God making His appeal as it were through us. We [as Christ's personal representatives] beg you for His sake to lay hold of the divine favor [now offered you] *and* be reconciled to God.

[21] For our sake He made Christ [virtually] to be sin Who knew no sin, so that in *and* through Him we might become [[a]endued with, viewed as being in, and examples of] the righteousness of God [what we ought to be, approved and acceptable and in right relationship with Him, by His goodness].

1. The Master Key

   a. There is a Master Key that unlocks everything in the Kingdom of God, here on earth.
   b. That Key is already in your possession. We must discover and learn to use the Master Key to be used by God in

these last days and to accomplish something significant for the Kingdom of God.

c. God has not hidden full understanding of this 'Master Key' from us. In fact, those who have accepted Jesus as Lord and Savior possess this key.

2. God has revealed this Master Key to us through His Word.

a. by correctly understanding how righteousness works in God's plan for man, we can more effectively use this master key to open the treasures of the Kingdom and receive all of the blessing of God's purpose in your life and others as you become a leader and a servant.

Romans 3:20-26
Amplified Bible (AMP)
[20] For no person will be justified (made righteous, acquitted, and judged acceptable) in His sight by observing the works prescribed by the Law. For [the real function of] the Law is to make men recognize *and* be conscious of sin [[a]not mere perception, but an acquaintance with sin which works toward repentance, faith, and holy character].

[21] But now the righteousness of God has been revealed independently *and* altogether apart from the Law, although actually it is attested by the Law and the Prophets,

[22] Namely, the righteousness of God which comes by believing *with* personal trust *and* confident reliance on Jesus Christ (the Messiah). [And it is meant] for all who believe. For there is no distinction,

[23] Since all have sinned and are falling short of the honor *and* glory [b]which God bestows *and* receives.

²⁴ [All] are justified *and* made upright *and* in right standing with God, freely *and* gratuitously by His grace (His unmerited favor and mercy), through the redemption which is [provided] in Christ Jesus,

²⁵ Whom God put forward [ᶜbefore the eyes of all] as a mercy seat *and* propitiation by His blood [the cleansing and life-giving sacrifice of atonement and reconciliation, to be received] through faith. This was to show God's righteousness, because in His divine forbearance He had passed over *and* ignored former sins without punishment.

²⁶ It was to demonstrate *and* prove at the present time (ᵈin the now season) that He Himself is righteous and that He justifies *and* accepts as righteous him who has [true] faith in Jesus.

b. We are justified by faith or not at all.

c. Justification means 'declared righteous' In other words we are righteous for no other reason than the fact that God declared us righteous.

d. Righteous by faith is like being born into a family. I did not have anything to do with the family I was born into.

e. I am a _____ based on my family's declaration. I did not have to do anything to become a part of my family. My parents simply declared me _____.

f. The same kind of dynamic is at work when we are born again. When we realize we need a Savior to forgive our sins and bring us into fellowship with God, and we ask Jesus to do those things, we are born again.

g. When we are born again, we are declared righteous and made members of the family of God. Being born again does not include instructions on how to do something to become righteous. They are not necessary. We are born again and declared righteous by the Word of God through our faith and belief in Jesus Christ.

3. The Action of Faith

    a. Often people will say they believe, yet until we understand the connection between belief and faith, we will wonder why our prayers remain unanswered. If it seems that our prayers are not being answered, God is not to blame.
    b. Belief can refer to the mental acceptance of something as truth, though absolute certainty may be absent. A problem arises when you believe something to be true and never act on it. This is where faith comes in.
    c. Faith is acting on what you believe. It is the appropriate, corresponding, suitable and proper action. For example, when you sit on a chair, you believe that the chair will provide support. Therefore, the appropriate corresponding action is to sit in the chair, with no thought concerning the chair's ability to support you!
    d. For years we have declared that we were standing in faith for healing when, in fact, we have only believed in God's ability to heal. We have also confessed God's delight in prosperity of his servant, yet we have never moved from that place of belief.

4. Faith requires corresponding action, not just any action.

James 2:17
Thus also faith by itself, if it does not have works, it is dead.

James 2:20
But do you want to know, O foolish man,
that faith without works is dead?

James 2:26
For as the body without the spirit is dead,
so faith without works is dead also.

a. If a person believes that God is going to heal them, there has to be some kind of action; otherwise, it is not faith.

b. We have to find an action that will correspond with the release of our faith. Many act improperly by doing things that do not correspond with their faith. [*For example, some would stop wearing glasses, if they were believing God for restored eyesight. That is not going to work if you cannot see without them. In a situation such as this, they should thankfully declare that their eyes are totally healed and put on their glasses!*]

5. Belief starts everything. Unbelief stops anything.

a. When you believe, something else is required. Abraham believed God, and God called it righteousness. Belief got it started. God showed up in Genesis 15 and made a covenant with him. In effect God said, "I have to persuade him to believe, he can begin the process."

Romans 10:10
For with the heart one believes unto
righteousness and with the mouth
confession is made unto salvation.

b. In order for Abraham to become the Father of Faith, his action had to correspond with what he said he believed; hence, the trip to Mount Moriah to slay his son (Gen. 22).

6. Wishing is not believing.

    a. There is no faith in wishing. In and of itself believing will not bring anything to pass; neither will wishing. At some point you have to believe what the Word of God says and begin to move forward with a corresponding action.

    b. Where you are still believing God for something and frustrated because you have not seen it, come out of the "belief mode" and get into the "action mode". When you believe it so much that you are willing to say it, and act on it, your faith becomes ignited. You then can expect God to do great things.

7. The test of belief is the movement it produces.

    a. The centurion's belief that Jesus could heal his servant moved him into the presence of Jesus. When Jesus heard the centurion say, "Speak the Word only and my servant shall be healed." He also heard great faith for healing. Then the man's servant was healed.

Matthew 8:5-10
Amplified Bible (AMP)
5 As Jesus went into Capernaum, a centurion came up to Him, begging Him,

6 And saying, Lord, my servant boy is lying at the house paralyzed and [a]distressed with intense pains.

7 And Jesus said to him, I will come and restore him.

8 But the centurion replied to Him, Lord, I am not worthy or fit to have You come under my roof; but only speak the word, and my servant boy will be cured.

⁹ For I also am a man subject to authority, with soldiers subject to me. And I say to one, Go, and he goes; and to another, Come, and he comes; and to my slave, Do this, and he does it.

¹⁰ When Jesus heard him, He marveled and said to those who followed Him [ᵇwho adhered steadfastly to Him, conforming to His example in living and, if need be, in dying also], I tell you truly, I have not found so much faith as this ᶜwith anyone, even in Israel.

b. When the angel Gabriel declared that Mary would have a son named Jesus, she chose to believe him. Her corresponding action was her statement, "Be it unto me according to your Word." (Luke 1:38)

c. If you believe that you are the righteousness of God, it will move you to begin exercising your rights.

d. If you believe God can remove your debt, you will begin to apply the principles that will release you from debt. If you believe God can heal your body, you will activate the principles that will bring healing.

LESSON FIFTY

Bible Purpose Driven:
Daily Wisdom Key for Today:

MY FAITH IS THE MASTER KEY

Verse to Remember: Romans 5:1
Therefore, having been justified by faith, we have
peace with God through our Lord Jesus Christ.

Question to Meditate On: <u>CONFESION OF FAITH:</u>

"Dear Heavenly Father, I declare now that my beliefs shall not stand alone. Your Word declares that I have been given a measure of faith, so right now I add that measure of faith to my beliefs. By faith I declare that I am justified. I am the righteousness of God by faith. I live by faith. Father, Lord, my belief moves me, and my faith has appeared. I walk by faith not by sight. I walk by the Word of God. This is my faith and I receive it now in Jesus' name! Doubt and unbelief Go! For I live by faith. In Jesus' name, Amen."

LESSON FIFTY-ONE

John 8:32
"And you shall know the truth, and the
truth shall make you free."

THE BELIEVER'S BILL OF RIGHTS

The truth shall make you free but If you don't know the truth about healing, deliverance, debt, protection and provision you will not be free. We have in the Constitution of the United States of America, what is called the *Bill of Rights*. As citizens, in the Bill of Rights, we are given certain guarantees – the right to assemble, the right to publish, freedom of speech, etc. Let's take a look at our spiritual rights endowed by our loving God.

1. We are citizens of the Kingdom of God.

Luke 12:32
Do not fear, little flock, for it is you Father's
good pleasure to give you the kingdom.

Ephesians 2:19
Now, therefore, you are no longer strangers and
foreigners, but fellow citizens with the saints
and members of the household of God.

Philippians 3:20
For our citizenship is in heaven, from which we also
eagerly wait for the Savior, the Lord Jesus Christ.

Hebrews 12:23
To the general assembly and church of the firstborn
who are registered in heaven, to God the Judge
of all, to the spirits of just men made perfect.

James 2:5
Listen, my beloved brethren: Has God not chosen the
poor of this world to be rich in faith and heirs of the
kingdom which He promised to those who love Him?

2. As a citizen of this Kingdom you have certain rights. As part of the family, we also have rights.

John 1:12
But as many received Him, to them He gave the right to
become children of God, to those who believe in His name.

Romans 8:15-16
For you did not receive the spirit of bondage again to fear
but you received the Spirit of adoption by whom we cry
out, "Abba, Father" The Spirit Himself bears witness with
our spirit that we are children of God, and if children, then
heirs – heirs of God and joint heirs with Christ, if indeed we
suffer with Him, that we may also be glorified together.

3. The Word of God is the believer's Bill of Rights.

   a. The Word guarantees certain things will happen if you believe and take corresponding action (faith).

4. A brief list of The Believer's Bill of Rights-

   a. You have a right to know that all your sins are forgiven and that have received the gift of eternal life

Romans 8:1
New International Version (NIV)
Therefore, there is now no condemnation
for those who are in Christ Jesus.

Isaiah 43:25
"I, even I, am He blots out your transgressions for
My own sake; and I will not remember your sins."

b. When the devil wants to bring up the old (failures; the past you lived in) you don't need to open the door or even answer the knock on the door. You don't have to let him torment you with the past. There is no past.

II Corinthians 5:17
Therefore, if anyone is in Christ, he is a
new creation; old things have passed away;
behold, all things have become new.

c. I am just as secure right now that my sins are forgiven as I will be when I stand before God. I have a right to know that I am forgiven!

d. It is not your worthiness that makes God receive you. It is the worthiness of the Lamb of God.

e. Your goodness or badness does not affect His worthiness. You Are accepted because of Jesus' completed work at Calvary.

f. You have a right to walk in health and conquer the powers of sickness and disease.

Jeremiah 30:17
New International Version (NIV)
Thus says the LORD: "I will give you back your health
again and heal your wounds. Now you are called The
Outcast and ,Jerusalem, the Place Nobody Wants."

g. Five points are illustrated:

    i)   I will restore your health,

    ii)   I will heal your wounds,

    iii) I will bring you out of captivity, and

    iv) I will restore your fortunes.

    v)   I will guide you in my purpose

h. If you are sick in your body you have a right to walk in Divine health. You have a right to conquer demons of sickness and disease.

i. He said, "I will restore your health." The word _restore_ means to 'take back the ground that you have lost.'

Proverbs 4:20-22
My son, give attention to my words; incline your ear to my sayings. Do not let them depart from your eyes; keep them in the midst of your heart; For they are life to those who find them, and health to all their flesh.

Isaiah 53:5
But He was wounded for our transgressions, He was bruised for our iniquities; The chastisement for our peace was upon Him, And by His stripes we are healed.

Matthew 8:16-17
When evening had come, they brought to Him many who were demon-possessed. And He cast out the spirits with a word, and healed all who were sick, that it might be fulfilled which was spoken by Isaiah the Prophet, saying: "He himself took our infirmities and bore our sicknesses."

I Peter 2:24
Who Himself bore our sins in His own body on
the tree, that we having died to sins, might live for
righteousness – by whose stripes you were healed.

Psalm 107:20
He sent His word and healed them, and
delivered them from their destructions.

Psalm 41:3
The LORD will strengthen him on his bed
of illness; who heals all your diseases.

Matthew 9:35
Then Jesus went about all the cities and villages,
teaching in their synagogues, preaching the
gospel of the kingdom, and healing every
sickness and every disease among the people.

Hebrews 13:8
Jesus Christ is the same yesterday, today and forever.

James 5:14-15
Is anyone among you sick? Let him call for the elders
of the church and let them pray over him, anointing
him with oil in the name of the Lord. And the prayer
of faith will save the sick, and the Lord will raise him
up. And if he has committed sins, he will be forgiven.

III John 1:2
Beloved, I pray that you may prosper in all and
be in health, just as your soul prospers.

Hebrews 4:16
Let us therefore come boldly to the throne
of grace, that we may obtain mercy and
find grace to help in time of need.

j. If you just received Christ last week, you have a right! Come boldly! Walk with your head held high. Know who you are. Know who He is. Know you are in covenant. You don't come feeling unworthy.

k. To the man who had been sick for 38 years, Jesus said, take up your bed and walk! To the man with the withered hand – stretch out your hand! To the leper – be clean and go show yourself to the priest.

l. You have a right to be debt free! You have a right to see all your needs met. You have a right to provision for yourself with enough extra to help others.

Genesis 12:2-3
I will make you a great nation; I will bless you
and make your name great; and you shall be a
blessing. I will bless those who bless you, and
I will curse him who curses you; and in you all
the families of the earth shall be blessed ".

Isaiah 30:21
Your ears shall hear a word behind you, saying,
"This is the way, walk in it." Whenever you turn to
the right hand or whenever you turn to the left.

Philippians 3:13-14
Brethren, I do not count myself to have apprehended;
but one thing I do, forgetting those things which
are behind and reaching forward to those things
which are ahead. I press toward the goal for the
prize of the upward call of God in Christ Jesus.

Philippians 4:15-19
Now you Philippians know also that in the
beginning of the gospel, when I departed from
Macedonia, no church shared with me concerning
giving and receiving but you only for even in
Thessalonica you sent aid once and again for my
necessities. Not that I seek the gift, but I seek the
fruit that abounds to your account. Indeed, I have
all and abound. I am full, having received from
Epaphroditus the things which were sent from you,
a sweet-smelling aroma an acceptable sacrifice, well
pleasing to God. And my God shall supply all your
need according to His riches in glory by Christ Jesus.

LESSON FIFTY-ONE

Bible Purpose Driven:
Daily Wisdom Key for Today:

THE BELIEVER'S BILL OF RIGHTS

Verse to Remember: John 8:32
"And you shall know the truth, and the
truth shall make you free."

Question to Meditate On: Petitional agreement prayer for you:

Dear Heavenly Father, we come to you with great thanks for all your goodness and for all that you have put into our hands. We thank you, Lord, that you have not given to us what we deserve, but rather, you have given to us out of your great love. We praise you for your mercy on us. We ask that you take our tithes and offerings and all that we give and use them as you please. We pray that you will continue to shower us with your blessings, and we commit to be faithful stewards of your goodness. Lord, we ask that you will bless the work of our hands and witness of our lives. We pray that the world may look at us and in some measure, see you and your goodness. In the name of Jesus our Lord, Amen.

LESSON FIFTY-TWO

Joshua 1:8
'This book of the law shall not depart out of thy mouth; but thou shalt meditate therein: for then thou shalt make thy way prosperous, and then thou shalt have good success.'

FINALLY, SOME SUGGESTIONS TO HAVE A DIRECT LINE WITH GOD

Now that you have come to the very end of these lessons and this book, we highly recommend that you get into a daily devotion, alone with God, and focus on practical, daily, bible purpose sowing and spending and watch the Lord begin to bless your labor and everything that your hand touches. Please review these points in this final lesson.

1. Get into the scripture.

    a. make a pledge that you will read the bible daily. We suggest that you make time and read it in the morning. You might say,

        "Brother Bruno, I don't have any time in the morning, I am busy with my family and business." Well, ok, read it in the afternoon.

        "But brother Bruno, I have to pick up my children and I have other commitments that do not allow me to be alone with the Lord in the afternoon." Well, then read it at night.

Romans 12:1-2
"I beseech you therefore, brethren, by the mercies of God, that you present your bodies a living sacrifice, holy, acceptable to God, which is your reasonable service. And do not be conformed to this world, but be transformed by the renewing of your mind, that you may prove what is that good and acceptable and perfect will of God.'

b. We see that Paul was speaking to the Christians in Rome because they had no direction and Paul began to lay the foundation of the principle of God to be successful.

Matthew 6:33
'But seek first the kingdom of God and His righteousness, and all these things shall be added to you.'

2. How to read the bible 3 times in 1 year - 4 steps

a. I Call this 2-2-1 & 2. Which added together make a total of 7 chapters of daily devotional reading enjoyment.

    i) Begin in the beginning. Read 2 chapters in Genesis. This is the foundation of the Old Testament.

    ii) Read 2 chapters in Psalms daily. Psalms is for healing.

    iii) Read one chapter in Proverbs for wisdom. Proverbs is the book of wisdom to make you an entrepreneur and a great leader.

    iv) Read 2 Chapters in the New Testament starting with the book of Matthew. The New Testament is resurrection.

If you follow this method daily, you will not fail because daily we need healing, daily we need to be baptized with the Holy Spirit and fire. Now, say to your friend or your wife, "2-2-1 & 2 is for YOU!" That make a total of 7 chapters a day and it will keep the doctor away. You will be making Jesus the doctor of healing, prosperity, financing and success.

3. Plug yourself into a solid, balanced, local church and get committed and involved.

   a. You need to find a church in your community that has some biblical teaching and sound faith that moves mountains.

      i) The church that inspires you with good preaching.
      ii) Sound teaching
      iii) Divine Healing.
      iv) Deliverance from demons.
      v) Prophetic
      vi) Worship
      vii) Prosperity.

   b. There are many balanced churches wherever you are. These 7 points are equal to 7 levels of anointing.
   c. WHY do we need this kind of Evangelical, Apostolic, balanced church? Because the church is a hospital and a healing center for the community, city and the nations. Prosperity is not an accident, it is a decision. This kind of church that moves in a high dimension stores up all the gifts of God and brings prosperity into your life.
   d. The church is God's calling of people who are of different nations and God has called them in, from darkness to light, and the church must be equipped to restore and repair the people. This is a process of elimination and restoration, ordained by God to make disciples.

e. The purpose of the church is to equip the saints, and to help them to evangelize the community and keep law and order and to get rid of all of the worldly, evil ideas of the devil and to be transformed in the divine power of God that all nations will know and experience our testimony and the evidence that we are being transformed in health, financially and with success.

f. In the church, you will find people who will help build you up, inspire you and encourage you and you will also find people who will proselyte and try and take people out of the church into their own doctrine. We must fellowship with one another and serve each other and to always walk in love. Jesus declares in:

John 13:35:
'By this all will know that you are My disciples,
if you have love for one another.'

4. Prayer that gives you a right relationship with God and men.

Matthew 6:9-15
'In this manner, therefore, pray: Our Father in heaven,
Hallowed by Your name. Your kingdom come. Your will
be done on earth as it is in heaven. Give us this day our
daily bread. And forgive us our debts, As we forgive
our debtors. And do not lead us into temptation, But
deliver us from the evil one. For Yours is the kingdom
and the power and the glory forever. Amen.'

We highly recommend that you get connected with men and woman of God who are Elders and who know how to pray. I remember when I came to the Lord 28 years ago, I would attend 3-5 meetings a day. I was so hungry for the Lord that I could not get enough. I discovered that prayer is unlimited with God.

a. What prayer is: Prayer is the offering up of our desires for lawful and needful things and things we want that are promised by God, with humble confidence that we will obtain them through Jesus Christ for God's glory and for our good. It is the pleading of our cause in God's court. Prayer is seeking help from God in matters that are beyond our power. It is the personal appeal to a personal and present God based upon His will and word and our lawful desires. It is cooperation with God's willingness to manifest His goodness to all those who have faith in Him and depend upon Him for help. Prayer is simply asking and receiving from God, and that is the theme of this final lesson.

i) Commands to pray – I Chronicles 16:11, II C Psalms 105:4, Matthew 7:7-11, Ephesians 6:18

ii) TIME TO PRAY – "Daily: In the morning" (Psalms 3:5, Psalms 88:13, Psalms 143:8) "Twice daily" (Psalms 88:1) "three times daily" (Psalms 51:17, Daniel 6:10) "Without ceasing" (I Thess. 5:17) "At night" (Mk. 1:35, Luke 6:12) "Night and Day", (Lk. 2:37).

iii) ATTITUDES IN PRAYER – "Standing" (Lk. 18:13) "Sitting" (Acts 1:14, Lk. 10:13) 'Lying" (II Samuel 12:16-20) "Kneeling" (Ps. 95:6, Dan. 6:10, Lk. 22:4, Acts 9:40) "Weeping" (Ezra 10:1, I Sam. 1:10) "Talking" (Gen. 18:23-33) "Meditating"

iv) (Psalms 5:1) "Agonizing" (Lk. 22:44) "Groaning" (Rom. 8:26-27) and "In the Spirit" (Eph. 6:18, Jude 20)

v) WHERE TO PRAY – "In the closet" (Matthew 6:6) "On the mountains" (Matt. 14:23) "In the homes", "In the temples" and "everywhere" (Acts 1: 13-14, Acts 2:46, 3:1, 12:12, I Tim. 2:8)

vi) HOW TO PRAY – "Jesus taught that men should not pray like the hypocrites, to be seen of men and not like the heathen who think that God hears from much speaking" (Matt. 6:5-8)

vii) THE PURPOSE OF PRAYER – The Chief end of all prayer should be to glorify God and to make full our joy. (John 14:13-15, 16:24)

viii) LEARN TO PRAY RIGHT – This is one of the greatest lessons to learn about prayer. One cannot get an answer unless he prays right. In Luke 11:1 we have a record of the disciples observing how Jesus prayed, they knew that God always heard him. There was such a absolute simplicity and assurance when He prayed and there came a hunger to them to know how to pray as He could. They asked Him, "Lord teach us to pray as John also taught His disciples", that should be the daily longing of every true child of God, the need of knowing how to pray right in the need of the hour.

PARTNERSHIP WITH GOD IN BUSINESS

The business man, <u>above many others</u>, should openly pray to God to help him in his many problems. He should learn to let God run his business by following the will of God concerning every move he makes. <u>God is interested in the success of every man</u>, and He will help everyone to be a success in life if he is consulted and obeyed. <u>God can run the business of any man better than any man himself can run it.</u> God knows the details of businesses worldwide and all of the problems that the businessman has to face and He can supernaturally work and accomplish things where all men fail. If a man wants to succeed in business he must not only make God his partner but he must be willing to follow the LAWS OF PROSPERITY discussed in the lessons above. As long as a man argues that it is not God's will to do this or that or certain things, they will come far short of God's blessings, it would seem to me that only one reading of the bible would be sufficient to correct most of the erroneous ideas that the average man has of God.

The purpose of these 52 lessons is to help such diluted people to see for themselves what God's will is and what they are missing out on concerning the good things in this life. <u>What should be done by every person is to read the bible for himself or for herself</u> and see what is plainly said in all of these questions we are teaching. Every man, by reading for himself, can see where he has been misled. The bible says one thing, and what men teach contrary to this is easily detected. There is no excuse for you that are reading these lessons, for you are having your eyes opened to see the infinite blessing that God has promised to them that love Him. You have no possible excuse to continue in unbelief and ignorance of what God wants you to have in life.

God has literally promised material wealth, physical health and spiritual freedom as well as sin from evil habits, and failure in life. In fact, there is not one phrase of life that God has ignored in His program. There is no want to them that fear God. There can be no failure in life to anyone who can tap the resources of God. It is the duty of every believer to learn what God has promised and to be bold and aggressive in attaining to the benefits provided. Let the reader enter whole-heartedly into fellowship with God and love and obey him, and he will see for himself that no good thing will be withheld from them who walk uprightly. (Psalms 84:11).

You have before you sickness or health, poverty or wealth, success or failure. You have before you the infinite resources of God and you can have in life what is good so forget the many false concepts of God and truth that you have been taught and lay hold of the abundance of life. You can have anything you want by simply asking and receiving from your HEAVENLY FATHER NOW AND FOREVERMORE!!

WHAT DOES PRAYER DO?

Prayer changes the atmosphere of every circumstance that you encounter day after day. When you pray right and intercede your intercession pushes back the evil and the stumbling blocks that the enemy puts in your life and your prayer causes God to release His glorious and powerful anointing on your very life and on your children and grand-children and <u>health, wealth & success transformation BEGINS to take place.</u>

FINALLY, in conclusion of these 52 lessons we will give you 7 points. I call them keys to WEALTH TRANSFORMATION that took place in the bible.

1.   The first one was Abraham,

Genesis 12:3
'I will bless those who bless you, And I will curse him who curses you; And in you all the families of the earth shall be blessed.'

2.   Isaac,

Genesis 26:12-14
'Then Isaac sowed in that land, and reaped in the same year a hundredfold; and the Lord blessed him. The man began to prosper, and continued prospering until he became very prosperous; for he had possessions of flocks and possessions of herds and a great number of servants. So, the Philistines envied him.'

3. Jacob,

Genesis 31:1
'Now Jacob heard the words of Laban's sons, saying, "Jacob has taken away all that was our father's, and from what was our father's he has acquired all this wealth."

4. Joseph,

Genesis 41:40-44
'You shall be over my house, and all my people shall be ruled according to your word; only in regard to the throne will I be greater than you." And Pharaoh said to Joseph, "See, I have set you over all the land of Egypt." Then Pharaoh took his signet ring off his hand and put it on Joseph's hand; and he clothed him in garments of fine linen and put a gold chain around his neck. And he had him ride in the second chariot which he had; and they cried out before him, "Bow the knee!" So, he set him over all the land of Egypt. Pharaoh also said to Joseph, "I am Pharaoh, and without your consent no man may lift his hand or foot in all the land of Egypt."

5. Israel through Moses,

Exodus 3:21-22
'And I will give this people favor in the sight of the Egyptians, and it shall be, when you go, you shall not go empty handed. But every woman shall ask of their neighbor, namely, of her who dwells near her house, articles of silver, articles of gold, and clothing; and you shall put them on your son and on your daughters. So you shall plunder the Egyptians.

6. Solomon,

I Kings 3:12-14:
'Behold, I have done according to your words; see, I have given you a wise and understanding heart, so

**that there has not been anyone like you before you,
nor shall any like you arise after you. And I have also
given you what you have not asked: both riches and
honor, so that there shall not be anyone like you among
the kings all your days. So, if you walk in My ways,
to keep My statutes and My commandments, as your
father David walked, then I will lengthen your days.'**

7.   THE 7ᵗʰ WEALTH TRANSFORMATION BELONGS TO
     YOU! ARE YOU READY FOR THAT? If the answer is
     YES shout HALLELUJAH.

III John 2:1
**'Beloved, I pray that you may prosper in all things
and be in health, just as your soul prospers.'**

Philippians 4:19
**'And my God shall supply all your need according
to His riches in glory by Christ Jesus.'**

II Corinthians 9:8
**'And God is able to make all grace abound toward you,
that you, always having all sufficiency in all things,
may have an abundance for every good work.'**

WOW, all grace, no lack, for every good work. When we tithe
and give offering to our local church and to the Mission work
and give offerings to others, so that the Gospel can go forth,
then and only then will God supply all of our needs. So, what
God is saying to you and I is that when we fulfill His demands
of being stewards to sponsor the Gospel of His Son, the Lord
Jesus Christ then God will supply all of our needs. Hallelujah.

95 % of people do not follow the laws of tithing and giving
because they operate externally and not internally. Externally

there is poverty, lack, sickness and fear of death but internally there is a unlimited storehouse when we operate in faith and take God for HIS word.

FINALLY, WE HAVE HIS PROMISES WHICH ARE YES AND AMEN – AS WE OBEY WE FLOW IF WE DISOBEY WE DON'T GO

As we come to the end of these 52 lessons in <u>Bible Financial Purpose Driven: Out of Debt and Poverty into God's Wealth</u>, please take ten minutes and meditate and evaluate whether you have been successful or not. If, after your evaluation you conclude that you have not been abundantly blessed as the Lord wants you to be, then you must see if there is sin in your life and give up the sin business totally and re-dedicate yourself over to the Lord and read the lessons over and over again. God cannot fail you. We highly recommend to read one lesson a week: meditating on the lesson daily, for seven days, until you become a walking miracle person with no lack within one year's time. Please, you must do this to protect your family, children and grand-children and the future generations.

LESSON FIFTY-TWO

Bible Purpose Driven:
Daily Wisdom Key for Today:

FINALLY, SOME SUGGESTIONS TO HAVE A DIRECT LINE WITH GOD

Verse to Remember: Joshua 1:8
'This book of the law shall not depart out of thy mouth; but thou shalt meditate therein: for then thou shalt make thy way prosperous, and then thou shalt have good success.'

Question to Meditate On: SUMMARY – ORDER OF SERVICE

God first, then family, then others. To serve and to be served, with the same measure that it is given to me, I will give it out in every area where God leads me because where God leads me, there, HE will feed me!

FINALLY, GET IT ALL, DO IT ALL AND GIVE IT ALL.

Psalms 121
'I will lift up my eyes to the hills- From whence comes my help? My help comes from the Lord, Who made heaven and earth. He will not allow your foot to be moved; He who keeps you will not slumber. Behold, He who keeps Israel Shall neither slumber nor sleep. The Lord is your keeper; The Lord is your shade at your right hand. The sun shall not strike you by day, Nor the moon by night. The Lord shall preserve you from all evil; He shall preserve you. The Lord shall preserve your going out from your coming in from this time forth, and even forevermore.'

EVERLASTING CHIP MINISTRY UNIVERSITY INTERNATIONAL

Mission FIRE Statement: To win 200,000,000 souls

1. Carry the saving and healing message of Jesus Christ to every nation and island on the earth.

2. Proclaim the whole gospel of Jesus Christ to every person on the earth in our generation.

3. Build-up, train, and strengthen believers in every nation by birthing the prophet in them.

4. Conduct schools of Ministry and open campuses for the purpose of passing the anointing God gave to Bruno Caporrimo, to us. So, we can reach their villages, communities, cities and nations for Christ.

5. Present the witness that Jesus is the Messiah to every creature; black, white or yellow.

6. Maximize technology, people and resources which God has provided for the spreading of the gospel.

7. Build God's mighty, active army of trained believers in every nation for the purpose of overtaking darkness and spreading the light of the gospel of Jesus Christ.

8. Establish a prayer covering over the entire earth with strategically located prayer centers which continually offer up prayer for the nations.

9. Provide prayer command centers in homes so that individuals and the hurting masses of the world will know that we are his disciples.

10. Recognize and support the unity in the body of Christ so the world will know that we are His disciples.

11. Operate, articulate and demonstrate to the world the 5-fold ministries of the church as outlined in Ephesians 4:11, for the perfecting of the saints, for the work of the ministry and edifying of the body of Christ.

12. To bring honor and glory to God in everything we do and say. In every action of the ministry.

I Corinthians 15:58

LIST OF BOOKS AVAILABLE BY DR. BRUNO CAPORRIMO

Honeymoon with the Holy Spirit
available in English, Chinese, Italian & Indonesian

From Mafia Boss to the Cross
available in English, Chinese, French & Indonesian

The Snake in the Glass
available in English, Chinese & Italian

A Heavenly Time: 365 Day Devotional
available in English

God's Plan for Man
available in English & Chinese

Birthing the Prophet in You
available in English & Indonesian

Understanding Your Spiritual Gifts
Available in English & Indonesian

The Invisible War
Available in English, Chinese, Italian, French & Indonesian

Deliverance & Healing for All
Available in English

Eye Opener: You Don't Have the Power to Bind the Devil
Available in English

The Sabbath? Not Saturday, Not Sunday!
Available in English

Please go to our website to place book orders or to
support the orphanages or 'Bibles for China':
drbrunocaporrimo.net & josephglobalinstitute.com

Contact us for speaking engagements,
seminars or to place book orders:

USA – (714) 331-5829
(626) 253-7674
echipministry@gmail.com

BIOGRAPHY

Dr. Bruno was born in Palermo, Sicily, Italy. He is the second youngest of a family of seven. During World War II his family lost everything and they immigrated to the United States. Dr. Bruno Caporrimo followed them to the USA at the age of eighteen in 1958. Within two years tragedy struck again and both of his parents died. Dr. Caporrimo slipped into a depression during which time he lost his identity and the values of life that he had learned from his family. He was then caught up in New York City's fast lane for twenty years, during which time, he became involved with the Italian mafia and became a habitual lawbreaker, breaking the laws of both country and God with his addiction of gambling. He was ordered by the courts to be on 5 years of probation with the condition that he was to leave New York. He and his family moved to California and he began to seek transformation yet, without a Godly mentor or attending church, he found addictions enter his life through family members to a point that he became suicidal. But then, God sent mentors to him.

At the age of 43, after experiencing more unhappiness and tragedy, he cried out to the Lord. In July of 1985 God heard his cries and opened the door to eternal life. Carlo Bruno had a supernatural encounter with the Lord. He gave Dr. Bruno a spiritual anointing, baptized him with the Holy Spirit, and transformed him with his love. Dr. Bruno was caught up in the heavens and was inspired and commissioned by God to build a spiritual army. More than 33 years have gone by and God has done incredible things in the life of Dr. Bruno Caporrimo. Following his radical conversion, in 1987 he became a Deacon and was Licensed and Ordained into the Assemblies of God Church.

From 1993-1997 Dr. Bruno attended Living Word Bible College in Pomona, California where he earned a Divinity degree with a dissertation on 'Fermentation and the Scriptures' which became his book, <u>The Snake in the Glass</u>. From 1997-2003 he worked and studied with the late Chancellor Dr. Samuel Kim and received a Doctorate in Theology from California State Christian University. At CSCU he studied deep theology and God inspired him to write a dissertation and a book called, <u>Honeymoon with the Holy Spirit</u> which became a best seller in Taiwan, Indonesia and America. He graduated from C.S.C.U. in 2003 and was appointed as Dean of International Discipleship in that same year. He also received a Certificate from Billy Graham's School of Evangelism. From 2007 to the present time Dr. Bruno has created and completed a full curriculum and International Discipleship & Training Center which is established globally through Long Distance and Correspondence Study for international students and Joseph Global Institute campuses with schools in Hong Kong with Dr. Samuel Long and a successful Egyptian campus as well as a campus in Bari, Italy under Pastor Saverio Corsini. He has published the curriculum into English, Chinese, Indonesian & Italian languages.

In 2011, after completing 80 Missions to China and Asia, Dr. Bruno stepped down from Shield of Faith Fellowship of churches due to doctrinal disputes and in the same year, while conducting a Mission to Taiwan, met and eternally linked with Dr. Henry Yeh, Founder and Board Chairman of South West International University (*swiu.edu*). ECM Discipleship & Training Center, with international headquarters in La Puente, California, is affiliated and associated with South West International University. Together, Dr. Bruno Caporrimo and Dr. Henry Yeh have set the goal of effectively reaching the nations through many local and international campuses to further train and equip Pastors, lay persons and the body of Christ, from every nation, so that they too can embrace God's plan for their lives. As such, Dr. Bruno and Dr. Yeh and a wonderful global staff and administrative team have discipled and ordained 1,000 men and women into the Ministry thus far.

Additionally, Dr. Caporrimo is a Board-Certified Psychotherapist and Counsellor by the Evangelical Order of Pastoral Counsellors of America. He received that title through his dissertation in a book entitled, <u>The Invisible War</u> which was completed after 11 years of research and writing. In this book, you will read how Dr. Bruno exposes 8 demons which are responsible for the breakup of family, marriages, homes, churches and cause people to run away. We recommend that you get a copy of this book as well as a copy of, <u>Birthing the Prophet in You</u>. Dr. Bruno was personally trained for more than 7 years, from Pastor Glenn Foster, about deep prophetic teaching. This book has the do's and don'ts and when to begin and when to stop when you move under the prophetic anointing. We highly recommend this book to everyone, which is a part of the curriculum, of ECM-JGI.

Also, he is an Ordained Rabbi and Board Member, appointed under the Association of Synagogues and Congregations by Beth Israel Jewish Ministries International and Rabbi Jeshurun Vargas. He and his wife Lydia Caporrimo have traveled throughout more than 40 nations as Speakers, Missionaries, Evangelists, Teachers and have established Campuses. He has conducted numerous conferences, seminars, workshops and healing crusades. God has blessed Dr. Bruno Caporrimo with a prophetic ministry to deliver God's Word and the saving knowledge of Jesus Christ to many multitudes of people. His own unique spiritual journey has touched the lives of millions of people through supernatural healings and life-changing prophecies. Now, in 2017, after completing this book we would like to share with you that we have traveled or taken over 245 Missions. Please stand with us in prayer and with your financial support. We want to train 1 million Missionaries to transform and build a new generation in high education and Biblical Theology.

PS: I am Dominic Contreras, the Administrator for ECM-JGI and his ghostwriter. I have worked side by side with Dr. Bruno more than 12 years and have travelled to many nations with Dr. Bruno and the team and prayed and fasted to the Lord to bring these inspirational books to all of you. I have been Ordained as a Assistant Pastor and Administrator by ECM-JGI and through all of the work books I have achieved a earned Bachelor, Master and Doctorate degree in Theology. We are delighted to share this with you and we hope that this book, <u>Bible Financial Purpose Driven</u> will inspire, encourage and build you up. This is our hope and prayer, that you will get God's calling and be a master in tool making, to train others, to build God's Army, to transform all the nations. We have a full curriculum and lifetime books to cover every area in 100% Biblical doctrine and personally I have seen with my own eyes the miracles in the Crusades where the blind see, the crippled walk and deaf ears open plus the Lord has used this ministry to raise 4 people from the dead. We have a video available which is a true story about a Woman who was in chains for more than 4 years and bound with legions and Dr. Bruno and the team went to the remote village and, after 10 hours of praying, she was totally redeemed by the Lord Jesus Christ. Plus, there was also a man in chains for 20 years in a dungeon in China too. He also carried legions of demons. Dr. Bruno found out later that, there were over 100 Missionaries in 20 years, who went to pray and liberate him and the man in chains beat them and they fled.

He could not be delivered. Again, Dr. Bruno and his team prayed all day and as he cried to the Lord he was determined not to leave until he saw this man set free. You can read much, much more of this true story in the book, <u>Honeymoon with the Holy Spirit</u>. We believe that we are in the end times and we are looking forward to the manifestation and glory of the fullness of the cloud glory which is nothing but the Lord Jesus Christ. We encourage you and your family to come on board, shoulder to shoulder with us, to bring the gospel all over the world. You can reach me personally through our email or website about our school. We have all the books you need to train you to be a business man, Ordained minister and 16 different other degrees to help you to discover God's calling in your life and equip you mentally, physically, financially and in every area of your life. This is the highest education that God has made available for you, your family and the next generations. From all of us, we want to thank you from the bottom of our hearts for reading this book.

Finally, Dr. Bruno and all of us, would like to give a heartfelt thanks to all of the mentors whom we have gleaned from and who have helped us to build this Ministry. And all the Christian TV and Radio Stations around the world who have partnered and linked with us. Thank you all from the bottom of our hearts.

Dominic Contreras,
your friend and servant
(626) 253-7674
echipministry@gmail.com

My Gift of Appreciation
TO YOU

A HEAVENLY TIME: 365 Day Devotional

A mini-bible treasure book

Unlock the Keys to God's Wisdom
in this 365 Day devotional and
receive the treasure of HIS storehouse

We thank YOU for partnering
with MANNA TV NETWORK in the
build-out and remodeling
of our new 5,000 sq. foot
production and training
facility located in
Los Angeles,California.We
have prayed and fasted and
believe that NOW is the time
for COMPLETION of this project

The total budget for this awesome
facility (5,000 sq. feet) is
$5 million(US$). This beautiful
leather bound devotional is my
newest release and is my gift
of APPRECIATION for your seed
of $100 or more towards this
project ($100 = 1 square foot)

Sow you best seed now as we take the
Gospel around the world 24-7 on our new
MANNA TV NETWORK!
B.C.M. - Chase bank
Swift code: Chas US33
Routing # - 322271627Account # - 8763504129
or on-line at:
    drbrunocaporrimo.net/bookstore.html

SEED of 1
Square foot
or more
Gift of Appreciation